Transitions

An Interactive Reading, Writing, and Grammar Text

Second Edition

Linda Bates

University of California–Davis

CAMBRIDGE
UNIVERSITY PRESS

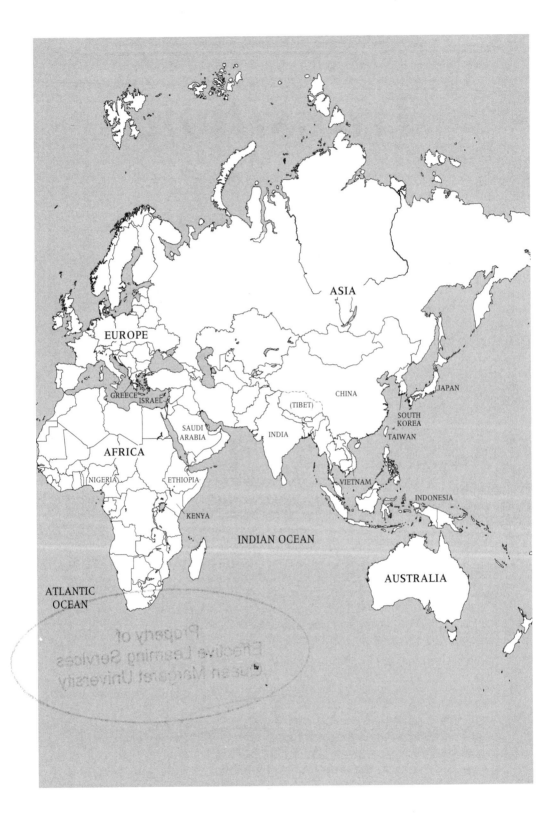

ASIA

EUROPE

GREECE
ISRAEL

SAUDI
ARABIA

INDIA

CHINA

(TIBET)

JAPAN

SOUTH
KOREA

TAIWAN

AFRICA

NIGERIA

ETHIOPIA

VIETNAM

INDONESIA

KENYA

INDIAN OCEAN

AUSTRALIA

ATLANTIC
OCEAN

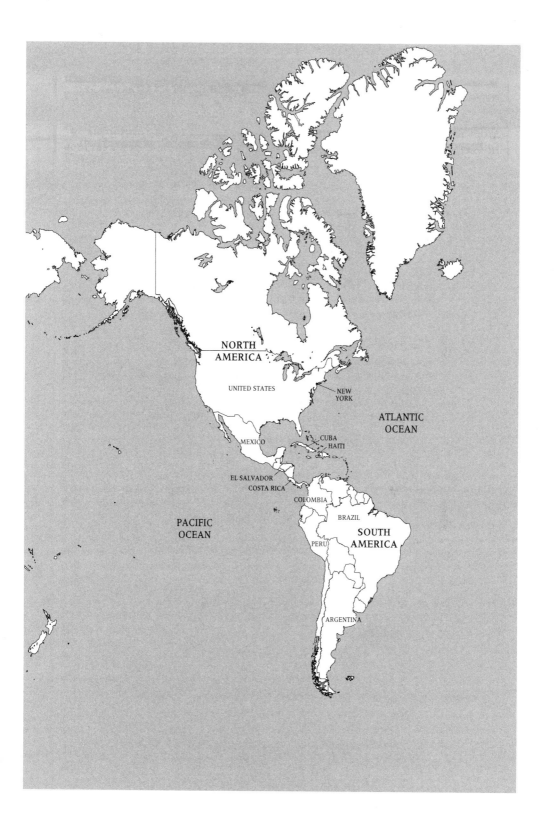

To Dale Neal (1908–1996)

PUBLISHED BY THE PRESS SYNDICATE OF THE UNIVERSITY OF CAMBRIDGE
The Pitt Building, Trumpington Street, Cambridge, United Kingdom

CAMBRIDGE UNIVERSITY PRESS
The Edinburgh Building, Cambridge CB2 2RU, UK
40 West 20th Street, New York, NY 10011–4211, USA
477 Williamstown Road, Port Melbourne, VIC 3207, Australia
Ruiz de Alarcón 13, 28014 Madrid, Spain
Dock House, The Waterfront, Cape Town 8001, South Africa

http://www.cambridge.org

First published by St. Martin's Press, Inc. 1997
4th printing 2001

Printed in the United States of America

Library of Congress Cataloging-in-Publication Data Available

A catalogue record for this book is available from the British Library.

ISBN 0 521 65782 2 Student's Book
ISBN 0 521 65781 4 Instructor's Manual

Acknowledgments are given on page 372.

Contents

V

PART II

Expository Paragraphs

3
Writing about a Favorite Activity or Hobby   43

6
Writing about a Family or Cultural Value — 112

PART III

Writing Essays

7
Writing about a Decision   **129**

9
Writing about Overcoming the Odds   **193**

10
Writing about the Way Males and Females Are Raised   **231**

Preface

The title of this text—*Transitions*—highlights two transitions the text will help students make: the transition from writing paragraphs to writing essays, and the transition from concrete to abstract writing topics. Overall, the text provides English as a Second Language (ESL) students with a transition into the world of academic writing.

Transitions, second edition, is designed primarily for academically oriented *intermediate* to *low-advanced* ESL students in colleges, universities, junior colleges, and intensive language programs, although it should be kept in mind that the meanings of the labels *intermediate* and *low-advanced* vary widely from program to program.

The text integrates reading, writing, and grammar, using a process approach, with emphasis on peer response. Several features make the text especially accessible and engaging to students: the hands-on workbook format, the extensive use of student writing samples, and a wide selection of multicultural readings that respect the native languages and cultures of ESL students. In addition, *Transitions* is intentionally designed to be flexible; it offers the instructor alternative applications to use with students of varying abilities and levels of preparedness.

Features of the Text

HIGH-INTEREST READINGS AND WRITING TOPICS WITHIN A THEMATIC ORGANIZATION

The second edition retains the very successful thematic organization of the first. Each chapter in the second edition is built around a theme introduced in the reading that begins the chapter and then is carried forward in the chapter's writing assignment. Students will find the readings, including the updated readings in this second edition, highly interesting and the writing topics engaging.

xvi

INTEGRATION OF READING, WRITING, AND GRAMMAR WITHIN THE CONTEXT OF CHAPTER THEMES

The text smoothly integrates reading, writing, and grammar by setting these components within the context of each unit's theme.

- **Reading.** The text's thematically oriented reading selections are written by a wide range of culturally diverse, international authors. The second edition adds more readings about scientists and even wider cultural diversity.
- **Writing.** The sections on writing guide students through all stages of the writing process—prewriting, drafting, revising, and editing.

  In the drafting and revising stages, students study models of student writing and take part in peer response activities. Assignment-specific Peer Response Sheets are included at the back of the text to guide students through this stage. In the editing stage, students study a grammar concept and then edit their drafts for the sentence problems they have just studied.

  In Chapters 1–6, the writing assignments focus on paragraph development. These writing assignments progressively take students from concrete to more challenging abstract writing topics. In Chapters 7–11, as students make the difficult transition from paragraph to essay, the five essay assignments begin once again at the concrete level and progress to the abstract.

  Although each chapter is thematically oriented, a number of common rhetorical modes, such as description, compare/contrast, cause-and-effect, and argument, are covered as part of the text's writing assignments.
- **Grammar.** Grammar, which is built into the editing stage, is presented within the context of the unit's reading and writing assignment. Many of the grammar sections, in fact, incorporate examples from the reading selection of the chapter. In the grammar section, students study a grammar concept and then immediately apply what they have learned to the editing of their own drafts.

  The text's grammar coverage is not comprehensive; instead, the text concentrates on helping students develop control of verb form, verb tense, logical connectors, and sentence structure. Intermediate ESL writers need to gain a measure of control in these key areas before moving on to eliminate less distracting sentence problems from their writing.

FLEXIBILITY

A wide range of materials gives instructors great flexibility in adapting the text to fit the needs of students of various skill levels and in different types of ESL programs.

- **Flexibility for Different Skill Levels.** Instructors can choose to use certain sections of the text according to the skill level of their students. For example, instructors may choose to primarily use the paragraph and early essay assignments in a class where students have little writing experience. With more experienced student writers, instructors can move quickly through the early paragraph assignments, treating them as review, in order to spend more time on the more challenging essay assignments in later chapters.

- **Flexibility for Different Programs and Classes.** The text's wide variety of materials fits the needs of many different types of programs, including intensive, junior college, and college or university programs. In addition, the integrated approach to reading, writing, and grammar gives instructors great flexibility in choosing from several possible emphases. An instructor in a composition class, for instance, can use the text to teach reading, writing, and grammar, with a primary emphasis on writing. If class time is limited, instructors can ask students to respond to the readings in a journal, rather than discuss the readings in class. For students in separate grammar classes, instructors can choose the appropriate grammar sections of the text. Finally, instructors in programs with separate reading, writing, and grammar components can use the corresponding sections of the text in those classes. In this way, students benefit from a well-integrated approach to learning English as a second language and also avoid the expense of separate texts for each course.

The *Instructor's Manual* provides useful suggestions for how to use the text, including sample course syllabi for different types of programs and for various lengths of terms (short intensive terms, two intensive terms, quarter terms, and semesters). Particularly helpful to new instructors are the sections of the *Instructor's Manual* that suggest ways to use the reading and grammar sections of the text and ways to guide students through the steps of the writing process. Both new and experienced instructors will find the additional generating activities, grammar exercises, and grammar "games" especially helpful.

THE SECOND EDITION

The second edition of *Transitions* retains features of the first edition that have proved successful—the text's thematic organization; its integration of reading, writing, and grammar; and its emphasis on the writing process and peer editing.

In response to surveys of instructors using the text, several changes have been made to strengthen the second edition:

- **The Number of Writing Assignments Reduced.** The ratio of paragraph to essay assignments has been reduced in order to allow students to move more quickly into essay writing. The second edition contains six paragraph assignments (rather than eight); this allows the text to give more emphasis to essay writing.

- **Readings Updated.** In the second edition, a number of longer, more recent reading selections have been added. Some of these readings are drawn from science and engineering, fields many of today's students are keenly interested in.

   1. The third chapter now includes a longer reading from the autobiography of evolutionary biologist E. O. Wilson. Students interested in science will find this reading intriguing.

   2. In response to user surveys, a number of longer readings replace short selections in the first edition. These longer readings, such as the excerpt from Mark Salzman's *Iron and Silk*, give students the opportunity for more extensive reading and fuller class discussion.

   3. In the interest of adding even more cultural diversity, a longer reading about a Cuban American student and her research in molecular biology has been added in Chapter 5.

   4. Chapter 9 now includes a fascinating account of the life and career of American astronaut Bonnie Dunbar. Students interested in engineering will eagerly read the section on Dunbar's involvement in ceramic engineering research and the space shuttles. Almost all ESL students, however, will identify with Dunbar's struggle to achieve success in her chosen field, despite the obstacles in her path.

   5. Chapter 10 now includes updated, longer, and more challenging readings on gender roles in Japan and Saudi Arabia. Students preparing to make the transition to the advanced level will benefit from these more academically oriented readings.

- **Supplemental Reading Lists Added.** Because research shows the great value of extensive reading in helping students improve their writing, supplemental reading lists have been added to most chapters. Students who want to do extensive reading to improve their writing and reading skills can find many of these interesting books and articles at their local or college library. Using the supplemental reading lists, students can follow up on an interest sparked by a reading selection in the text. They might read, for example, further accounts of Apollo astronauts, the science section of the Tuesday *New York Times*, an immigrant physician's story of practicing medicine in a small town, or the fiction of the young Haitian American author Edwidge Danticat.

- **Grammar and Editing Sections Revised.** In just a few chapters, a small number of editing activities have been added. These include areas that commonly give intermediate-level students problems, such as comma splice/fragments and pronoun reference/agreement. The grammar sections on present and past tense are now consolidated in the first chapter. Presenting these sections together as review makes the text more appropriate for the intermediate level.

Acknowledgments

I would like to thank the following reviewers for their contributions to the book: Nancy M. Fletcher, English Language Institute, Texas A&M University; Joanne Grumet, Baruch College–CUNY; R. Kay Hart, Texas A&M University; Lynne Henson, Palomar College; Christine Meloni, George Washington University; Rosa Brefeld Schuette, Washington University; Linda M. Silvestri, IELI, State University of New York at Buffalo; and Dona Stein, Gavilan College.

I would like to thank Emily Berleth of St. Martin's Press and Nancy Benjamin of Books By Design for their expert help in guiding this book through the production process. It is indeed a privilege to be a part of St. Martin's Press and those who work with St. Martin's.

I would also like to give special thanks to my family—Bob, Cynthia, Adam, and Melanie—without whose loving support I could not have produced this text. In addition, I am grateful to my friend and ESL colleague, Ellen Lange, whose great support and extensive ESL expertise have proved invaluable to me as I completed this text.

I dedicate this second edition of *Transitions* to my father, Dale Neal, who taught me the value of taking on new challenges and pushing forward into new frontiers, while remaining strong and brave in the face of difficulties and adversity.

CHAPTER 1

Writing about a Treasured Possession

In this chapter, you will write a paragraph about a possession that is special to you. Before you begin your paragraph, you will read the following selection about a treasured possession. Reading this selection will give you ideas for the paragraph you will write later in the chapter.

The reading that follows is from *A Place for Us*, a book written by the Greek American writer Nicholas Gage in 1989. In an earlier book, *Eleni* (1987), Gage told of his mother Eleni's struggle to save her children during Greece's civil war in the late 1940s. Eleni's husband (Gage's father) had immigrated from Greece to the United States in 1910. During a return visit to Greece in 1926, he met and married Eleni. Although he promised to send for Eleni and the children, he never fulfilled that promise. Gage says that by 1948 "it was too late" for his father to keep his promise because Communist guerillas had taken control of the village. Eleni resisted the guerillas' attempts to send her children to Communist "re-education" camps in Eastern Europe. Yet before Eleni could carry out her escape plan to save herself and her children, she was imprisoned and tortured. Finally, as Gage says, his mother's

READING PROCEDURE

In each reading selection throughout this text, you will see the more difficult vocabulary words highlighted in **bold.** This means that each of these words is defined in the Glossary at the back of the book. As you read through each selection, try to guess the meanings of words you do not understand. Then discuss with your classmates the meanings of words you cannot guess or look them up in the Glossary or in your dictionary. If there are other words that you do not know, underline them and discuss them with your classmates or look them up in the dictionary. Then write the definition of each word in the outside margin of the selection.

"bullet-riddled body [was] tossed into a shallow grave with other victims" and only later reburied by her father in the village churchyard. Eleni's fifteen-year-old daughter Glykeria was driven at gunpoint into Albania.

In the following selection, Gage describes how he felt in 1949 when he and his three sisters, without any money, boarded a ship in Athens to leave their homeland and begin a journey across a vast ocean to the United States. As nine-year-old Gage stood with his three older sisters (aged ten to twenty) on the deck of the ship as it pulled away from Athens, his thoughts turned to the few treasured possessions he was able to bring with him.

▶ *BEFORE YOU READ*

1. Can you locate Greece on the map that appears in the front of this book? How far do you think it is from Greece to the East Coast of the United States?

2. Young Gage and his three sisters must have been relieved that they had successfully escaped from their Communist-controlled village in Greece and had avoided being sent to re-education camps in Eastern Europe. Yet leaving behind their homeland and the village where their mother was buried must have been difficult for them. How do you think they might have felt about this?

3. Have you ever been in a situation similar to the one experienced by Gage and his sisters as they left Greece? Did you also leave your home country to immigrate to the United States or to study in the United States? Or, if you have been in the United States most of your life, did you leave your family and friends to study at a college or university? In either case, how did you feel about leaving your home country or your family?

from *A PLACE FOR US*

NICHOLAS GAGE

I put my hands in my pockets to **take stock** of the treasures I had with me—**amulets** to protect me against the uncertain future. There was the cross-shaped box on a chain that my mother had hung around my neck in the last moment we were together. It was her most magical possession, because it held a **splinter** of a bone from a **saint,** and it was the only thing she could give to protect me from being shot or stepping on a **land mine** during our escape. I had promised her I would be brave, and the cold hardness of the cross made me feel braver now.

I **inventoried** my other treasures. First, a white handkerchief my **godmother** had given me on the day between the wars when she left the village with her son to join her husband, Nassio, in America. Nassio hadn't **procrastinated** like my father. While we were being

Nicholas Gage (right front), *his sisters, and relatives at the harbor in Piraeus, Greece, before boarding the ship for America on March 3, 1949.*

starved and bombed in the village, his son was in America, no doubt playing with wonderful toys like the wind-up airplane his father had once sent him. I had always hoped my godmother would give me that airplane when she left, but the handkerchief was what I got, and now I touched it to **ease** my **transition** from one culture to another.

I fingered the **reed whistle** that my Uncle Andreas had **whittled** for me when he taught me to make birdcalls. Andreas had always been the kindest man in my life, not like my **stern, irascible** grandfather. Uncle Andreas was the one who cried when we left the **refugee** camps, as my ten-year-old sister Fotini ran to comfort him, giving him a tiny, nearly worthless coin that she had been **hoarding.**

Then my fingers touched something cold and smooth, and I pulled it out of my pocket. It was the small black stone that I had picked up outside my house on the night of our escape, because my mother had ordered me to throw one behind me so that I would never return to the place that gave us so much **suffering.** I had kept that stone in my pocket for eight months, and now it was time to toss it into the sea.

My mother had often told us the story of how my father, an **itinerant tinker** of seventeen, when he boarded the ship for America, **triumphantly** tossed over the rail the **fez** that the Turkish **occupiers** of northern Greece forced men to wear in those days as a symbol of their **subjugation.** When the fez disappeared into the waves, she said, my father felt like a free man for the first time in his life.

Now it was my turn to throw this stone from my village into the same sea, to insure that I would never be pulled back to this land of war and **famine,** bombs, **torture** and **executions.** My mother had said that any one of her children who came back would receive her **curse.** Throwing the stone was the way to turn my back **irrevocably** on Greece and my face toward America, where my father waited.

But my mother's body was still in Greece, in the church only a few yards below our ruined house. They had called her the _Amerikana_ and all her life she had dreamed of America, but she would never leave our mountains. My sister was still somewhere behind those mountains too, unless she was dead.

It was the only country I knew, and I loved the cruel beauty of the mountain peaks, the sound of the goats' bells in the thin air, the smell of wood smoke, and the annual **transfiguration** of the gray hillsides when the Judas trees and wildflowers burst into **paschal** colors in the spring. I wasn't sorry to be leaving Greece, but **despite** my mother's orders, I couldn't make myself throw that stone **overboard** and cut myself off from my native land forever. It was the only place I had ever felt I belonged, until the war killed my mother and washed my sisters and me away like the **swells** of the sea that frightened me so when I first saw its **vastness.**

I slipped the stone back into my pocket and turned to follow my sisters, who were **descending** the steel stairs into the **bowels** of the ship, crying out in **dismay** at the **dizzying sway** beneath their feet.

▶ _AFTER YOU READ_

1. At the beginning of the reading, Gage calls the treasures in his pockets "amulets." What are amulets? How could they "protect [Gage] against the uncertain future"?

2. Gage tells us that his mother "had said that any one of her children who came back [to Greece] would receive her curse." What is a curse? Why do you think Gage's mother threatened her children with a curse if they returned to Greece?

3. As nine-year-old Gage considered tossing the stone overboard, he thought of both Greece and the United States. What do you think the young boy's feelings were about going to the United States? What might have caused him to feel that way? Why do you think he did not want to toss the stone overboard? What did the stone mean to him?

SUPPLEMENTAL READING LISTS

In this and the following chapters, you will find lists of additional books and articles that you may want to read. These additional readings will often be on the theme of the chapter. Doing this kind of additional, extensive reading outside your class will help you develop reading, as well as writing, skills.

Supplemental Reading List—Chapter 1

Berthelson, John. "Flying High: First Chinese-American Astronaut Is Set to Blast Off into Space Next Month," *Far Eastern Economic Review*, June 30, 1994, p. 62.

This article tells of the prized possessions that astronaut Leroy Chiao, the first Chinese American astronaut, took with him into space.

Goldberg, Jeff. "Lunar Reflections," *Omni*, July, 1989, pp. 35–88.

This article describes the various prized possessions that each of the Apollo astronauts took to the moon—from rings and golf balls to medallions. Each astronaut was allowed eight ounces of personal mementos.

✏️ WRITING ASSIGNMENT: *Writing about a Treasured Possession*

In this chapter, you will first review the basics of paragraph writing and then work through the stages of the writing process to develop a paragraph about your most prized possession. Before beginning your prewriting (the first stage in the writing process), discuss the following question with your classmates. Your answer to this question will become the focus of your paragraph.

Question: What is your most treasured possession, and why is it special to you?

Write a paragraph about your most prized possession. Include specific details to describe the possession and explain to your reader why it means so much to you.

Before you begin writing your paragraph, study the following guidelines on paragraph writing.

Guidelines on Paragraph Writing

WHAT IS A PARAGRAPH?

A *paragraph* is a group of sentences that develops one central point. A writer often directly states this point in a sentence near the beginning of the paragraph; this statement is called a *topic sentence*. The writer then develops the topic sentence more fully within the body of the paragraph.

❑   *ACTIVITY 1.1:*   **DEVELOPING THE CENTRAL POINT**

Have one member of the class read aloud this student paragraph about a prized possession. Then discuss the questions that follow it:

My most treasured possession is an old-fashioned gold pocket watch. My father gave me this watch when I left home to come to the United States to study. When I open the cover of the watch, I see the clock face with its numbers written in faded black roman numerals: I, II, III, and so forth. After I snap the cover shut, I look at the scratched and dull gold cover. Then I can faintly see the engraved picture of a bird in flight on the watch's cover. As I hold the watch in my hand, it reminds me of my grandfather Nemo, who first owned the watch. Most of all, it makes me think of my father, who with tears in his eyes, placed the watch lovingly in my hand as I prepared to make my first flight from home.

DISCUSSION QUESTIONS

1. What is the central point of this paragraph?

2. How does the writer develop the central point in the body of the paragraph?

PARAGRAPH UNITY

The first principle of paragraph writing is *unity,* which means that the entire paragraph should focus on one central point. As you write and then revise your paragraph on a prized possession, make certain that all of the sentences within it relate to the central point you are making.

When you are writing, your mind may not always stick to one point. As you begin writing about one idea, other related thoughts usually occur to you. Yet these related thoughts are sometimes not focused exactly on the central point you are trying to make in a paragraph. Instead, these *digressions* only lead you away from the central point.

In conversation, digressions are often acceptable. Your listeners will wait patiently, for instance, when you wander away from the point you are making, perhaps to tell a funny story that is not directly related to your central point. Most readers, however, and especially those in the academic world, are not as patient as listeners. Readers expect you to write unified paragraphs in which you stick to one central point throughout each paragraph.

❑ *ACTIVITY 1.2:* **LOOKING FOR PARAGRAPH UNITY PROBLEMS**

As you read the following student paragraph, look for problems with unity. For example, can you find any sentences that do not stick to the central point of the paragraph? If so, how would you solve the problem? Discuss the unity problems you find in the paragraph as well as your solutions with your classmates.

> Whenever I look at the mirror in my room, I also turn to my most important possession next to the mirror. It is a 16-inch × 20-inch picture of my high school track team. The picture is neatly fitted into a clear plastic frame that I especially purchased to protect it from getting stained or being covered by dust. In the picture, all forty-four members of our track team are lined up into six rows, smiling, and looking very happy. As I look at the picture, I remember the favorite memories and exciting moments I had during track season, such as the tough practice, bitter losing, and sweet winning. Later, I also played football on the same field where we practiced track. Every single great time I shared with my teammates is inside the picture and in every one of my teammates' smiles, and their smiles bring me back my own smile when I am feeling down.

Overview of the Writing Process

As you write paragraphs and essays in this and the other chapters of this text, you will learn that *writing* is a *multi-staged process*. You will also learn various techniques that successful writers use to move through the stages of the writing process to produce academic papers. You will work through these stages to complete your own paragraphs and essays. The following overview of the writing process will help you understand the stages.

THE PREWRITING STAGE

In the *prewriting stage,* successful writers take some time to gather their ideas and to focus those ideas before they begin writing. After focusing the question that will be answered in a paragraph or essay, the writer takes the time to generate or gather a wealth of ideas in response to that question. The writer then focuses this wealth of ideas and draws up a rough plan for the paragraph or essay.

THE DRAFTING STAGE

After generating a wealth of ideas and drawing up a rough plan for the paragraph or essay, the successful writer then sits down to *draft* the piece of writing. For a short piece, drafting may be done in one sitting; for a longer piece, the first rough draft may take several sittings to complete.

THE REVISING AND EDITING STAGES

After producing the first rough draft, the writer is ready to begin revising. Revising takes place in two stages: first, the writer *revises* or *reworks* the organization and the content of the draft; second, the writer *edits* or reworks sentences and words throughout the draft. When revising, the writer makes many changes in the early draft and often writes more than one draft. Once the writer is satisfied with the organization as well as the ideas of the latest draft, the next step is the editing stage. Here the writer works to improve the sentences in the draft.

As part of the revising stage, writers often share their drafts with other readers, asking for suggestions for how to improve their drafts. As part of each writing assignment in this text, you will work with a group of students in your class, commenting on each person's draft and making suggestions for improvements.

Keep in mind that the writing process is flexible. You should *not* think of writing as a step-by-step process that requires you to complete step one before moving on to step two. Rather, when you write, you will often find yourself moving both forward and backward through the stages of the writing process. You might, for example, complete a draft and then, when revising the draft, decide to move back to the planning stage to draw up a new plan. Or, as you are revising a draft, you might instead decide that you need to take time to generate or gather more ideas about the topic.

Prewriting: Gathering Ideas

DESCRIPTIVE DETAILS

To describe your prized possession in a paragraph, you want to use words that paint a sharp, clear picture of the object in the reader's mind. You can create these word pictures by using concrete and specific words and by avoiding abstract words.

Concrete versus Abstract Words

Concrete words appeal to one of our five senses: sight, smell, taste, touch, or hearing. Unlike abstract words, concrete words bring to mind real things that exist in the physical world around us. Here are some examples of concrete words:

cloud   nose   door   cat   leaf   chair   smoke   rain

Abstract words, in contrast, do not appeal to our senses of sight, touch, smell, and so on. Instead, they relate to our thoughts and feelings by describing things that do not exist in the physical world. Here are some examples of abstract words:

education   loyalty   love   jealousy   competition

Specific versus General Words

Specific and *general words* can be used to describe the same things, but specific words make the description clearer for readers. As shown in the following diagram, general words (*food*) are least descriptive and specific words (*chocolate ice cream*) are most descriptive.

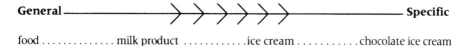

General $\longrightarrow$ $\rangle$ $\rangle$ $\rangle$ $\rangle$ $\rangle$ **Specific**

food . . . . milk product . . . . .ice cream . . . . .chocolate ice cream

The more specific the word you choose, the more of a clear, sharp picture you will paint for your reader.

Descriptive Details in the Gage Reading

What specific, concrete details do you remember about the possessions Gage describes in the reading at the beginning of the chapter? Why do you think these details are important to the writer's central point?

❏ *ACTIVITY 1.3:* **USING CONCRETE AND SPECIFIC DETAILS**

Here again is the student paragraph you read in Activity 1.1. As one class member reads the paragraph aloud, circle all of the concrete and specific words that the writer uses to paint a vivid picture of a pocket watch. Then discuss the questions following the paragraph with your classmates.

My most treasured possession is an old-fashioned gold pocket watch. My father gave me this watch when I left home to come to the United States to study. When I open the cover of the watch, I see the clock face with its numbers written in faded black roman numerals: I, II, III, and so forth. After I snap the cover shut, I look at the scratched and dull gold cover. Then I can faintly see the engraved picture of a bird in flight on the watch's cover. As I hold the watch in my hand, it reminds me of my grandfather Nemo, who first owned the watch. Most of all, it makes me think of my father, who with tears in his eyes, placed the watch lovingly in my hand as I prepared to make my first flight from home.

DISCUSSION QUESTIONS

1. What concrete and specific words did you find in the preceding description of a pocket watch?

2. What senses—touch, taste, smell, and so on—do these words appeal to?

3. Does the use of concrete and specific words paint a clear, sharp picture of the pocket watch in your mind? Choose several words from the paragraph and tell how they make the pocket watch vivid for you.

CLUSTERING

Before you begin writing your paragraph about a treasured possession, try the prewriting technique of *clustering* to help you think of descriptive details about your possession. First, write the name of your possession in the middle of a blank piece of paper. Then think of specific and concrete words that describe the possession and write them down. Draw lines or branches out from your central point to your specific and concrete words and enclose the words in bubbles or circles.

The accompanying diagram shows how the student writer of the paragraph about a pocket watch used clustering to gather specific and concrete words to describe his prized possession.

An Example of Clustering

EXPLAINING THE POINT OF YOUR PARAGRAPH

Before you write your paragraph, jot down a few notes about how you will explain to your reader why your prized possession is special. Think for a moment about the Gage reading at the start of the chapter. Does Gage explain why the stone and the other possessions were important to him? How does knowing what the possession meant to Gage make the selection a more powerful piece of writing?

Drafting

Now that you have a rough idea of what you want to say in your paragraph about a treasured possession, you are ready to begin drafting. Your instructor may either set aside some class time for writing the first draft of your paragraph or ask you to write it at home. Whether you write in the classroom or at home, find a place where you feel comfortable writing. Gather all the materials you need—paper, your favorite pen or pencil, and any other writing tools that you like to use. If you are using a computer to write, make yourself comfortable at the computer.

As you begin to write your paragraph, remember that you do not need to concentrate on perfectly written sentences during the drafting stage. This is the time to focus on getting your ideas down on paper. Later you will discuss your rough draft with your writing group and then reshape and rewrite it during the revising stage.

Revising

Now that you have completed the rough draft of your paragraph, you are ready to begin revising it. In the revising stage, you direct your attention to larger, more overall problems, such as how you have organized and developed your ideas in the paragraph.

THE IMPORTANCE OF PEER RESPONSE

Peer response is an important part of the writing process for many writers, especially student writers. Your peers, who are also writers, are a valuable source of information on how to improve your writing. For each paragraph and essay you write in this text, you will work with your peers in the classroom as a writing group. Whether your group contains only yourself and a partner or a team of three to six students, the group will listen as you read your drafts aloud and then will give you suggestions on how to strengthen your writing. Your peers are your audience, your readers; they can help you see things about your writing that are very difficult for you alone to judge.

In order to make peer response a valuable experience, you need to work with your writing group to develop the best possible approach. It is important to be courteous to other writers when you respond to their drafts, keeping in mind that they may be sensitive about what they have written. Still, you need to be honest in judging the strengths and weaknesses of your peers' writing. Thus, work with your group to keep a good balance between courtesy and honesty. You and the other members of your writing team will then find peer response a valuable experience.

❏ *ACTIVITY 1.4:* EVALUATING A STUDENT'S PARAGRAPH

Before you and the other students in your writing group begin looking at each other's draft paragraphs, practice on the following student paragraph, if time permits. Read the paragraph aloud and then discuss the questions that follow it with your classmates.

My most treasured possession is just a common, old letter whose four corners are all marked by my fingerprints with many holes. My grandfather, who was a kind and honest man, gave me this letter when I was eleven years old. At that time, I did not realize how valuable it was, so I just kept it in my ordinary letter box. A few years later, after my grandfather passed away, I found out that he was an illiterate person. I also found out that he had to copy all the letters of words one by one to give the letter to me. Now, every time I read the letter, I can see my grandfather's generous eyes and charitable smile through its letters. The letter does not look clean and neat anymore, but it is my most meaningful possession because it brings so many memories of my grandfather back to me.

DISCUSSION QUESTIONS

1. Is the paragraph *unified* around one central idea that is clear to the reader? What is the central idea?

2. Does the writer use enough *concrete, specific details* in describing the object to give the reader a sharp, clear picture of the possession?

3. Does the writer *explain* to the reader why the possession is special to him or her?

4. What makes this description appealing?

❏ *ACTIVITY 1.5:* PEER RESPONSE

You will now share the rough draft of your paragraph with your group and give one another ideas about improving the drafts. Use the following procedure:

1. One group member should begin by reading aloud his or her draft paragraph. Another member should record the group's answers to the questions on the Peer Response Sheet for Activity 1.5 on page 337. These answers will give the writer ideas about the strengths and weaknesses of the paragraph.

2. After you are finished filling out the sheet, give it to the writer so that he or she can use the ideas when revising the draft.

3. Repeat the procedure for each group member.

4. Then revise your own paragraph, keeping in mind the suggestions of your writing group.

Editing: Present Tense and Past Tense

Now that you have revised your draft paragraph and are satisfied with its development, you are ready to begin editing. During the editing stage, you make changes in your sentences, correcting problems in grammar, usage, punctuation, and spelling.

One of the most important steps in the editing process is making sure your verbs are correct in terms of form and tense. The following discussion of tense will help you determine whether your use of verbs is correct. In addition, the sections on the present and past tenses will be important to you in editing your paragraph about a possession because you probably used either mostly present or mostly past tenses.

WHAT IS TENSE?

What is *tense* and how does it differ from *time*? You can think of time as a line along which the past, the present, and the future are located (see the diagram that follows).

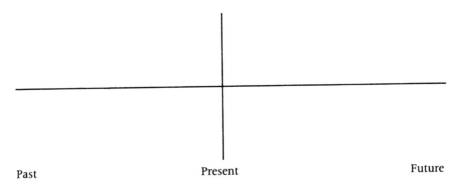

Past   Present   Future

Tense, however, does not always fall into the three precise groups of past, present, and future. Tense is unlike time in the following two ways:

1. Tense can span or include more than one time period:

Saudi Arabia *is* a country in the Middle East.

In this example, the present tense verb *is* includes all three time periods, suggesting that Saudi Arabia has existed and will exist in the Middle East in past, present, and future times.

2. Tense can carry messages about an event other than just its time:

Last week my cousin Hurran *bought* a pickup truck.

Here the past tense verb *bought* tells us not only that this event (the purchase of a truck) occurred in the past but also that the event is completed or ended.

Last year Hurran *rode* the bus to school.

In this example, the past tense verb *rode* tells us that this event (the riding of the bus) was habitual or repeated.

Thus, you can see why tense is not exactly the same as time. As a result, you should concentrate on the messages or meanings that each tense can convey in your writing, as well as on the time period a tense may cover.

Tense and tense-like forms fall into three groups: the *past tense,* the *present tense,* and *future verb forms.*

| Past Tense | Present Tense | Future Verb Forms |

However, keep in mind that these groups do not necessarily fit neatly into the three groups of time. You will be studying verb tenses in the editing sections throughout this book. In this chapter, we will look more closely at present tense and past tense.

USING PRESENT TENSE OR PAST TENSE IN YOUR PARAGRAPH

In writing your paragraph about a possession, you will want to use mostly present tense to describe a possession that is now important to you. If you are writing about a possession that was important to you earlier in your life, you will want to use mostly past tense.

USING THE PRESENT TENSE

If the present tense does not necessarily tell us the time of an event or only the time, what does it tell us? Let's examine a few sentences from the following student paragraph to determine what the present tense can tell us. In this paragraph, the writer describes a favorite possession of his cousin, a Bedouin tribesman who lives on the Saudi Arabian peninsula. Bedouins are an ethnic group of Arabs who live in the deserts of Arabia, North Africa, and Syria.

❏ *ACTIVITY 1.6:* **LOOKING FOR PRESENT TENSE VERBS**

1. Can you locate Saudi Arabia on the map that appears on the inside front cover of this book?

2. As you read the following paragraph, underline the present tense verbs. Also take note of how heavily this description relies on present tense verbs.

> My cousin Hurran's favorite possession is his red Datsun pickup truck. A truck is an important part of desert life for Hurran and other Bedouin tribesmen in Saudi Arabia. Hurran uses his truck to bring food and water to his large family where they are camped in tents on the desert. Since the desert receives very little rainfall each year, Hurran often has to make a trip into town and then fill the back of his truck with fifty-gallon drums of water. When sandstorms make the roads difficult for cars to travel, Hurran feels proud that he can get through in his truck. Hurran's truck can even serve as an ambulance when it is needed to take a sick camel to the veterinarian clinic in town.

By looking at the sentences in the preceding paragraph, we can determine that the present tense can tell us a number of different things.

State of Being Present
Present tense can describe *a state of being* (a state, not an action). It can suggest that this state of being is one of the following:

- *a general statement of fact or truth that is a "timeless truth"* (such as a scientific truth):

    A desert *receives* only a few inches of rainfall each year.

    Saudi Arabia *is* a country in the Middle East.

These kinds of general statements of fact or truth are "timeless" in that they do not refer to a specific time period. Instead, the present tense here suggests that this truth is "forever" true—it was true in the past, it is true now, and it will be true in the future. A "timeless truth" could be, for example, a proverb, a scientific truth, or a geographic truth.

- *a general statement of fact that has a more limited time span* (one that is not necessarily "forever" true):

    My cousin's most valued possession *is* his truck.

Here the present tense is used to describe a general statement of fact without reference to any specific time period. This statement of fact holds true now, before now, and after now (but not necessarily "forever").

Habitual Present

Present tense is also used with active verbs to describe *something that happens routinely or habitually.* Like the present tense that is used for general statements of fact, the habitual present tense does not limit routine or habitual activities to a particular time span. Instead, it suggests a timeless quality; that is, the habit or routine that happens regularly also did so in the past and will do so in the future.

Hurran *uses* his truck to carry food and water to his family's tent camps in the desert.

When the present tense is used to describe a habitual or routine activity, it may have an adverb of frequency with it.

Each Saturday, Hurran drives into town to get food and water supplies.

He washes and waxes his truck *each week.*

FORMATION OF THE PRESENT TENSE

With regular verbs, use the *base form of the verb* for the present tense. (The base form of the verb is the dictionary entry for the verb or the infinitive without the word *to.*) Here is how the present tense verb *to love* is formed:

	Singular	**Plural**
First person	I love	We love
Second person	You love	You love
Third person	He/she/it loves	They love

Subject-Verb Agreement

Subject-verb agreement is when the verb ending correctly matches (or "agrees with") the subject. Note that in the present tense, for the third-person singular (*he/she/it*), you add *-s* or *-es*. For example:

My cousin love*s* his truck.

USING THE PAST TENSE

You may have noticed in the Gage reading that the author uses mostly past tense verbs to describe the possessions that were important to him when he was a child. If you are writing your paragraph about a possession that was important to you at an earlier time, you will also want to use mostly past tense verbs.

The Meaning and Use of Past Tense Verbs

In the following activity, you will examine sentences drawn from the Gage reading to determine the several meanings of the past tense.

❏ *ACTIVITY 1.7:* **DISCOVERING THE MEANINGS OF THE PAST TENSE**

Examine the following sentences and think of what the past tense verb in each sentence means.*

1. A cross-shaped box from my mother was in one pocket.
2. I put my hands in my pockets to inventory my treasures.
3. Mother often told us the story of my father's journey to America.

Next, read the following three questions and determine which one of the preceding sentences is the answer to the question.

1. Which sentence refers to a *single, definite event in the past?* _____

2. Which sentence refers to a *state of being in the past?* _____

3. Which sentence refers to a *sequence of events in the past—something that oc-*
curred habitually or regularly? _____

As you determined, the past tense has several different meanings. A writer can use the past tense to refer to:

- *a single, definite event in the past*

    I *put* my hands in my pockets to inventory my treasures.
    I *fingered* the reed whistle from Uncle Andreas.

In using the past tense here, the writer indicates that he is thinking of a definite, specific time in the past when this event occurred. The writer may indicate this specific, definite time with a time signal (*once, yesterday, last year*) or may only suggest it.

---

*The information in the sample sentences and exercises in this grammar section is taken from Nicholas Gage, *A Place for Us* (1989).

- *a state of being in the past*

  A cross-shaped box from my mother *was* in one pocket.

  I *had* a white handkerchief from my godmother in another pocket.

- *a sequence of events in the past—something that occurred habitually or regularly*

  Mother often *told* us the story of my father's journey to America.

  People in the village *called* mother *Amerikana*.

In the preceding examples, something took place in the past, and a period of time passed between the past event and the present moment.

FORMATION OF THE PAST TENSE

For regular verbs, you form the simple past tense by adding *-d* or *-ed* to the base form of the verb.

live   liv*ed*

ask   ask*ed*

(See Appendix B for the past tense of irregular verbs.)

PROBLEMS WITH THE PAST TENSE

One common problem writers have with the past tense is that they fail to use it where it is needed. Instead, they use the present or another tense to describe something that actually occurred in the past. If your first language does not have a tense system that distinguishes between past and present in the same way that English does, then you will need to look carefully at your verbs to make certain that you are using the past tense, not the present or another tense, for events that happened in the past.

Using the Past Tense in Describing Past Events

In describing a possession that was important to you at an earlier time, you will want to use mostly past tense verbs. You should avoid the present tense unless you have a good reason for using it. Think of your description as being centered in what we will call the "world of the past." In looking at the accompanying diagram, imagine that this "world of the past" is a world of people and events that stands completely in past time—it is over and has nothing to do with what is happening *now* in the present. Note that the centering point of this world is in past time—that is, the axis that now runs down the middle of the globe rests on a centering point in past time.

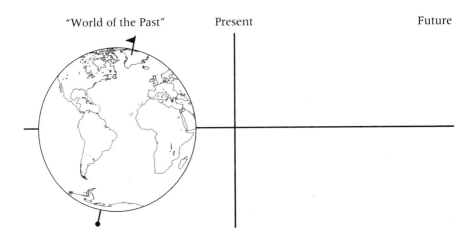

To describe events within this "world of the past," you use mostly past tense verbs. (In Chapter 5, you will learn about one other tense that you can use in the "world of the past"—the past perfect. Now, however, you should focus on mastering the past tense.)

Using the Present Tense while Describing Past Events

Only rarely should you use the present tense when describing a past event.

DO USE the present tense to show a present perspective on past events:

PRESENT TENSE   PAST TENSE
I *remember* when I *left* Greece in 1949.

DO USE the present tense within a past description or narration when you describe a "timeless truth":

PAST TENSE   PRESENT TENSE
I *realized* that people sometimes *have* different views about leaving their homeland.

However, reserve this use of the present tense in past narration for those statements that would sound awkward or be misleading if changed to the past tense:

Awkward: I *learned* from reading science books that water *froze* at 32°F.

(Suggests that water no longer freezes at 32°F.)

Clear: I learned from reading science books that water *freezes* at 32°F.

DO NOT USE the present tense to refer to habitual or regular occurrences in the past when describing past events, even though the habits or regular occurrences still may be true now. Instead, stay with the past tense because you are focusing the reader's attention on events that took place in the "world of the past"—in a world that is completely over with and thus all in past time. If you bring in the present tense, you will confuse your readers, making them wonder whether you are describing events that are happening now (in the present).

Incorrect within Description of Past Events:

I *realized* upon leaving that I *love* the beauty of Greece.

Correct within Narration of Past Events:

I realized upon leaving that I *loved* the beauty of Greece.

DO NOT USE the present tense in the analysis portion of your paragraph to describe how you felt or thought then, at that time in the past, about your possession. Instead, use the past tense. For example:

I *felt* that the stone *was* my link with Greece.

While analyzing a past event, maintain past tense verbs, even when what you are explaining is still true now:

Incorrect: I *realized* that Greece *holds* a special place in my heart.

Correct: I realized that Greece *held* a special place in my heart.

DO USE the present tense in some cases to analyze how you feel *now* about a past incident. However, if you choose the present tense for all or part of your analysis, be certain to use *a time signal (now, at this time, today)* to tell the reader that you are moving into the present tense to analyze.

Time Signal: My mother advised me to throw the stone overboard. I realize *now* that she wanted me to cut my ties with my homeland.

❏ *ACTIVITY 1.8:* **USING TIME SIGNALS**

In the following passage, the student uses time signals to indicate shifts from the past to the present tense. Underline the time signals and discuss the shifts with your classmates.

My most treasured possession is my bike, which is an efficient, two-wheeled transportation. Before my college classes started this year, my dad ran around town for approximately one month just to find this suitable, comfortable, and lasting bike for me. When I first saw it, I was disappointed because it was used, and its tires were torn. My dad, however, said that he would fix everything so that it would look brand new. He replaced the tires, cleaned the whole bike, and repainted the frame a shiny black. He also bought and attached metal "saddlebags" onto the back so I could carry my heavy books and backpack. When I ride my bike around campus now, I think of how fancy it looks. I also hear my father saying, "Ride carefully and watch out for incoming bikes and pedestrians."

❏ *ACTIVITY 1.9:* **EDITING PRACTICE FOR PRESENT AND PAST TENSES**

If time permits, identify and correct tense problems in the following two paragraphs. Notice that the first is centered in the present (with some description of past events), while the second is centered in the "world of the past." Discuss your corrections with your classmates.

Paragraph Centered in the Present

My most prized possession is a gold necklace. The necklace has a chain with the writing "Maria" on it. My mother give the necklace to me as a present for my fifteenth birthday. In my country when your age is fifteen, it means that you are not a girl or boy anymore. When you are 15, you can pass for an adult, so my mother present the necklace to me as something to remind me that I am not a child anymore. Now my mother lives far away from me, so every time I look at the necklace I remember all my mother did for me, especially her advice about being an adult.

Paragraph Centered in the "World of the Past"

When I was in high school, my favorite possession was an expensive gold pen, which my uncle gave me because I had all A's in my high school grades. Since my uncle lived in Hong Kong, he was too far away to visit me, so he send me this pen. He asked that I think of him when I used the pen. In school, if I used the pen to write an essay, I used to get a very good grade because the pen bring me confidence. At home, if my brother wanted to borrow my pen, he had to sign a special contract in order to use it. While my brother was writing with my pen, I keep my eyes on him because I am afraid that my brother would break it. When I wanted to sleep, I hid my pen in a secret place because I didn't want my brother to take it. Although it was just a pen, it helped me solve a lot of difficult problems, and it was my most prized possession.

❏ *ACTIVITY 1.10:* **EDITING PRACTICE FOR SUBJECT-VERB AGREEMENT**

If time permits, underline and correct any problems you see with subject-verb agreement in the following paragraph.

One of my most treasured possessions is a classic gold mirror compact. My friend Ji-Sook gave it to me before I left Korea because she wanted me to think of her during the time she could not be with me. When she gave me a surprise present, I couldn't say any words. I was speechless because of her thoughtful thinking and because of the beautiful gold mirror compact. On the outside of the compact, there is a picture of a girl holding many pink flowers. The picture is a little dark with gray and pink colors, and gold surround the picture. When I open the compact, I can hear a song, "Yesterday," by the Beatles. Inside, I can see my friend's picture beside a gold rose on the edge of the mirror, while my face appear inside the mirror. Whenever I see it, open it, or hear the song, it remind me of Ji-Sook, and it make me miss her a lot.

 EDITING CHECKLIST

Before revising the last draft of your paragraph about a treasured possession, check each verb carefully in terms of the following:

☐ Check that you are correctly using *present tense* to describe a possession that is important to you now: Use the present tense for each verb that describes a state of being (a general statement of fact or truth) or something that happens routinely or habitually.

☐ Check for *subject-verb agreement:* For each third-person singular subject (*he/she/it*) with a present tense verb, be certain that you have added an *-s* or *-es* to the base form of the verb.

☐ Check that you are correctly using *past tense* to describe a possession that was important to you in the past: Use the past tense for each verb that describes a single, definite event in the past; a state of being in the past; or a sequence of events in the past. Be sure that you have used the present tense within the "world of the past" only in those rare instances where it is justified (see pages 20–21).

CHAPTER 2

Writing about a Special Place

In this chapter, you will write a descriptive paragraph about a place that is special to you. In the reading that follows, writer Ved Mehta describes a place that was special to him—a broom closet at the boarding school he attended as a young boy. Reading Mehta's vivid description of the broom closet will help you learn more about what makes descriptive writing so powerful and interesting. It will also help you gather ideas for your descriptive paragraph about a special place.

In 1949, fifteen-year-old Mehta, blind since age four, left his native India to attend the Arkansas School for the Blind in Little Rock, Arkansas. After graduating from that school, he went on to study at Pomona College, Oxford University, and Harvard University. Mehta, a contributor to the *New Yorker* since 1959, has written numerous books and has received several awards for his writings, including the MacArthur Prize Fellowship, two Guggenheim Fellowships, and a Ford Foundation Grant.

In the following selection from *Sound-Shadows of the New World* (1985), Mehta describes the boarding school's broom closet, which was his special place as a young man. During his stay at the school, Mehta wrote to his father (Daddyji) in India, asking his father to urge the headmaster of the Arkansas school to provide Mehta with a small private room where he could listen to Indian music and work quietly on his writing and reading. Although the school officials were not able to offer Mehta his own dormitory room, they did offer him an old broom closet, "the size of a telephone booth," just outside the boys' sleeping hall.

▶ *BEFORE YOU READ*

1. Can you locate India on the map that appears in the front of this book?

2. Do you think it is a good idea for a school administrator to offer a blind student a broom closet as his own private space? Why or why not?

3. In the reading that follows, Mehta mentions some of the resources that were available to him—a "Talking Book" from the Library of Congress and a Braille book. He also mentions Edward R. Murrow. With your classmates, discuss what Talking Books and Braille books might be, as well as who Edward R. Murrow was.

from *SOUND-SHADOWS OF THE NEW WORLD*

VED MEHTA

The broom closet was emptied out, but the smell and the **cobwebs** seemed to **cling** to it, as if they were part of the four imprisoning walls. I at once wanted to set up my radio-phonograph, but there was no electrical **outlet.** The only electrical connection was a bulbless light **socket** dangling from the ceiling, and it didn't immediately occur to me that I could use the socket as an outlet. Moreover, I found that I couldn't set up my typewriter, because there was no **spare** table to be had in the whole school. I **concentrated** on getting a chair.

. . . I got permission . . . to move my chair [from next to my dormitory bed] into the broom closet. After that, I would slip into the closet, close the door, sit in my chair, and read a **Braille** book or just think. . . .

Although I didn't need a light, I bought a bulb and put it in the light socket.

One evening I wasn't feeling well and I went straight upstairs from supper without going to the night **session** of study hall. Someone had forgotten to switch off the radio in the lounge, and a man was speaking on it. His voice was so **hypnotic** that it drew me the way the **magnet** I used to play with as a child drew steel **pellets.** The man was giving a few items of the news of the day. He went on to **comment** on one of them in sensible but **foreboding** tones. At first, his voice reminded me of the rising of the east wind in the **Himalayas** during my early-childhood walks, then of the grave, **regal** voice of the **BBC** newsreader speaking about the worsening war as if he were the King himself, broadcasting from under the weight of his crown. Perhaps it is really Daddyji's voice speaking to me through the vastness of oceans and deserts that now separate us, I thought dreamily.

There was a **commercial** for Campbell's soup, and the man signed off with a **quotation** for the day from Mark Twain and a sort of **benediction:** "Good night and good luck." The announcer came on and invited the audience to "listen to [**Edward R.] Murrow** tomorrow."

Since the broadcasts of Edward R. Murrow **clashed** with the night session of study hall, I could hear them only on Fridays. Still, I came to think of those Friday broadcasts as my private weekly newspaper and would feel sad if I missed a word between the opening "This . . . is the news" and the closing "Good night and good luck." Murrow came to fill a **vacuum** in my life in Arkansas which I hadn't realized existed until I started listening to him. I came to hear in his broadcasts **echoes** of servants and neighbors, family and friends of my childhood discussing the crash and bang of the world war, the rumble and tumble of the British Empire, the rise and fall of **Hitler, Hirohito, Churchill, Gandhi, Jinnah.** In Arkansas, I realized, until I began listening to Murrow I had been—except for Mr. Chile's world history class—cut off from world events, almost like a boy on the moon. Now, thanks to Murrow, instead of thinking about my own problems and my own failures I came to think about world problems and world failures. I came to believe that Murrow's **sombre** comments and light **grace notes** were a perfect way to describe the world. I came to **honor** and **venerate** him, **idealize** and **identify with** him to the point where I wouldn't know what to think of a **flash bulletin** on the radio, for instance, until I had heard him discuss it. After listening to him, I would sit in my broom closet feeling the **burden** of the world on my shoulders and thinking **solemn** thoughts and wondering how I could become another Murrow. . . .

I threw myself **furiously** into **transforming** the broom closet into an **electronic listening post** [with] **dictation**-and-typing room. I bought some **planks** from a lumberyard and **lugged** them to the school's shop, where I sawed them into shelf lengths and **cleats;** I then **installed** the shelves in the broom closet in **tiers**—one broad shelf at table height for equipment, a narrower shelf above it for tape-recorder accessories, and a third, still narrower, above that for typing paper and other **stationery.** I bought from Woolworth's some electric wire, some **male and female plugs,** and some switches and switch boxes; brought an electric line down from the light socket in the broom closet; and built myself a **veritable** panel of half a dozen outlets and switches. I bought the latest-model Revere portable tape recorder, which had two tracks, took a five-inch **spool,** and ran at a speed of three and three-quarter inches a second, and along with it I bought a foot control, earphones, a tape **splicer,** and tapes. I ordered and received the special clock [timer] from New York. After what seemed like an **interminable** time—I could do my shopping and carpentry work only on weekends—I was able to hook up all my equipment through the clock and arrange my typewriter on the tablelike shelf beside the tape recorder so that I could operate both of them at once.

At all hours of the day and night, I would slip into the transformed broom closet, sit among a network of dangling wires and cables, listen to tape-recorded Murrow, and, with the aid of the foot control and the earphones, type his interesting comments into my journal. The journal grew rapidly, not only with Murrow but with quotations from other radio programs, with my own comments, and with passages from **Talking Books;** I had moved my Talking Book player into the broom closet, too, because when I was listening to books in bed I frequently dropped off to sleep, but when I sat up in my chair I was able to keep myself awake, no matter how sleepy I was. I could, in addition, tape Western classical music (something never heard in the lounge) off the air and listen to it and to my Indian records over the earphones—and nobody would know what I was doing. (I had hardly ever played my Indian records when my radio-phonograph was in the lounge, because the other boys laughed at the "**caterwauling.**") I felt that my broom closet was now a little spaceship, like the ones on the "Dimension X" radio program, and that I, its captain and sole passenger, was **surveying** events in the present world and back in history and, as it were, **logging** them for unknown generations.

▶ *AFTER YOU READ*

1. What concrete and specific details does Mehta use to describe the broom closet? Do these details create for you a vivid picture of his special place?

2. Why do you think the broom closet became Mehta's special place?

3. In what ways do you find Mehta's description of the broom closet interesting?

Supplemental Reading List—Chapter 2

Bass, Rick. *Winter: Notes from Montana.* Boston: Houghton Mifflin/Seymour Lawrence, 1991.

In *Winter,* environmentalist Bass describes winter in a small valley town in Montana. Bass, known for his descriptive, evocative style, brings the wilderness and its inhabitants to life.

✍ WRITING ASSIGNMENT: *Writing about a Special Place*

In this chapter, you will first learn more about descriptive writing and then work through the stages of the writing process to develop a paragraph about your special place. Before you begin writing, discuss the following question with your classmates. Your answer to this question will become the focus of your paragraph.

Question: What place is special to you, and why is it special?

Write a paragraph about your special place. It might be a place where you like to go to be alone or to study. Or, like Mehta's special place, it might be a place that was special to you as a child. In your paragraph, include concrete, specific details to describe the special place. Also, think about the one central point you want to make in describing the place. This central point will help you develop and arrange the details of your description.

Before you begin work on your paragraph, study the following guidelines about descriptive writing.

Guidelines on Descriptive Writing

THE CENTRAL POINT

As noted in Chapter 1, a paragraph is a group of sentences that develops one central point. In planning your descriptive paragraph about a special place, you need to think about the central point you want to convey to your reader—that is, what makes the place special to you. Perhaps the place is important to you because of the memories attached to it or because it makes you feel comfortable when you go there to read or be alone.

DESCRIPTIVE DETAILS

Much of your central point can be communicated to the reader through descriptive details. As noted in Chapter 1, concrete and specific details appeal to the reader's five senses; they also bring to mind feelings. Thus, you want to choose selectively those descriptive details that convey your central point by bringing to the reader's mind vivid images, smells, tastes, and sounds, as well as feelings associated with the details.

CONVEYING YOUR CENTRAL POINT TO THE READER

Announcing the Central Point Directly

One way to convey the central point of your descriptive paragraph is to state directly why the place is special to you. You can do this by announcing the subject of your description early in the paragraph in a topic sentence—a sentence placed near the beginning of the paragraph that announces the topic or central point of the paragraph. Later in the paragraph, you can analyze or explain to the reader why the place is special.

❏   *ACTIVITY 2.1:*   **USING A DIRECT STATEMENT OF THE CENTRAL POINT**

Read this student paragraph and discuss the questions that follow it with your classmates:

> When I became seven years old, my father made for my birthday a small playhouse that is now the most memorable place of my childhood in Korea. My father worked hard to build the house for three days, and I helped him as an assistant by looking for tools or holding a board while he drove a nail into it. After we finished putting the playhouse together, we painted the outside blue and made a little white door with a tiny bell hanging on it for visitors. Also, we covered its floor with green, soft carpet and opened two windows on each side of the walls. I loved to look through the windows to the outside world. Finally, I moved into the playhouse all of my favorite things, such as sketchbooks, color pens, comic books, and a bear doll. At that time, I really thought that nobody could get in my playhouse, so I felt very comfortable and secure when I was inside its shelter. When I felt sad or lonely, my playhouse was always there, so I ran into it. Now, I cannot have my playhouse anymore because of my age, but I keep the memories of my old playhouse in my heart.

DISCUSSION QUESTIONS

1. In which sentence early in the paragraph does the writer announce the subject (the special place) to be described?

2. In which sentences does the writer explain why this place is special to him?

3. What is the central point the writer is making about the playhouse?

4. What details in the paragraph help convey the central point?

Suggesting the Central Point

Another way to convey the central point of your paragraph is to suggest it rather than announcing it directly. Early in the paragraph, you can tell your reader about the subject to be described; throughout the remainder of the paragraph, you then let the details convey your central point about the place, using only a small amount of explanation.

❏   *ACTIVITY 2.2:*   **LETTING THE DETAILS SUGGEST THE POINT**

After reading this student paragraph, discuss the questions that follow it with your classmates:

As a child growing up in China, I lived on a farm with my grandmother during the first seven years of my life. The main entrance to her two-story brick house was just one and a half blocks away from the rice fields; therefore, the adults and the children usually gathered around the front lounge eating meals, telling stories, and resting from work. The large apple tree, famous for its cool shade during the long hot summer, stood just a few feet away from the front of the house. Little kids like myself always sat under the shade of the tree while playing stones and cards. We loved to climb the apple tree to see if there were any apples to pick or birds' eggs to take home. A very attractive part of my grandmother's house was the open ceiling in the middle of the living room, which had a built-in pool just beneath it. Although the pool was used to save water for washing clothes, I liked to jump in it and pour water all over myself. Living on the farm allowed me to realize that the most precious and valuable things about living are to enjoy life and appreciate a happy family. Even though picking flowers, climbing trees, and running around the rice field may seem silly and awkward to some people, I feel that these were some of the best experiences I had to help identify myself.

DISCUSSION QUESTIONS

1. In which sentence does the writer announce the subject of the paragraph?

2. What is the central point the writer is making about this subject?

3. In what ways do the specific details help convey the central point?

4. In which sentences does the writer directly explain why this place is special?

Conveying the Central Point with an Image

Yet another way to convey the central point of your description is by comparing two seemingly unlike things. This comparison should help the reader see more clearly the point you are making. The following are two types of comparisons: similes and metaphors.

With a *simile,* you compare two dissimilar things by using the word *like* or *as* to say that *A* is *like B.* With a *metaphor,* you also compare two unlike things, but instead of saying that *A* is *like B,* you say that *A is B.*

❑   *ACTIVITY 2.3:*   **USING A SIMILE**

Read this sentence from Mehta's description of the broom closet, in which he uses a simile to describe his situation in Arkansas. Then discuss the questions that follow with your classmates.

In Arkansas, I realized, until I began listening to Murrow I had been—except for Mr. Chile's world history class—cut off from world events, almost *like a boy on the moon.*

DISCUSSION QUESTIONS

1. What two dissimilar things does Mehta compare with this simile?

2. What picture does the simile bring to your mind? What feelings does it suggest?

3. What central point does the simile convey about Mehta's situation in Arkansas?

❑ *ACTIVITY 2.4:* **USING A METAPHOR**

In the last paragraph in the Mehta reading on pages 26–27 (the one that begins "At all hours"), Mehta uses a metaphor to bring together the central point of his description. Read this paragraph again and then discuss the following questions.

DISCUSSION QUESTIONS

1. First think of the picture you had of a broom closet before you read Mehta's description. How do you now imagine what the broom closet looked like? What did it smell like? What feelings does it bring to your mind?

2. In the central metaphor, what does Mehta say the broom closet became for him? What pictures and feelings does the metaphor bring to mind?

3. What is the central point of Mehta's description—the one he uses a metaphor to convey?

Prewriting: Gathering Ideas by Freewriting

Before you begin writing your paragraph about a special place, try the prewriting activity of *freewriting* to help you discover the details you will use as well as the central point you will make in your description. First, plan to spend about ten to fifteen minutes on freewriting. After choosing the special place you will describe, write these two questions at the top of a blank piece of paper:

1. In describing this place, what descriptive details will I include?

2. What is the overall point I want to make about the place?

Next, write nonstop on these questions, noting all of the answers that come to mind. Do not be concerned about sentence structure, grammar, or spelling. Instead, try to get down on paper all of the ideas you can think of to describe your special place. Most of all, do not stop writing. If your mind goes blank, repeat the last word you wrote down. If you cannot think of the English word, write it in your first language.

After freewriting for ten to fifteen minutes, read over what you have written. Look for concrete details you can use in your paragraph, as well as for the overall point you might make about your special place.

Drafting

Once you gather ideas about your special place and have a sense of the central point of your description, you are ready to write the first draft of your paragraph. Before you begin writing, decide whether you want to announce your central point in a topic sentence or suggest it through details or an image. Also consider which specific and concrete details will most successfully convey your central point.

Now, find a place where you feel comfortable writing and try to write your first draft in one sitting.

Revising

After completing the first draft of your paragraph about a special place, you are ready to begin revising it. Remember that during the revising stage you should not be concerned with correcting errors in sentence structure, spelling, or grammar. Rather, you should look at the paragraph as a whole, especially in terms of the overall point you are making and your development of that point.

❑ *ACTIVITY 2.5:* **PEER RESPONSE**

Working with your writing group, read each other's draft paragraphs aloud and share ideas for improving them. Use the following procedure:

1. One student should begin by reading aloud his or her draft. The group should then discuss the draft in terms of the questions listed on the Peer Response Sheet for Activity 2.5 on page 339. Another group member should record the group's comments on the sheet.

2. After you are finished filling out the sheet, give it to the writer so that he or she can consider the comments when revising the draft.

3. Repeat the procedure for each group member.

4. Then revise your own draft paragraph, keeping in mind the suggestions of your writing group.

Editing: Sentence Structure

After revising the first draft of your paragraph about a special place, you can begin editing your sentences. In addition to examining your use of verb tenses, you will need to look at the structure of your sentences. The following sections on *sentence structure* will help you detect sentence problems in your writing.

In addition, you need to focus on strengthening your writing style. One way to do this is by aiming for *sentence variety*. Whether in a paragraph or a longer piece of writing, using a variety of sentence types and lengths makes writing more interesting and easy to read.

On the following pages, you will review the basics of sentence structure and practice one type of sentence structure—coordination. This will help you achieve greater sentence variety in your writing. In later chapters, you will practice other types of sentence structure.*

WHAT IS A SENTENCE?

A *sentence* is a group of words that can stand by itself as a complete thought. For a sentence to be complete and structurally correct, it must have at least one *independent clause*, which consists of a subject and a finite verb. A sentence containing one independent clause is called a *simple sentence*.

Independent Clause		
Subject	*Finite Verb*	
Mehta	opens	the broom closet door.
He	feels	the cobwebs on the wall.
He	will need	a chair in his closet.

*The information in the example sentences and exercises in this grammar section is taken from Ved Mehta, *Sound-Shadows of the New World* (1985).

The *subject* of an independent clause may be a noun, a pronoun, a noun clause, or a nonfinite verb.* Notice that a prepositional phrase (a group of words that begins with a preposition—*in, on, at, before,* and so forth) may not serve as the subject of a sentence.

The *verb phrase* in an independent clause must contain a *finite verb.* A finite verb is a verb form that most often has a subject (which it agrees with in person and number), as well as tense or mood.

A PROBLEM WITH SENTENCE STRUCTURE: FRAGMENTS

A group of words that is punctuated as a sentence (with a period at the end) but that cannot actually stand alone is called a *fragment.* A fragment might be a clause that does not have the necessary elements to be an independent clause—a subject and a finite verb. Or, a fragment might be a dependent clause or a phrase. In the following example, the fragment is italicized:

Mehta cannot set up his radio. *Because the closet does not have an electrical outlet.*

❑ *ACTIVITY 2.6:* **CORRECTING FRAGMENTS**

Find and correct any fragments in the following paragraph about a special place.

First, look at each group of words punctuated as a sentence. Then, after identifying the fragments, revise the sentences. You may combine the fragment with another sentence that it belongs with logically, or you can add the essential elements that are missing (a subject or a finite verb). Share your revisions with your classmates.

My favorite place on campus is the grass hill overlooking Putah Creek. Just behind the administration building. The hill is covered with soft green grass and lovely oak shade trees. Families of ducks live on the creek shore. Waiting patiently for students or faculty members to bring them pieces of bread. Next to the water, there is a redwood bench; you can sit and study there. Or just watch the children playing on the edge of the water. I like to go to this grassy hillside in the late evening. When the sun is just setting. After I have spread my blanket

---

*The following are nonfinite verbs: the infinitive (as in *to walk*), the *-ing* verb form, and the *-ed/-en* verb form. The base form of the verb (the infinitive without the word *to*) may be finite or nonfinite. A nonfinite verb does not have a true subject that it agrees with in person or number, nor does it have tense (though some nonfinite verbs, such as infinitives and *-ing* or *-ed/-en* verb forms, may signal time).

on the cool grass, I lie on my back and watch the clouds overhead. After a short while at this peaceful spot. I feel relaxed and ready to go back to my studies.

SENTENCE VARIETY

In addition to correcting sentence structure problems during the editing stage, you want to vary the length and structure of your sentences. If most of your sentences are short and simple, for instance, your writing will sound monotonous because you are using too much of the same type of sentence structure. Too many short, unrelated sentences in a paragraph also make it hard for the reader to see the connections between your ideas.

❑ *ACTIVITY 2.7:* **VARYING SENTENCE STYLE**

Read aloud and then compare the two paragraphs that follow. Which is the more effective paragraph? Why?

PARAGRAPH A

My dormitory room is on the second floor of Campo Hall. It reflects my personality. First, you open the door. You can see arranged furniture and books. The small desk stands beside the door. On the white painted wall, there are some characteristic decorations. There is a "Welcome" sign with balloons. There is a Korean flag with a cross and calendars. Second, on the left-hand wall, a bookshelf stands beside the bed. Here I keep my books. I have science and religion books. Behind the door are two calendars. They are a Korean folkways calendar and a Chinese calendar. I am a person who is conservative on religion and speculative. My culture is important to me. This is seen in the decorations of my room. My room shows my neatness.

PARAGRAPH B

My dormitory room, on the second floor of Campo Hall, reflects my personality. First, as you open the door, you can see arranged furniture and books. The small desk stands beside the door. On the white painted wall, there are some characteristic decorations: a "Welcome" sign with balloons, a Korean flag with a cross, and two calendars. Second, on the left-hand wall, a bookshelf stands beside the bed. Here I keep my books, which are science and religion books. Next, behind the door are two calendars, which are a Korean folkways calendar and a Chinese calendar. I am a person who is conservative on religion and speculative; my culture is also important to me. All this, as well as my neatness, is seen in the decorations of my room.

VARYING SENTENCE STRUCTURE

To achieve sentence variety, you need to vary your sentences in terms of both their length and structure. You can vary the length of your sentences simply by making some long and others short. You will also want to use a variety of sentence structures. The following are three types of sentence structure: simple sentences, compound sentences, and complex sentences.

1. *Simple Sentence.* A *simple sentence* has one independent clause:

Independent Clause		
Subject	*Finite Verb*	
Mehta	opens	the broom closet door.

2. *Compound Sentence (Coordination).* A *compound sentence* contains two independent clauses that are joined together:

Independent Clause		Independent Clause
Mehta can smell the broom	, and	he can feel the cobwebs.

This type of joining of clauses is called *coordination.* In a compound sentence, both clauses have the same weight or importance.

3. *Complex Sentence (Subordination).* A *complex sentence* contains at least one independent clause and one dependent clause. This type of structure, called *subordination,* allows you to form a sentence in which you "subordinate" one clause (the dependent clause) to another (the independent clause).

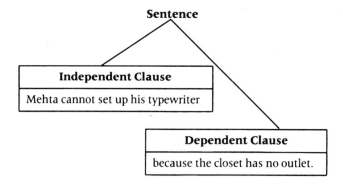

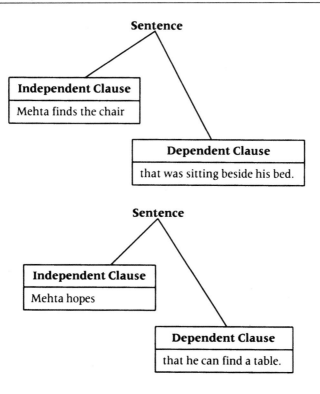

Now that you have just reviewed the simple sentence, which consists of one independent clause, and the compound sentence, which contains two independent clauses, you are ready to review coordination more fully. Coordination is used to build compound sentences. (In later chapters, you will practice building other kinds of compound sentences, as well as complex sentences.)

As you develop your writing style, you will want to build for yourself a storehouse of sentence structures by practicing and mastering different types of sentences. Having a storehouse of many sentence structures at hand will allow you to add variety to your sentences as you write and edit.

COORDINATION: FORMING COMPOUND SENTENCES

As noted earlier in the chapter, too many short, unrelated sentences in a paragraph make writing boring; they also make writing hard to read because the connections between the ideas are not clear to the reader. One simple way to solve this problem is to use coordination when joining two logically related independent clauses. The result is a compound sentence in which the two clauses have equal weight.

You can build a compound sentence by joining two logically related independent clauses in any one of the following three ways:

1. By using a semicolon:

| Independent Clause | ; | Independent Clause |

Mehta loved to listen to Murrow's voice; it reminded him of the wind in the Himalayas.

2. By using a transition:

| Independent Clause | ; transition, | Independent Clause |

Mehta could not listen to Murrow every day; *therefore,* he taped the nightly broadcasts.

3. By using a coordinate conjunction (*and, but, for, nor, or, so, yet*):

| Independent Clause | , coordinate conjunction | Independent Clause |

Mehta was alone in the broom closet, *but* he didn't feel isolated.

Joining Two Independent Clauses with a Semicolon

In some cases, you can join two logically related independent clauses with only a *semicolon(;):*

Mehta loved to listen to Murrow's voice; it reminded him of the wind in the Himalayas.

❏ *ACTIVITY 2.8:* **BUILDING COMPOUND SENTENCES**

The following compound sentences have independent clauses joined with only a semicolon. Discuss with your classmates the kinds of clauses that you think are best joined with only a semicolon. What is the logical relationship between the two clauses in each of these examples?

1. Mehta loved to listen to Murrow's voice; it reminded him of the wind in the Himalayas.
2. Listening to "Talking Books" in bed put Mehta to sleep; listening to them in the closet kept him wide awake.

Joining Two Independent Clauses with a Transition

You can also join two logically related independent clauses with a *transition* (see page 150 for a list of transitions). Notice the punctuation in this type of sentence:

Mehta could not listen to Murrow every day; *therefore,* he taped the nightly broadcasts.

Here the transition serves as a *logical connector*—a word that informs the reader of the logical relationship between the two clauses.* (You will practice forming compound sentences using transitions in Chapter 7.)

Joining Two Independent Clauses with a Coordinate Conjunction

You can also use a *coordinate conjunction* to join two logically related independent clauses. Like transitions, coordinate conjunctions serve as logical connectors. The following chart lists several coordinate conjunctions. Each conjunction tells the reader precisely what the logical relationship is between two independent clauses.

Logical Relationship	Coordinate Conjunction
Addition	*and*
Contrast	*but, yet*
Choice	*or, nor*
Cause	*for*
Result	*so*

Mehta was alone in the closet, but he didn't feel isolated.

The Coordinate Conjunctions *for, so,* and *nor*

Although *for* is rarely used in informal writing or conversation, it may be used in formal written English:

Formal: Mehta could not listen to his "Talking Books" in bed, *for* he would drop off to sleep.

Instead of using *for* in a sentence like this, writers sometimes use a subordinate conjunction like *because* or *since:*

Less Formal: Mehta could not listen to his "Talking Books" in bed *because* he would drop off to sleep.

(For more information on subordinate conjunctions, see Chapter 3.)

The coordinate conjunction *so* is used primarily in spoken English because of its informality. Therefore, you should avoid using *so* in written English for a clause that explains the result of something:

---

*If you look at the list of logical connectors in Appendix A (pages 303–304), you will see that transitions are only one type of logical connectors; other types include coordinate conjunctions and subordinate conjunctions.

Informal: The other boys laughed at Mehta's Indian music, *so* he listened to it in the broom closet.

Instead, you can use a transition—*therefore, thus, consequently*—to introduce a result clause:

The other boys laughed at Mehta's Indian music; *therefore,* he listened to it in the broom closet.

(For more on transitions as logical connectors, see Chapter 7.)

Another way to avoid the informal use of *so* is to subordinate the "cause" clause with a subordinate conjunction such as *because* or *since:*

CAUSE
Because the other boys laughed at Mehta's Indian music,

RESULT
he listened to it in the broom closet.

Note that after the coordinate conjunction *nor,* you use *question word order* * in the *nor* clause:

Mehta did not feel alone in the broom closet,

AUXILIARY VERB + SUBJECT + MAIN VERB
   nor did   *he*   *feel* cut off from the world.

❑ *ACTIVITY 2.9:* **USING COORDINATE CONJUNCTIONS**

For each of the following sentences, join the independent clauses with an appropriate coordinate conjunction and the necessary punctuation.

Coordinate Conjunctions: yet for and nor but or

1. A school administrator offered Mehta the broom closet _____ he immediately took it.

2. The broom closet was smelly and dirty _____ this did not discourage Mehta.

3. Mehta could listen to his Indian music in the closet _____ he could just think.

4. Mehta wanted to finish the closet quickly _____ he could only work on it on the weekends.

Note: Just as you do not want to overuse simple sentences, you also want to be careful about not using too many compound sentences because this too can lead to monotonous, dull writing:

*In question word order, you put the auxiliary or helping verb before the subject of the sentence. In normal word order, the subject comes before all verbs.

Mehta bought wood at the lumberyard, and he brought it to the closet. He sawed the wood into shelf lengths, and he nailed the shelves to the walls.

Instead, use compound sentences in combination with other types of sentence structures to give your writing variety and interest.

More Sentence Structure Problems: Comma Splices and Run-on Sentences

As you edit your sentences, look for two problems in forming compound sentences: comma splices and run-on sentences.

A *comma splice* occurs when two independent clauses are joined only by a comma:

Comma Splice: Mehta could listen to his tapes of Murrow's broadcasts, he could listen to his Talking Books.

Correct: Mehta could listen to his tapes of Murrow's broadcasts, *or* he could listen to his Talking Books.

A *run-on sentence* occurs when two independent clauses are joined or "run together" without any punctuation or a logical connector:

Run-on Sentence: The broom closet began as a dirty, smelly place Mehta turned it into a very special place for himself.

Correct: The broom closet began as a dirty, smelly place, *but* Mehta turned it into a very special place for himself.

(See Appendix E for further explanation of editing strategies for correcting comma splices and run-on sentences.)

❏ *ACTIVITY 2.10:* **EDITING FOR COMMA SPLICES, RUN-ONS, AND FRAGMENTS**

Find and correct any fragment, comma splice, or run-on sentence problems in the following paragraph. Share your revisions with your classmates.

My favorite spot is my hammock in the sunshine on my balcony it is a nice place to relax for a change. The mid-afternoon sunlight still dazzles me very much, even though the green leaves on the trees are beginning to change their colors. Being on this hammock is like being in the air, this small terrace seems to cling to the outside of my dormitory's second floor. The hammock makes my mind and body float wonderfully in the fine air. Whenever I am tired. Although this place is too simple to be equated with a balcony from *Romeo and Juliet,* I find it to be an especially pleasing place where I can enjoy the peaceful atmosphere. I relax on the hammock and look up into the blue sky, I can hear the jet sound of an airplane, which makes me happy. I like it. When I hear the sound, I suddenly think about where that airplane came from and where it is going. Watching the airplane and swinging in my hammock make me very relaxed and help me forget the cares of my schoolwork.

 EDITING CHECKLIST

Before revising the last draft of your paragraph about a special place, check your sentences in terms of the following:

☐ Check for *fragments:* Does each sentence have all the elements of an independent clause?

☐ Check for *sentence variety:* If you have used several simple sentences one after another, can you join any logically related sentences by using coordination?

☐ Check compound sentences for *comma splices* or *run-ons.*

☐ Check for correct use of *verb tense:*
  • mostly *present tense* for a place that is special to you now.
  • mostly *past tense* for a place that was special to you at an earlier time. (Check that you have only rarely used the present tense within this "world of the past," as noted in Chapter 1.)

CHAPTER 3

Writing about a Favorite Activity or Hobby

In Chapters 3–6, you will write *expository* paragraphs. In this type of paragraph, you state a point and then go on to explain or analyze that point.

In this chapter, you will write an expository paragraph about your favorite leisure-time activity or hobby. Before beginning your paragraph, you will read the following selection about a favorite hobby. In reading this selection, you will see the techniques a professional writer uses in vividly describing a favorite activity. What you learn from the reading will help you write your own paragraph about a favorite activity or hobby later in this chapter.

The reading is from *Naturalist* (1994), the autobiography of Edward O. Wilson. Wilson is a professor of entomology (the scientific study of insects) at Harvard University and curator of the Museum of Comparative Zoology. He is the author of a number of books, including *Insect Societies* and *The Diversity of Life*. He won two Pulitzer prizes for *The Ants* and *On Human Nature*. In *Naturalist*, Wilson describes how he became a naturalist and how he developed his ideas about evolutionary biology and biodiversity.

In this reading, Wilson describes his childhood in the mid-1930s spent exploring the waters of Florida's Gulf coast. In these early years, Wilson's favorite activity was studying the many fascinating species of animals that lived in the Gulf waters. This hobby, as Wilson explains, later led to his choice of a career as a naturalist. Events that occurred in this early time also led him to his chosen specialty within entomology—the study of ants.

▶ *BEFORE YOU READ*

1. In the reading, Wilson tells how his parents—who were getting a divorce—arranged for him to spend the summer when he was seven years old with a family living on the Gulf coast of Florida. How would you

43

imagine a seven-year-old boy would feel to be "parked," as he says, with an unfamiliar family while his parents were arranging their divorce?

2. Wilson describes in the reading several sea animals that particularly fascinated him—the jellyfish, stingray, and porpoise. Do you know what each of these animals looks like? If so, draw a picture of each on the board for your classmates.

3. Many of the animals Wilson describes in the reading are very large sea creatures. Have you ever seen a large sea creature or a large fish in a lake or ocean? If so, how did you feel about seeing it?

from *NATURALIST*

Edward O. Wilson

What happened, what we *think* happened in distant memory, is built around a small collection of **dominating** images. In one of my own from the age of seven, I stand in the **shallows** off Paradise Beach, staring down at a huge jellyfish in water so still and clear that its every detail is **revealed** as though it were trapped in glass. The creature is **astonishing.** It existed outside my previous imagination. I study it from every angle I can manage from above the water's surface. Its **opalescent** pink bell is divided by thin red lines that **radiate** from center to circular edge. A wall of **tentacles** falls from the rim to surround and partially **veil** a feeding tube and other organs, which fold in and out like the fabric of a drawn curtain. I can see only a little way into this lower **tissue** mass. I want to know more but am afraid to **wade** in deeper and look more closely into the heart of the creature.

The jellyfish, I know now, was a **sea nettle,** formal scientific name *Chrysaora quinquechirrha,* a scyphozoan, a **medusa,** a member of the **pelagic fauna** that drifted in from the Gulf of Mexico and paused in the place I found it. I had no idea then of these names from the **lexicon** of **zoology.** The only word I had heard was *jellyfish.* But what a **spectacle** my animal was, how **demeaning,** the **bastard** word used to label it. I should have been able to whisper its true name: *scy-pho-zo-an!* Think of it! I have found a scyphozoan. The name would have been a more fitting **monument** to this discovery.

The creature hung there **motionless** for hours. As evening **approached** and the time came for me to leave, its **tangled undermass** appeared to stretch deeper into the darkening water. Was this, I wondered, an animal or a collection of animals? Today I can say that it was a single animal. And that another outwardly similar animal found in the same waters, the **Portuguese man-of-war,** is a **colony** of animals so tightly joined as to form one smoothly functioning **superorganism.** Such are the general facts I recite easily now, but this sea nettle was special. It came into my world **abruptly,** from I knew not where, radiating what I cannot put into words except—*alien purpose and dark happenings in the kingdom of deep water.* The scyphozoan still **embodies,** when I **summon** its image, all the mystery and **tensed malignity** of the sea.

The next morning the sea nettle was gone. I never saw another during that summer of 1936. The place, Paradise Beach, which I have revisited in recent years, is a small settlement on the east shore of Florida's Perdido Bay, not far from Pensacola and in sight of Alabama across the water.

There was trouble at home in this season of **fantasy.** My parents were ending their marriage that year. Existence was difficult for them, but not for me, their only child, at least not yet. I had been placed in the care of family that **boarded** one or two boys during the months of the summer vacation. Paradise Beach was **paradise** truly named for a little boy. Each morning after breakfast I left the small shorefront house to wander alone in search of treasures along the **strand.** I waded in and out of the dependably warm **surf** and **scrounged** for anything I could find in the **drift.** Sometimes I just sat on a rise to **scan** the open water. Back in time for lunch, out again, back for dinner, out once again, and finally, off to bed to relive my continuing adventure briefly before falling asleep.

I have no remembrance of the names of the family I stayed with, what they looked like, their ages, or even how many there were. Most likely they were a married couple and, I am willing to suppose, caring and warmhearted people. They have passed out of memory, and I have no need to learn their **identity.** It was the animals of that place that **cast** a lasting **spell.** I was seven years old, and every **species,** large and small, was a wonder to be examined, thought about, and, if possible, **captured** and examined again.

There were **needlefish,** foot-long green **torpedoes** with slender beaks, **cruising** the water just beneath the surface. Nervous in **temperament,** they kept you in sight and never let you come close enough to reach out a hand and catch them. I wondered where they went at night, but never found out. Blue **crabs** with skin-piercing **claws scuttled** close to shore at **dusk.** Easily caught in long-handled nets, they were boiled and cracked open and eaten straight or added to gumbo, the spicy seafood stew of the Gulf coast. Sea trout and other fish worked deeper water out to the nearby **eelgrass flats** and perhaps beyond; if you had a boat you could cast for them with bait and **spinners. Stingrays,** carrying threatening **lances** of bone flat along their muscular tails, buried themselves in the bottom sand of hip-deep water in the daytime and moved close to the surf as darkness fell.

One late afternoon a young man walked past me along the beach **dangling** a **revolver** in his hand, and I fell in behind him for a while.

He said he was hunting stingrays. Many young men, my father among them, often took guns on such **haphazard excursions** into the countryside, mostly .22 pistols and rifles but also heavier handguns and shotguns, **recreationally** shooting any living thing they **fancied** except **domestic** animals and people. I thought of the stingray hunter as a kind of **colleague** as I trailed along, a fellow adventurer, and hoped he would find some exciting kind of animal I had not seen, maybe something big. When he had gone around a bend of the **littoral** and out of sight I heard a gun pop twice in quick **succession.** Could a bullet from a light handgun **penetrate** water deep enough to hit a stingray? I think so but never tried it. And I never saw the young **marksman** again to ask him.

How I longed to discover animals each larger than the last, until finally I caught a **glimpse** of some true giant! I knew there were large animals out there in deep water. Occasionally a school of **bottlenose porpoises** passed offshore less than a stone's throw from where I stood. In pairs, **trios,** and **quartets** they cut the surface with their backs and **dorsal fins, arced** down and out of sight, and broke the water again ten or twenty yards farther on. Their repetitions were so **rhythmic** that I could pick the spot where they would appear next. On calm days I sometimes scanned the glassy surface of Perdido Bay for hours at a time in the hope of spotting something huge and **monstrous** as it rose to the surface. I wanted to at least see a **shark,** to watch the **fabled** dorsal fin **thrust** proud out of the water, knowing it would look a lot like a porpoise at a distance but would surface and sound at irregular intervals. I also hoped for more than sharks, what exactly I could not say: something to **enchant** the rest of my life.

Almost all that came into sight were clearly porpoises, but I was not completely disappointed. Before I tell you about the one **exception,** let me say something about the **psychology** of **monster** hunting. Giants exist as a state of mind. They are defined not as an **absolute** measurement but as a **proportionality.** I **estimate** that when I was seven years old I saw animals at about twice the size I see them now. The bell of a sea nettle averages ten inches across, I know that now; but the one I found seemed two feet across—a grown man's two feet. So giants can be real, even if adults don't choose to **classify** them as such. I was **destined** to meet such a creature at last. But it would not appear as a **swirl** on the surface of the open water.

It came close in at dusk, suddenly, as I sat on the dock leading away from shore to the family boathouse raised on **pilings** in shallow water. In the failing light I could barely see to the bottom, but I stayed **perched** on the dock anyway, looking for any creature large or small that might be moving. Without warning a gigantic **ray,** many times larger than the stingrays of common experience, **glided** silently out of the darkness, beneath my dangling feet, and away into the depths on the other side. It was gone in seconds, a circular shadow, seeming to **blanket** the whole bottom. I was thunderstruck. And immediately seized with a need to see this **behemoth** again, to capture it if I could, and to examine it close up. Perhaps, I thought, it lived nearby and cruised around the dock every night.

Late the next afternoon I **anchored** a line on the dock, **skewered** a live **pinfish** on the biggest hook I could find in the house, and let the bait sit in six feet of water overnight. The following morning I rushed out and pulled in the line. The bait was gone; the hook was bare. I repeated the **procedure** for a week without result, always losing the pinfish. I might have had better luck in **snagging** a ray if I had used shrimp or crab for bait, but no one gave me this beginner's advice. One morning I pulled in a Gulf toadfish, an **omnivorous** bottom-**dweller** with a huge mouth, **bulging** eyes, and **slimy** skin. Locals consider the species a trash fish and one of the ugliest of all sea creatures. I thought it was wonderful. I kept my toadfish in a bottle for a day, then let it go. After a while I stopped putting the line out for the great ray. I never again saw it pass beneath the dock.

Why do I tell you this little boy's story of medusas, rays, and sea monsters, nearly sixty years after the fact? Because it **illustrates,** I think, how a naturalist is **created.** A child comes to the edge of deep water with a mind prepared for wonder. He is like a **primitive** adult of long ago, an **acquisitive** early *Homo* arriving at the shore of **Lake Malawi,** say, or the **Mozambique Channel.** The experience must have been repeated countless times over the thousands of **generations,** and it was richly rewarded. The sea, the lakes, and the broad rivers served as **sources** of food and **barriers** against enemies. No **petty boundaries** could split their flat **expanse.** They could not be burned or **eroded** into **sterile gullies.** They were **impervious,** it seemed, to change of any kind. The waterland was always there, timeless, **invulnerable,** mostly beyond reach, and **inexhaustible.** The child is ready to **grasp** this **archetype,** to **explore** and learn, but he has few words to describe his guiding **emotions.** Instead he is given a **compelling** image that will serve in later life as a **talisman, transmitting** a powerful energy that directs the growth of experience and knowledge. He will add **complicated** details and **context** from his **culture** as he grows older. But the **core** image stays intact. When an adult he will find it **curious,** if he is at all **reflective,** that he had the urge to travel all day to fish or to watch sunsets on the ocean horizon.

Hands-on experience at the **critical** time, not systematic knowledge, is what counts in the making of a naturalist. Better to be an **untutored savage** for a while, not to know the names or anatomical detail. Better to spend long **stretches** of time just searching and dreaming. Rachel Carson, who understood this principle well, used different words to the same effect in *The Sense of Wonder* in 1965: "If facts are the seeds that later produce knowledge and wisdom, then the emotions and the **impressions** of the senses are the **fertile** soil in which the seeds must grow. The years of childhood are the time to prepare the soil." She **wisely** took children to the edge of the sea.

The summer at Paradise Beach was for me not an educational exercise planned by adults, but an accident in a haphazard life. I was parked there in what my parents **trusted** would be a safe and **care-free environment.** During that brief time, however, a second accident **occurred** that determined what kind of naturalist I would **eventually** become. I was fishing on the dock with **minnow** hooks and rod, **jerking** pinfish out of the water as soon as they **struck** the bait. The species, *Lagodon rhomboides,* is small, **perchlike,** and **voracious.** It carries ten needlelike **spines** that stick straight up in the **membrane** of the dorsal fin when it is threatened. I carelessly **yanked** too hard when one of the fish pulled on my line. It flew out of the water and into my face. One of its spines **pierced** the **pupil** of my right eye.

The pain was **excruciating,** and I suffered for hours. But being anxious to stay outdoors, I didn't complain very much. I continued fishing. Later, the host family, if they understood the problem at all (I can't remember), did not take me in for medical treatment. The next day the pain had **subsided** into mild discomfort, and then it **disappeared.** Several months later, after I had returned home to Pensacola, the pupil of the eye began to cloud over with a **traumatic cataract.** As soon as my parents noticed the change, they took me to the old Pensacola Hospital to have the **lens** removed. The **surgery** was a **terrifying** nineteenth-century **ordeal.** Someone held me down while the **anesthesiologist,** a woman named Pearl Murphy, placed a **gauze** nose **cone** over my nose and mouth and **dripped ether** into it. Her fee for this **standard** service, I learned many years later, was five dollars. As I lost **consciousness,** I dreamed I was all alone in a large **auditorium.** I was tied to a chair, **unable** to move, and screaming. Possibly I was screaming in **reality** before I went under. In any case the experience was almost as bad as the cataract. For years afterward I became **nauseous** at the smell of ether. Today I suffer from just one **phobia:** being trapped in a closed space with my arms **immobilized** and my face covered with an **obstruction.** The **aversion** is not an ordinary **claustrophobia.** I can enter closets and elevators and crawl beneath houses and automobiles with **aplomb.** In my teens and twenties I explored caves and underwater **recesses** around **wharves** without fear, just so long as my arms and face were free.

I was left with full sight in the left eye only. Fortunately, that vision proved to be more **acute** at close range than average—20/10 on the **ophthalmologist's** chart—and has remained so all my life. I lost **stereoscopy** but can make out fine print and the hairs on the bodies of small insects. In **adolescence** I also lost, possibly as the result of a **hereditary defect,** most of my hearing in the **uppermost registers.** Without a hearing aid, I cannot make out the calls of many bird and frog species. So when I set out later as a teenager with Roger Tory Peterson's *Field Guide to the Birds* and **binoculars** in hand, as all true naturalists in America must at one time or other, I proved to be a **wretched** birdwatcher. I couldn't hear birds; I couldn't **locate** them unless they **obligingly fluttered** past in clear view; even one bird singing in a tree close by was **invisible** unless someone pointed a finger straight at it. The same was true of frogs. On rainy spring nights my college **companions** could walk to the **mating** grounds of frogs guided only by the high-**pitched** calls of the males. I managed a few, such as the deep-voiced barking tree frog, which sounds like a soul on its way to **perdition;** but from most species all I **detected** was a **vague buzzing** in the ears.

In one important respect the turning wheel of my life came to a **halt** at this very early age. I was destined to become an **entomologist, committed** to **mute** crawling and flying insects, not by any touch of **idiosyncratic genius,** not by **foresight,** but by a **fortuitous constriction** of **physiological** ability. I had to have one kind of animal if not another, because fire had been lit and I took what I could get. The attention of my **surviving** eye turned to the ground. I would thereafter **celebrate** the little things of the world, the animals that can be picked up between thumb and **forefinger** and brought close for inspection.

▶ *AFTER YOU READ*

1. As Wilson stood in the water or above the water watching animals in the Gulf, how did he feel? Why did the sea creatures fascinate him? Why do you think looking for and observing sea creatures was his favorite activity as a young boy?

2. In the reading, Wilson says that a "child comes to the edge of deep water with a mind prepared for wonder." The powerful images the child receives there, according to Wilson, are the most important factors in making the child a naturalist. Do you agree with Wilson that it is best for a child to begin with "hands-on experience" of nature, or do you think it is best for children to gain systematic knowledge of names, facts, and anatomical detail before exploring nature?

3. Wilson describes how a fishing accident caused loss of sight in one eye, while heredity led to loss of hearing in the upper registers. This ultimately meant that he was limited in his choices of a field of study within zoology. How would you expect a young boy or a young man choosing a career to feel about losing sight in one eye and part of his hearing? What do you think was Wilson's attitude toward these limitations in his life?

4. Do you think this is an interesting and powerful reading? If so, why?

Supplemental Reading List—Chapter 3

Bonner, John Tyler. *Life Cycles: Reflections of an Evolutionary Biologist.* Princeton: Princeton University Press, 1993.

If you are interested in science, you will enjoy reading Bonner's book about his life and his developing interest in biology.

The New York Times—Tuesday Science Section.

If you are interested in science, you will also enjoy reading the science sections in Tuesday's edition of *The New York Times* (which you will most likely find in your library). The Tuesday science section contains articles on the latest science topics. These articles are written for non-science readers.

✏️ **WRITING ASSIGNMENT:** *Writing about a Favorite Activity or Hobby*

In this chapter, you will first study expository writing and then work through the stages of the writing process to develop your own expository paragraph. Before you begin writing, discuss the following question with your classmates. Your answer to this question will become the focus of your expository paragraph.

Question: What is your favorite activity or hobby, and why do you enjoy it?

Write a paragraph about the one thing that you like most to do during your free time. Be sure to use specific and concrete details to develop for your reader a word picture of the activity. Also remember to analyze the point of your expository paragraph by explaining to the reader why the activity is your favorite.

Guidelines on Expository Writing

In an expository paragraph, you explain or analyze a central point. In this section, you will learn how to state the point of your expository paragraph in a topic sentence and to develop that point with evidence and analysis.

TOPIC SENTENCE

In earlier chapters, you learned that a paragraph is a group of sentences unified around a central point. When you wrote your descriptive paragraphs, you chose either to state the point of the paragraph directly (by announcing it in a topic sentence near the beginning of the paragraph) or indirectly (by suggesting it).

In expository paragraphs, academic writers usually state their central point near the beginning of the paragraph in a topic sentence. You may think of a *topic sentence* as the sentence in which you directly announce or state the point of your paragraph to the reader, rather than only suggesting the point within the paragraph. In the topic sentence, you are saying to the reader: "Here is the point I am going to prove in this paragraph." Once you announce your point, the reader then knows what to expect in the remainder of the paragraph. By keeping this point in mind, the reader can more easily read the paragraph.

For example, one student announced his central point in a topic sentence in this way:

Topic Sentence: My favorite hobby is playing Mah-Jong, which is a Chinese game played with tiles.

This topic sentence brings many questions to the reader's mind: "What is Mah-Jong?" "Why does the writer like to play Mah-Jong?" and "Why is it the writer's favorite hobby?" The reader then expects the writer to answer these questions in the remainder of the paragraph. After reading the paragraph, the reader is satisfied because the questions have been answered.

❏ *ACTIVITY 3.1:* **LOCATING THE TOPIC SENTENCE**

As you read this student paragraph about a favorite hobby, identify the writer's topic sentence by putting it in brackets: [   ]. Then discuss the questions that follow the paragraph with your classmates.

My favorite hobby is going fishing with my best friend Tan on Saturdays. We wake up at the crack of dawn, as the thick darkness is turning into daylight. We then begin to drive up to Folsom Lake, which is a very peaceful place. There we can see the fog floating above the lake's surface, revealing the clear blue water. Once in a while, we cast a fishing line. As soon as the weight hits the water, it makes a splashing sound. Sometimes we have to sit there for hours before a fish finally bites the bait. When I begin to pull it in, the pole starts to bend as my arms are shaking, but I still keep on turning the wheel. The exciting part is feeling my body react like a baby who just got a new toy, while the challenging part is keeping the trout from escaping my hook. Fishing at Folsom Lake makes me forget about school and all my distressing problems. Whenever I am out on the lake, I feel no pressure or demands, and it is very relaxing. When Monday morning classes come, the day goes by fast because the memories of my hours fishing on Folsom Lake are still fresh in my mind.

DISCUSSION QUESTIONS

1. Which sentence is the writer's topic sentence?

2. Does the topic sentence help you, as the reader, to understand the central point of the paragraph? Why or why not?

At first, including a topic sentence near the beginning of a paragraph may seem too direct to you. You may feel that stating your point so directly to the reader seems impolite or rude. Or, you may have been taught in your culture that announcing a point directly may offend readers, suggesting that they are not able to see the point themselves. However, in academic and other types of writing, readers often expect to know the point of a paragraph early on. Readers want to know your central point at the start of a paragraph because it helps them understand what follows in the paragraph.

EVIDENCE AND ANALYSIS

After you state the central point of your expository paragraph in a topic sentence, you then go on to develop that point through evidence and analysis.

Evidence

Evidence is the specific detail or "proof" that you use to support or "prove" the overall point of your paragraph. Evidence includes, for instance, specific and descriptive details, examples, facts, figures, and quotations.

You need to think about your reader's expectations when choosing your evidence. That is, once you announce your central point in a topic sentence, what will the reader then expect to hear about that point in the remainder of the paragraph? For example, if your topic sentence states that Mah-Jong is your favorite hobby, then the reader will expect you to describe all the details about Mah-Jong: What is Mah-Jong? How do you play it? What is it like when you play Mah-Jong with friends? Why do you enjoy playing Mah-Jong?

Above all, evidence is *specific*, not general. It includes:

Specific, concrete descriptive words

Specific examples from your experience or observation

Specific facts, data

Specific quotations

❏ *ACTIVITY 3.2:* **LOCATING THE EVIDENCE**

Reread the student paragraph in Activity 3.1, this time underlining the specific evidence (descriptive words, examples, facts) that the writer uses to develop the central point and to create in the reader's mind a vivid picture of the hobby. Then answer the following questions.

DISCUSSION QUESTIONS

1. Does the paragraph have enough specific evidence (details, facts, examples, quotations) to give the reader a clear picture of the activity or hobby?

2. Does the writer need to add more specific evidence?

Analysis

In addition to evidence, you need to support the central point of the topic sentence with *analysis*. Think of evidence as the "proof" and analysis as the explanation of your central point. Thus, in an expository paragraph, you (1) state your point, (2) present your evidence to support the point, and (3) analyze or explain the evidence in terms of the central point.

To decide what you need to discuss in your analysis, you need to think about the overall point of your paragraph. Consider again the question you are answering for this chapter's Writing Assignment: What is your favorite activity or hobby and why do you enjoy it? Note that you are being asked to do more than simply write a paragraph describing one of your hobbies; you are also being asked to *explain why* that hobby is your *favorite* hobby. Thus, in your analysis, you need to explain to your reader why this hobby is your favorite one, why it is enjoyable to you.

❏ *ACTIVITY 3.3:* **LOCATING THE ANALYSIS**

Read again the student paragraph in Activity 3.1. This time, though, look for the writer's analysis. Circle the phrases or sentences in which the writer explains the evidence—telling the reader *why* fishing is his favorite leisure-time activity. Remember that evidence includes specific, concrete details (words that appeal to the five senses), whereas analysis consists of more general, abstract ideas (in this case, ideas about what makes fishing enjoyable for the writer). Try to identify the abstract ideas that make up the writer's analysis, even though these abstract ideas may be accompanied by specific details.

Prewriting: Gathering Ideas
by Tree Diagraming

Now that you have a sense of how to develop an expository paragraph, you are ready to begin work on your paragraph about a favorite hobby. To generate ideas about your topic, try the prewriting technique of *tree diagraming.*

Like the clustering technique discussed in Chapter 1, tree diagraming involves drawing a picture of your ideas. With tree diagraming, however, you allow your ideas to branch out over half the page. First, write the controlling question you are answering at the top of a blank piece of paper. Then write down everything that comes to mind about your favorite activity or hobby and draw lines or "branches" as shown in the accompanying example.

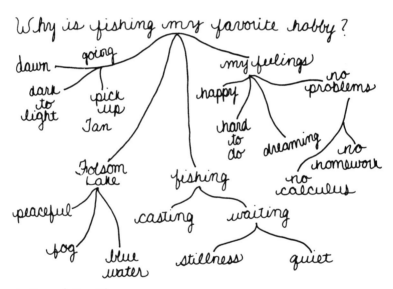

An Example Tree Diagram

USING A BOX DIAGRAM TO ORGANIZE YOUR IDEAS

After you have generated ideas about your topic with a tree diagram, you are ready to plan by focusing and organizing those ideas. Some writers like to do a great deal of planning before they begin drafting, while others prefer to make only a simple, rough plan of their ideas before writing. With practice, you will develop a style of planning that works best for you.

First, look over your tree diagram and decide which ideas you will use. Then create a rough plan of what you will say in the paragraph. One way to plan a paragraph involves drawing a *box diagram* like the one in the accompanying example. Here the student wrote the topic sentence at the top of the box and then jotted down a few ideas about specific evidence and a few notes about analysis.

T. S. My favorite hobby is fishing with my friend Jan.

Evidence:
wake up, drive to Folsom
fishing — casting, waiting,
struggling with a fish

Analysis:
peaceful
exciting.
challenging
relaxing - wipes out
problems

An Example Box Diagram

Drafting

Now that you have a rough plan for your paragraph about a favorite activity, you are ready to begin drafting it. Try to work in a quiet place and to complete the first draft in one sitting. This will help you arrange the ideas in your paragraph so that they follow smoothly, one after another. If you try to write your paragraph in more than one sitting, it will be more difficult to arrange your ideas logically.

Revising

Before sharing your rough draft with your writing group, practice evaluating the two student drafts that follow in Activity 3.4.

❏ *ACTIVITY 3.4:* **EVALUATING TWO STUDENTS'**
     PARAGRAPHS

One member of your writing group should read paragraph A aloud. Then the group should discuss the paragraph in terms of the following questions. Repeat the same procedure for paragraph B.

DISCUSSION QUESTIONS

1. *Topic Sentence:* Does the paragraph contain a topic sentence near the beginning that announces the central point? If not, is the point of the paragraph clear? Is the central point of the paragraph an answer to the controlling question of the writing assignment? Discuss your suggestions for improvement.

2. *Specific Evidence:* Does the paragraph have enough specific evidence (details, facts, examples, quotations) to give the reader a clear, sharp picture of the activity or hobby? Discuss your suggestions for improvement.

3. *Analysis:* Does the paragraph contain enough analysis to explain the evidence? In other words, does the writer explain why the hobby is a favorite? Discuss your suggestions for improvement.

PARAGRAPH A

My favorite hobby is playing the guitar. For me, my classical guitar is special and differs from others. First, it is handmade, and the sound is very clear and sharp. Second, the guitar's strings never get too loose; you just need to set the chords to the right tune, and then you can play as long as you want. At night, after my family goes to bed, I take it out from its box and lock myself into my room. I usually start by playing "Romance d'Amour," which is an old song written in the Middle Ages. It is a love song and consists of guitar melodies only. After "Romance d'Amour," I usually exercise my fingers by moving them on the guitar's frets, which are ridges across the fingerboard. I also like to find new melodies and new sounds on the guitar.

PARAGRAPH B

My favorite leisure-time activity is camping in the Santa Cruz forest, which is located along the coast of California. Although it takes me about an hour by car to get to the camping area, I still am willing to drive there because camping in this forest is one of the most enjoyable things in my life. I usually go there in the early morning because I do not want to miss any part of the camping day. In the early morning, I go hiking up to a mountain. During my hiking, I can breathe the fresh air in the redwood forest, which is incomparable to the polluted air in the city where I live. Hiking is a challenging and healthy exercise. I find it a very interesting activity because it requires a lot of courage, strength, and patience to arrive at my destination, which is the top of a very high mountain. However, the reward is worth it. Standing or sitting on the top of the very high mountain, I can see the beauty of the sunrise. On the way back, I just take my time to look at the natural, colorful landscapes and to listen to the singing of different kinds of birds. The many bird songs create a very special symphony. After I have finished my hike, I enjoy my breakfast cooked on a rock oven over firewood. In the afternoon, I go swimming in a clean and peaceful river with a beautiful beach of pale beige sand. In the late afternoon, I go fishing at the creek. I love camping there because I enjoy being out in nature and getting away from all of my responsibilities.

❏   *ACTIVITY 3.5:* **PEER RESPONSE**

Now share your draft paragraph with your writing group. Use the following procedure:

1. One group member should begin by reading aloud his or her rough draft. The group should then discuss the paragraph in terms of the questions listed on the Peer Response Sheet for Activity 3.5 on page 341. Another member should record the group's comments on the sheet.

2. After you are finished filling out the sheet, give it to the writer so that he or she can consider the comments when revising the draft.

3. Repeat the procedure for each group member.

4. Then revise your own draft paragraph, keeping in mind the suggestions of your writing group.

Editing: Adverbial Clauses

In Chapter 2, you learned about three basic ways of building a sentence and the importance of using different types of sentence structure to give your writing variety. Here again are three basic types of sentence structure:

1. *Simple Sentence* = One independent clause:

Sharzad loves to ride her bike on weekends.

2. *Compound Sentence* (coordination) = Two or more independent clauses:

Independent Clause		Independent Clause
Sharzad loves to ride her bike	, but	her sister likes to walk.

3. *Complex Sentence* (subordination) = One independent clause (minimum) + one dependent clause (minimum):

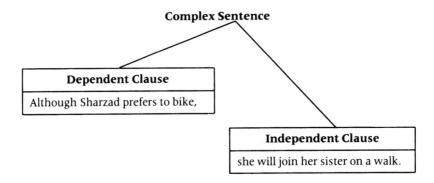

With *subordination,* you join together at least one dependent clause and at least one independent clause to form a complex sentence. That is, you "subordinate" one clause (the dependent clause) to another (the independent clause). For example, you can subordinate one clause to another by using an adverbial clause, an adjective clause, or a noun clause. In this chapter, you will learn how to use adverbial clauses. (Chapters 8 and 10 will show you how to use adjective and noun clauses.)

WHAT IS AN ADVERBIAL CLAUSE?

One way to subordinate one clause to another clause is by using a *subordinate conjunction as a logical connector* to connect the two clauses. Subordinate conjunctions (*because, since, although, while, when,* and others) show the reader the logical relationship between the independent and the dependent clauses in a sentence. When you use a subordinate conjunction to begin a dependent clause, the resulting dependent clause is called an *adverbial clause* because it works like an adverb in modifying the verb of the main clause or the entire main clause.

Punctuating Adverbial Clauses

First look at the two following example sentences. What do you notice about the punctuation of adverbial clauses?

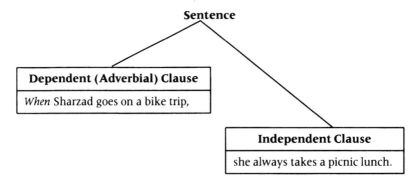

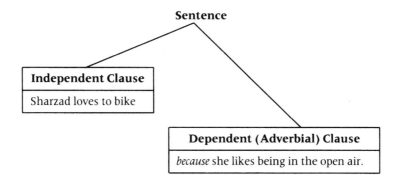

Now circle the correct punctuation in the parentheses:

When the dependent clause comes first, you put (*a comma, no comma*) after it.

When the dependent clause comes last, you put (*a comma, no comma*) before it.

Why Use Adverbial Clauses?

Adverbial clauses are particularly helpful in building the analysis of expository paragraphs and essays. In expository writing, you analyze and explain your point to the reader. Thus, instead of simply bringing in the facts of the evidence, you also explain what that evidence means. Adverbial clauses allow you to build this kind of analysis into your writing because such clauses answer the questions that your reader is most likely to ask about the evidence. For example, if you are writing about fishing as your favorite hobby, the reader will probably want answers to these questions:

When?

As soon as the sun rises, we wake up to go fishing.

Where?

We like to fish *where* there are no other people fishing.

How?

Tan baits the hook *as* I have shown him in the past.

Why?

I love fishing *because* all my problems disappear when I'm on the lake.

Adverbial clauses also give you an additional means of achieving sentence variety and thereby help the reader see the connections between your ideas. Rather than presenting one simple sentence after another and expecting the reader to make the connections between your ideas, you can use subordinate conjunctions to tell your reader precisely what those connections are.

SUBORDINATE CONJUNCTIONS AS LOGICAL CONNECTORS

As noted earlier, in building an adverbial clause, you use a subordinate conjunction as a logical connector to make the logical relationship between independent and dependent clauses clear to the reader. Here is a list of subordinate conjunctions and the logical relationships they convey:

Logical Relationship	Subordinate Conjunction
Time	when whenever since while before after until as as soon as as long as once
Place	where wherever
Contrast	although though even though while whereas
Manner	as
Cause	because since as

Subordinate Conjunctions Signaling Time

Logical Relationship	Subordinate Conjunction
Time	when whenever since while before after until as as soon as as long as once

Subordinate conjunctions that signal time are divided into the following groups:

Time Before:

Before Luis and Jorges have a party, they clean their apartment.

They keep cleaning *until* the apartment is spotlessly clean.

Same Time:

When Luis and Jorges have finished cleaning, they make up a guest list.

While Luis thinks of friends' names, Jorges writes them down.

As they are making up the guest list, they also begin thinking of music for the party.

As long as Luis and Jorges have been roommates, they have enjoyed having parties on the weekends.

Time After:

After Luis and Jorges make a list of food for the party, they decide to call Maria to help out.

They have known Maria *since* she moved next door one year ago.

Time Immediately After:

As soon as Maria arrives, the three friends start telephoning people on the guest list.

Once they have called everyone on the list, they decide to take a break.

Anytime:

Whenever Luis and Jorges have a party, everyone invited seems to come.

Note: When the dependent clause refers to future time, you usually use the present tense (not the future tense) in the dependent clause:

Incorrect:

Jorges and Luis will clean their apartment when they *will have* time.

Correct:

Jorges and Luis will clean their apartment when they *have* time.

Complete the following sentence by adding a clause that fits logically with the connector *when*. Be careful of tense.

Luis will buy the food *when* _____

_____.

If the verb in the independent clause is a past tense verb (past, past progressive, or past perfect), the verb in the dependent clause usually must also be a past tense verb (not a present tense verb):

Correct:

PAST PROGRESSIVE   PAST

Maria *was baking* a cake when the phone *rang.*

❏ *ACTIVITY 3.6:* **SIGNALING TIME**

Complete each of the following sentences by adding a clause that logically fits the other clause in the sentence:

1. *When* she heard that Luis and Jorges were having a birthday party for Ina, Maria _____.

2. Luis and Jorges like to have a party *whenever* _____

_____.

3. Mia has lived next door to Luis and Jorges *since* _____

_____.

4. For Ina's birthday party, Mia arrived at Luis and Jorges's apartment *before* _____.

5. *After* Chang and Bryant had blown up the balloons, they_____

_____.

6. Chad decided not to light the fire for the barbecue *until* _____

_____.

7. *As* Hamon cut up the lettuce for the salad, Ingrid_____

_____.

8. Luis said, "We will serve dinner *as soon as* _____

_____."

9. *As long as* everyone was enjoying the music, Luis_____

_____.

10. Jorges said, "We can cut the cake *now that*_____

_____."

11. *Once* the cake was finished, _____

_____.

12. *While* Aldo served the ice cream, Jong _____

_____.

13. *By the time* the party was over, _____

_____.

Subordinate Conjunctions Signaling Place

Logical Relationship	Subordinate Conjunction
Place	where wherever

The subordinate conjunctions *where* and *wherever* are used to signal place. *Where* refers to a definite place:

Maria likes to play tennis *where* the court is made of clay.

Wherever refers more generally to any place:

Maria and her friends will play tennis *wherever* there is an empty court.

❑ *ACTIVITY 3.7:* **SIGNALING PLACE**

Complete each of the following sentences by adding a clause that logically fits the other clause in the sentence:

1. Maria wants to live *where* _____

_____.

2. *Wherever* her friends choose to play tennis, Maria _____

_____.

Subordinate Conjunctions Signaling Contrast

Logical Relationship	Subordinate Conjunction
Contrast	although though even though while whereas

Subordinate conjunctions of contrast fall into two groups. First, *although, though,* and *even though* signal a mild or only partial contrast to the reader:

Although Bachmai needs to save her money, she often spends it on her favorite activity of going to the movies.

Though she likes all kinds of movies, comedies are her favorite.

Second, *while* and *whereas* signal a stronger contrast and sometimes even complete opposition:

While Bachmai prefers comedies, her brother Wing loves horror films.

Her cousin Wai thinks theater is the best entertainment, *whereas* Bachmai believes movies provide more entertainment for your money.

As noted earlier, when the dependent clause comes first in the sentence, you put a comma after it. When the dependent clause comes last in the sentence, you put no comma before it. However, when a subordinate conjunction of contrast introduces a dependent clause that comes last in a sentence, you often do need a comma before the dependent clause:

Bachmai likes to watch videos at home, *although* she would rather see a movie in the theater.

❏ *ACTIVITY 3.8:* **SIGNALING CONTRAST**

Complete each of the following sentences by adding a clause that logically fits the other clause in the sentence. Be sure to include punctuation where it is necessary.

1. *Although* Bachmai prefers comedies, she also _____

_____.

2. *Even though* horror films are her brother's favorites, she _____

_____.

3. *While* Wing thinks the best evening's entertainment is a Stephen King horror film, his cousin Wai believes _____.

Subordinate Conjunction Signaling Manner

Logical Relationship	Subordinate Conjunction
Manner	as

As you learned earlier, *as* can signal time in terms of "same time":

Maya and her cousin Sami like to take a picnic lunch to the beach on Saturdays. Maya unpacks the picnic basket *as* Sami lays out the beach blanket.

Here *as* means the same thing as the logical connector of time *while*. Yet *as* can also signal manner, meaning "in the manner or way that":

Maya carefully packs the picnic basket *as* her mother has shown her.

❏ *ACTIVITY 3.9:* **SIGNALING MANNER**

Complete each of the following sentences by adding a clause that logically fits the other clause in the sentence:

1. Maya _____

as her swimming instructor has taught her.

2. Maya _____

as Sami is getting out of the water.

Subordinate Conjunctions Signaling Cause

Logical Relationship	Subordinate Conjunction
Cause	because since as

The subordinate conjunctions *because, since,* and *as* signal cause. Use these subordinate conjunctions to introduce the "cause" clause in a sentence that has one "cause" and one "result" clause.

In the following sentences, put brackets [ ] around the independent and dependent clauses. Then label the clauses, showing which clause is the "cause" clause and which is the "result" clause. The first example is done for you.

Every afternoon, [Shumeye likes to run on the school's track] [since most runners on the track team run there.]

Shumeye likes to run with other runners because he can talk with them about running and other things.

He tries to run six to seven miles since this is what his coach suggests.

❏ *ACTIVITY 3.10:* **SIGNALING CAUSE**

Complete each of the following sentences by adding a clause that logically fits the other clause in the sentence. Also, be sure to include punctuation where it is needed.

1. *Because* it is hard to exercise alone Shumeye _____

_____ .

2. Shumeye will be in good shape by the end of the year *since* _____

_____.

3. Shumeye doesn't think he is ready for the varsity track team *as* _____

_____.

❏ *ACTIVITY 3.11:* **USING SUBORDINATE CONJUNCTIONS**

For each pair of sentences that follows, use an appropriate subordinate conjunction to join them into one sentence. Refer to the list of subordinate conjunctions on page 60 as needed. Be sure to punctuate the new sentences if necessary. In some cases, you may need to change words or add words in order to combine the sentence pairs.

The following sentences are about two Nigerian students, Albert and Aloo, who are attending a college near Boston, Massachusetts. On weekends, their favorite activity is to go into Boston and see the sights.

1. Albert and Aloo were visiting Boston last week. They decided to attend a play.

_____

_____

_____

2. They chose the play *No Exit.* Aloo's roommate had recommended it.

_____

_____

3. Aloo and Albert had a limited budget. They decided to take the subway to the play.

_____

_____

4. The play was good. They wished they had gone to the Boston Red Sox baseball game.

_____

_____

_____

5. Next, Aloo located the Boston Museum of Science on the map. Albert looked up the bus schedule.

_____

_____

_____

6. They arrived at the Museum of Science. They saw an ocean-sailing film shown on a four-story-high movie screen.

_____

_____

_____

7. Outside the museum, Albert leaned out into the street to look for a bus. Aloo looked in his change purse for the necessary change.

_____

_____

_____

8. Aloo tried to be careful of the drivers in Boston. His roommate had suggested this.

_____

_____

_____

9. Aloo and Albert walked down to Pier 4 on the wharf. They hoped to get on an excursion boat there.

_____

_____

_____

10. They were very happy with their dinner at "Jimmy's" restaurant. They had their first tastes of clams and lobster there.

_____

_____

_____

EDITING CHECKLIST ─────────────────────────

After considering the suggestions of your writing group and revising your paragraph about a favorite activity, you are now ready to edit the draft. Check your draft in terms of the following:

☐ Check each verb for the correct use of the *present* and *past tenses.*

☐ Check sentence structure for *variety.* If you find that you have too many simple or compound sentences one after another, join those that are logically related. Use the appropriate subordinate conjunctions to create adverbial clauses.

CHAPTER 4

Writing about a Custom

In this chapter, you will write a paragraph about a custom of your family or culture. A *custom* is a practice common to a particular group of people, usually a specific act or a series of actions handed down from one generation to the next. A custom might be a manner of greeting someone or the practice of serving elders at the table first.

Some customs are of such minor importance that people may choose whether to follow them. In Saudi Arabia, for instance, one traditional Arab custom for women is decorating their hands with spidery designs in henna (a reddish-brown dye). Other customs are considered so important that violating them may result in disapproval or even punishment. In some Arab countries, for example, certain customs backed up by laws forbid women from driving, boarding airline flights, or checking into hotels without written permission from a male member of their family.

The most important customs of a group of people are usually based on philosophical or religious beliefs. The traditional Arab custom that requires women to wear veils, for instance, is based on a passage in the Koran, the holy book of Islam.

Before beginning your paragraph about a custom, you will read the two selections that follow. Reading these selections will give you ideas for your own paragraph. In the first reading, from "The South Koreans" published in *National Geographic* (August 1988), author Boyd Gibbons describes the Korean custom of grave tending as practiced by his interpreter, Jong.

▶ *BEFORE YOU READ*

1. Can you locate South Korea on the map that appears in the front of this book?

2. How do people in your culture go about honoring a family's ancestors?

3. In the reading, the author mentions both Confucianism and Buddhism.

69

Share your knowledge of the Buddhist religion and Confucian philosophy with your classmates.

from *THE SOUTH KOREANS*

BOYD GIBBONS

My interpreter, Jong, and I drove into the hills north of Kwangju to visit the grave sites of his father and **ancestors.** When Jong was a boy, his grandparents had wanted to have a grandson come live with them, and as he was the **eldest** of four boys, he was sent out to their farm for a couple of years.

"My grandparents loved me in the Korean way," Jong said. "That means I got spoiled."

Following the **Buddhist** tradition, on the 49th day after his father's death, Jong's family prepared at the family altar fish, beef soup, and fruit wine—all foods his father had enjoyed—to keep his memory alive. Then for a year, in the **Confucian** way, they prepared the same foods on the 1st and 15th of each month.

At his father's grave Jong knelt on some pine **boughs** he had snapped off and bowed twice. He poured a little soju, a liquor, in three places around the mound ("Three is a good number in Korea"), then we sat and shared the rest of the soju, some dried **squid,** and a few ripe **persimmons.** "We share this as though my father were alive," Jong said.

"My brother sometimes goes to the Christian church, and Christians aren't supposed to bow to others' **idols.** But I tell him that he better respect this family tradition."

▶ *AFTER YOU READ*

1. How have Jong and his family combined several traditions to create a way of honoring the family's ancestors?

2. Do you think it is a good idea to honor ancestors in a customary way, as the Koreans do with grave tending? Why or why not?

3. What are the strengths of this piece of writing?

The second reading is from *Iron and Silk* (1986), by American author Mark Salzman. Salzman writes about the two years he spent in the city of Changsha, in the Hunan Province of China, teaching English to medical students. In the reading, Salzman tells of two visits he made to families of fishermen on the Xiang River.

▶ *BEFORE YOU READ*

1. In the reading, Salzman tells of the Chinese tradition of gift giving. In your culture, do you have any special customs about gift giving?

from *IRON AND SILK*

Mark Salzman

Early one morning a heavy fog fell over the city. Right away I thought of going down to the river to see what it looked like. I put a few pieces of steamed bread into a small covered pot, got on my bicycle and rode down to the end of Anti-Imperialism Road. I parked the bicycle against a tree, went down the stone steps of the flood wall to the riverbank and sat on a **discarded** tire.

I hoped that I might see the fog rise, or at least have the sun burst through an opening and light it all up, but nothing like that happened. I ate my steamed bread and was getting ready to leave when something caught my eye. Out of the fog slipped a tiny boat with a fisherman standing in it, rowing slowly and singing to himself. Chinese rowboats, unchanged for many centuries, are shaped like cigars and have a curved roof of woven **bamboo** at one end. The **oars** are longer than Western oars, crossing in front of the oarsman to form an X. The oarsman stands at the **rear** of the boat, facing forward, with the oars in front of him. He pushes them through the water, pulling them for the return stroke. The fisherman stopped not far from me and took out his net, which was folded neatly into a ball and had several round metal weights **dangling** from it. He walked to the front of the boat, got his footing, wound up and threw the net. It spun in the air, and the weights went their separate directions, opening the round net like a flower before it hit the surface of the water and disappeared. After waiting a few minutes he pulled it in, taking a few **wriggling** fish out and dropping them into a bucket. He folded the net carefully and prepared to move on. Just as he took the oars in his hands, he saw me.

I cannot imagine what goes through a Chinese fisherman's or **peasant's** mind when he sees a white man for the first time, but I can describe the physical reaction: **paralysis,** and the mouth drops open. This is what happened that morning, and only when the current started to spin his boat around did he come to and start rowing. He rowed slowly past me, his mouth still open, close enough that I could see that he was barefoot, in the winter, and that his hands were dark and swollen from all the time they spent in the cold water. I smiled at him and he **beamed** back, waving so **vigorously** he nearly fell out of the boat. I said hello and asked him if he wasn't cold without shoes on, and he dropped both oars, **clapping** his hands with delight. It was **obvious** that he simply could not believe that I spoke Chinese. He picked up the oars, rowed **frantically** over to where I stood and stretched out his hand to help me into the boat. "Jump on!" he yelled, "I have to show you to my family!" At first I **hesitated,** but then I remembered that I was not in New Haven anymore and would probably not be **mugged,** so I took his hand and got on.

We rowed downstream for about half an hour, talking the whole way, though he often had to say things a few times for me to understand him. He tried to speak **Mandarin** for my benefit, but his Changsha accent made it almost **incomprehensible.** He seemed most interested in hearing songs from my country. I sang a few lines of this and that as he rowed and asked him if he liked them. "They're not bad, but not as good as Hunan folk songs!" "Would you sing one for me?" "Of course!" I leaned back in the boat and put my arms behind my head while he sang. His broken voice was the perfect instrument for the **exquisitely frail melodies,** and certainly I could not have heard them under better **circumstances.**

He stopped singing to point something out to me. Near the river bank, not far ahead, a **cluster** of five or six boats like his floated together, connected by ropes. "My family!" he said, then urged me to **crawl** under the bamboo roof. "Don't come out until I tell you!" He rowed up to the **flotilla,** tied his boat to one of the others and exchanged a few words with someone before **winking** at me and telling me to come out. I crawled out and stood up. Ten or eleven men and women, young and old, sat together around a **portable** charcoal stove eating a mid-morning **snack.** One by one they looked up, and I could see the paralysis hit like a wave until it reached the youngest child, not more than three years old, who burst into tears. My friend **doubled over** with laughter, and as soon as he could speak he **blurted** out, "There's more—he talks!" This time I hit them with the smile and the speech all at once, and the effect was **stupendous.** Before I knew it, I had more food than I could eat in a week set in front of me, the men crowding around me shaking my hands and slapping my shoulders with joy, the women asking me questions all at the same time, and the children fighting to get in line to touch me.

My friend, who called himself Old Ding, was the only one among them able to **approximate** the sounds of Mandarin, so I couldn't understand a word anyone was saying. I smiled a great deal, though, and that was enough. I became their new friend, and they **indicated** with **sincerity** that what was theirs was now also mine. That morning I learned to row their boats, cast a "flower net," as they called it, and set up the larger nets that are pulled shut by two, three, or sometimes six boats.

Around noon I reminded Old Ding that I had a two-thirty class, so I should be getting back. He, one of his brothers and I **hopped** into the smallest boat, and after I had said goodbye to the family and promised to return, we started upstream. The Xiang River runs fast, so even with the brothers taking turns rowing vigorously, it took us an hour and a half to get back to the city limits, where my bicycle was parked. The brother had a huge barrel chest, a **scarred** face and a **moustache** that made me think of **Fu Manchu.** He didn't speak so much as **growl,** or so it seemed to me, and every once in a while he leaned forward to **slap** me on the shoulder, nearly **propelling** me out of the boat. He smiled at me, **gnashed** his teeth and growled. "What is he saying?" I asked Old Ding. "He says he likes you and wants to **wrestle!** My brother likes to wrestle!"

Before letting me ashore, they **insisted** that we have one more adventure. A big river boat was **anchored** in the middle of the river, **dredging** up **silt** from the riverbed and dropping it onto flat **tug-boats** that carried it to shore. Old Ding knew the **crew** and suggested that we stop by and say hello. We rowed alongside the boat and got on quietly. None of the crew saw us, for they were all in the cabin relaxing during **xiuxi.** The three of us walked into the cabin, me last of all. The captain was the first to look up. He opened his mouth but was **unable** to speak, and his cigarette fell from his lower lip into his bowl of rice, where it **sizzled** loudly. Once the **initial** shock and **frenzy** died down, the captain gave me a tour of this boat. He told me that he remembered the American soldiers from the Second World War very well. With great **emotion** in his voice, he repeated over and over how good it was of them to help China. At last, he managed to say "USA!" in English, and gave me the **thumbs-up sign.**

Eventually we left the river boat and the brothers took me to where I had first gotten on. Only after I agreed to accept the two biggest fish in the **hold** did they let me ashore. They stood in the boat waving for as long as I could see them, yelling after me that I should come back soon to play, that all I had to do was walk by the river and I would find them. To avoid arriving late for class, I rode directly to the classroom, where I had a difficult time explaining to my doctor students how I came to possess two giant fish that still breathed when I set them on my desk. Every few minutes, just as the **curious** whispering had died down and we began to go over the lesson, one of the fish would **leap** into the air and land with a loud snap on the floor. On my way home, I gave the fish to Teacher Wei and told her of my day with the fisherman. She **nodded** slowly as I told it, and when I had finished, she smiled. "The fishing people are very honest, and very kind. You see how well they treat you? That is the Chinese way. They are common people, but they understand manners better than we **intellectuals,** who are now cautious and tired."

Two hours later she walked into my room with a covered pot and put it on my desk. It contained one of the fish, cooked to perfection in a spicy Hunan sauce. "Of course," she said as she hurried out, "we intellectuals can still do a pretty good job." . . .

I had walked along the river many times since meeting the fisherman that day in winter, but I did not see him again until spring. It was late afternoon, and I had bicycled to a point along the river about a mile downstream from where we had met, hoping to find a deserted spot to draw a picture. I found a **niche** in the sloping flood wall and started drawing a **junk moored** not far from me. Half an hour passed, and just as I finished the drawing, I heard someone calling my Chinese name. I looked down to see Old Ding **scrambling** up the flood wall, his boat anchored behind him. I noticed that he limped badly, and when he got up close I could see that one of his legs was shorter than the other and set at an odd angle. Such was his balance and skill in the boats that I only saw his **deformity** when he came ashore. He squatted down beside me and explained that he had just returned from a long fishing trip on Dong Ting, a **sprawling** lake in North Hunan. "Big fish up there," he said, **gesturing** with his arms. Then he asked me what I was doing. I showed him the drawing, and his face lit up. "Just like it! Just like the boat!" He cupped his hands to his mouth and yelled something in the direction of the junk, and right away a family appeared on deck. "Let's show it to them!" he said, and dragged me down to the water. He exchanged a few words with the family, and they leapt into action, the women going into the sheltered part of the junk to prepare food and the men rowing out to meet us in one of two tiny boats **lashed** to the side. We got in the little boat and returned with them to the junk. We ate a few snacks of different kinds of salted fish, had tea, and then I showed them the drawing. They seemed delighted by it, so I tore the sheet out of my block. I handed it to the oldest member of the family, a man in his sixties, who opened his eyes wide with surprise and would not take it, saying, "How can I take this? It is a work of art; what do I have to offer you in return?" I laughed, saying that it was only a drawing, and I would be happy if he would take it just for fun. But he was serious; when at last he accepted it, putting it down carefully on the bed, he began **negotiating** with Old Ding to choose an **appropriate** gift for me.

Fifteen minutes of vigorous discussion, all in **dialect,** produced a decision: they would give me one of the rowboats. I looked at Old Ding and said that that was absolutely **ridiculous,** that of course I would not take a boat from a poor fisherman's family in return for a **charcoal sketch.** "Oh, but it's no problem! They can get a new one!" I **realized** that the situation was serious, for if I refused and left, they would no doubt carry the rowboat to my house and lay it on the front porch. I looked at the old man. "That is a very fine gift, it is worth thousands of drawings like that one, but we Americans have a custom, and that is we speak directly. If we want something, we say so." Many Chinese people **appreciate** "talking straight," perhaps because **convention** almost never allows it, so they **applauded** this and told me by all means to speak up. "The boat is very fine, but there is something I want more." They all smiled and nodded and said that of course I could have whatever I wanted, but I could see they were deeply nervous. I believe they expected me to ask for the junk. "In my country, we have a **supersti-**

tion. If someone gives you a piece of art, like a painting or a poem, you must give him a piece of art in return, or the feeling will be spoiled. If I take the boat, I will feel sad. I would **prefer** that a member of your family sing a folk song from your hometown." The family, almost **hysterical** with **relief,** cheered my decision, saying it had "true spirit," and each of them sang something for me.

After we left the junk, Old Ding asked me if I would have dinner with his family that night. I wasn't feeling up to it just then: the **encounter** with the family on the junk had tired me out, so we made a date for a week from that day, a Saturday. I was to wait by the river in the afternoon, and he would pick me up in his boat.

▶ *AFTER YOU READ*

1. On Salzman's visit to the first family of fishermen, how did the family show their welcome for him?

2. How did Salzman feel about giving the drawing to the second family of fishermen? After accepting the drawing, what did the old man feel obligated to do? Why? What would you say is the Chinese custom of gift giving that this example illustrates?

3. What kind of problem did this custom create for Salzman? How did he resolve the problem? Did Salzman truly describe an American custom of gift giving?

4. Have you ever been with people of another culture who had different customs from those of your culture? Have you ever been in a situation where a difference in customs caused problems? If so, how did you resolve the problems?

Supplemental Reading List—Chapter 4

Nimmo, Harry Arlo. *The Songs of Salanda and Other Stories of Sula.* Seattle: University of Washington Press, 1994.

In this book, anthropologist Nimmo describes the culture and customs of the Bajan, nomadic boat-dwellers in the waters off the Philippines.

Morris, Mary. *Wall to Wall: From Beijing to Berkline by Rail.* New York: Penguin, 1991.

This exciting tale by travel writer Morris tells of her discoveries about the people of China, the Soviet Union, and Eastern Europe as she traveled on the Trans-Siberian rail express.

Scot, Barbara J. *The Violet Shyness of Their Eyes: Notes from Nepal.* Corvallis, OR: Calyx Books, 1993.

Scot vividly recalls the time she spent in a small village in Nepal. Her description of the Nepalese, their customs, and the land itself will make you want to visit this unique country set in the midst of the Himalayas.

✐ Writing Assignment: *Writing about a Custom*

In this chapter, you will first learn more about using description and analysis in your writing and then work through the stages of the writing process to develop your own paragraph about a custom. Before you begin work on your paragraph, discuss the following question with your classmates. Your answer to this question will become the focus of your paragraph.

Question: What custom does your family or culture follow, and why?

Write a paragraph about a custom commonly practiced by your family or by the people of your culture. The custom may be one common practice (such as the Arab female custom of painting the hands with henna) or it may be a series of ritual practices (such as the Korean grave-tending custom of Jong and his family).

Near the beginning of your paragraph, you may want to announce the central point—the custom—in a topic sentence. Next, include enough concrete, specific details and other types of evidence to give your reader a clear understanding of the custom. Also, analyze your evidence by explaining the custom to your reader—what it means, how it was passed down, and/or what its importance is to your family or people.

Guidelines on Descriptive and Analysis Writing

In writing your paragraph about a custom, you want to pay close attention to both *description* and *analysis.*

DESCRIPTION

In presenting evidence for your custom, be certain to use descriptive details—concrete and specific words that give the reader a clear understanding of the custom. (For more on concrete and specific words, see Chapter 1.)

❏ *ACTIVITY 4.1:* **IDENTIFYING DESCRIPTIVE WORDS**

As one class member reads aloud the description of Jong and his family's grave-tending custom in the reading on page 70, underline the specific and concrete words that the author uses to describe the custom. Then discuss the questions that follow with your classmates.

DISCUSSION QUESTIONS

1. What specific and concrete words does Gibbons use to describe the custom—its origins, its timing, the place where it is practiced, and the foods used?

2. Are there enough descriptive details in the reading to create in your mind a vivid picture of the custom?

3. Look back on page 9 at the scale of general to specific words. Where on the scale would you put Gibbons's use of descriptive details? Explain your response.

ANALYSIS

In addition to descriptive details, you need to include analysis of your custom. As you learned in Chapter 3, by announcing the central point of a paragraph in the topic sentence, you set up certain expectations in the reader's mind. Your description as well as your analysis should fulfill these expectations. For example, if you announce in your topic sentence that the paragraph is about Arab women's custom of painting their hands with henna, your reader expects you to describe and analyze that custom in the remainder of the paragraph. Other questions may also arise in the reader's mind:

Why do women in Arab countries paint their hands with henna?

What is the origin of this custom—its roots?

In analyzing your evidence—explaining it to the reader—consider answering one or more of the following questions. These are the types of questions a reader will have once you announce your central point.

Analysis Questions:

Who practices the custom?

How do they practice the custom?

What is the origin of the custom?

Why do people practice the custom?

How important is the custom to these people?

When is the custom practiced?

Of course, you cannot answer all of these questions in a single paragraph, but you should try to focus on one or two of them when analyzing your evidence.

❑   *ACTIVITY 4.2:*   **IDENTIFYING EVIDENCE AND ANALYSIS**

In the following paragraph from "Peoples of China's Far Provinces," published in *National Geographic* (March 1984), author Wong How-Man tells how the manager of a hotel in a remote part of China described the greeting customs of Tibetan nomads. (Nomads are members of a tribe that wanders from place to place, especially in desert areas.)

As one class member reads the passage aloud, underline the specific evidence (the descriptive details about the custom) in the paragraph. Then reread the paragraph, this time placing brackets around the analysis (the explanation of the custom). Discuss the questions that follow.

Before you read, see if you can locate Tibet on the map that appears on the inside front cover of this book.

"Tibetan gestures are different from ours," the manager continued. "When addressing you for the first time, a Tibetan may stick out his tongue at you and show his open **palms** at waist level. This is an ancient and very **courteous** form of Tibetan greeting. The outstretched hands show that no weapon is hidden, and thus no harm is intended. The **display** of the tongue dates back to an old **superstition** that one who poisons others has a black tongue."

DISCUSSION QUESTIONS

1. Which parts of the passage are evidence, and which are analysis?

2. Which of the analysis questions listed on page 77 does the paragraph answer?

❑   *ACTIVITY 4.3:*   **EVALUATING A PARAGRAPH ABOUT A CUSTOM**

Also in "Peoples of China's Far Provinces," Wong How-Man describes another custom of people in a remote area of China. In the following passage, he describes a custom practiced by a tribe of Tibetans known to outsiders as the "White Horse Tibetans" and to themselves as the "Di" people. According to How-Man, the Di people practice the unique custom of singing to their oxen as the oxen plow the fields. (Oxen are adult male cattle whose sexual organs have been removed.)

After one class member reads the passage aloud, discuss the questions that follow.

Though the Di have no written language, they enjoy a colorful **oral** history. Chen Yuanguang, a Chinese **authority** on the Di, told me a delightful **legend purporting** to explain the people's habitual singing.

In ancient times, runs the legend, heaven **bestowed** on humans an **abundance** of rice covering the entire earth like snow. But a woman accidentally stepped on some grains of rice, thereby offending God. God sent the ox to earth to announce His punishment for mankind: Each person was to comb his or her hair three times a day and eat but one meal a day.

By mistake the ox ordered combing of the hair once a day and eating of three meals a day. God was much angered and **banished** the ox to earth to **toil** and **repent.** The ox begged for **mercy.** First, he claimed he would be ill-treated on earth. God therefore gave the ox horns to defend himself. Second, the ox worried about insect bites. God gave him a tail to drive the insects away. Third, the ox was afraid of being punished if he was to oversleep. So God asked the people to sing to the ox to keep him awake. To this day, the Di always sing whenever they **plow** the fields with their oxen.

DISCUSSION QUESTIONS

1. What are the strengths of this reading? That is, what makes it appealing to you as a reader?

2. Which of the analysis questions listed on page 77 does the paragraph answer?

3. What does the legend seem to say about women?

Prewriting: Generating Ideas

If you have not yet chosen a custom to write about, take a few minutes to generate some ideas about several possible topics. Try brainstorming a list of all the possible customs you might write about. Then choose the one custom that is most important or interesting to you.

Next, generate some ideas about the custom by using one of the prewriting techniques you learned in earlier chapters—clustering (pages 10–11), freewriting (pages 31–32), or tree diagraming (page 54). As you work through the prewriting activity, think about the details of the custom. Also think about what the custom means, how it has been passed down, and what its importance is to your family or people.

Drafting

After generating some ideas about your custom, you are ready to begin drafting your paragraph. Before you start writing, make sure you have a rough plan of how you will develop the paragraph. Some writers like to include quite a lot in their prewriting plan, while others simply make a rough mental plan of the paragraph. In your plan, you might include a rough topic sentence, the details you want to include about the custom, and your ideas for analyzing the custom.

As you write your first draft, concentrate on writing your ideas down, not on the form of your sentences.

Revising

If time permits, before sharing your draft paragraph with your writing group, practice evaluating the two student paragraphs that follow in Activity 4.4.

❏ *ACTIVITY 4.4:* **EVALUATING TWO STUDENTS'**
   PARAGRAPHS

Although both student paragraphs that follow describe the Vietnamese Lunar New Year, each takes a different approach to analyzing the custom.

After one student has read paragraph A aloud, discuss the paragraph in terms of the following questions. Repeat the same procedure for paragraph B.

DISCUSSION QUESTIONS

1. *Topic Sentence:* Does the writer clearly announce the point of the paragraph in a topic sentence—what the custom is and who practices it?

2. *Evidence:* Does the writer include enough specific, concrete evidence to build in your mind a detailed picture of the custom?

3. *Analysis:* Does the writer thoroughly analyze the evidence? Which of the analysis questions listed on page 77 does the writer answer in analyzing the custom?

4. What are the strengths of this paragraph? What are its weaknesses (areas needing improvement)?

5. What does paragraph B seem to say about women?

PARAGRAPH A

In Vietnam, the fifteenth of August of the lunar calendar is the mid-autumn festival, which is a holiday for children. The idea of this festival is to teach children about their culture and customs and to give them a chance to play all day with friends. The day before the festival, my father usually buys four paper lanterns for my brother, my sisters, and me. Each lantern has a different shape, such as a bird, an airplane, a boat, or a butterfly. My mother prepares some cookies, jam, and special cake for this occasion. The celebration of the festival is often at night, just after sunset. It's like Halloween night in the United States, but we don't wear makeup or go from house to house to ask for candy. Instead, we dress nicely and light our lanterns with candles to join other kids walking around our neighborhood. We sing our folk songs and dance as we pass through the streets. After having fun with our friends, we return to our house and sit around our grandparents and other family members. As we eat cake and drink tea, our grandfather tells us the story about the festival. The festival is eventually over as we fall asleep. Even though we live in the United States now, my family and many other Vietnamese still celebrate this festival to remind us of our customs and our culture.

PARAGRAPH B

The Moon New Year

The moon new year is one of the happiest holidays for Vietnamese children due to the fun that it gives them and its popular legend. Back in the old time, a man named "Chu Coi" by luck found a tree that could cure any kind of sickness. However, there was a rule that forbade urinating at the foot of this tree; bad things would happen if someone broke this law. Unfortunately, his wife, the beautiful lady "Chi Hang," forgot this rule and urinated at the tree's foot. The tree then began shaking, which made it start to fly. This tree kept on flying up into the sky with Chu Coi and Chi Hang hanging onto it until it hit the moon and settled there. Since that time, on every night of August 19th of the Vietnamese lunar calendar, Vietnamese people have a chance to see this couple again because the moon is at its fullest and brightest on this night. Elders usually drink tea and eat moon cakes, which are made of flour, sugar, egg, and different kinds of peas, while they behold the legendary couple and the beautiful moon. Some even create some poems while they gaze at the moon. Similarly, the children have their own fun. They carry their lanterns of different shapes and colors in their hands around the town streets and sing Moon New Year's songs at the same time. The children play as if they are playing around the fairy couple.

❏ *ACTIVITY 4.5:* **PEER RESPONSE**

Now share your draft paragraph about a custom of your family or culture with your writing group. Use the following procedure:

1. One group member should begin by reading aloud his or her draft paragraph. The group should then discuss the draft in terms of the questions listed on the Peer Response Sheet for Activity 4.5 on page 343. Another member should record the group's comments on the sheet.

2. After you are finished filling out the sheet, give it to the writer so he or she can consider the suggestions when revising.

3. Repeat the procedure for each group member.

4. Then revise your own draft paragraph, keeping in mind the suggestions of your writing group. Pay particular attention to any problems with your topic sentence, evidence, and analysis.

Editing: More on Verb Tense and Sentence Structure

After you have revised your draft paragraph and are satisfied with its content, you are ready to begin editing your sentences. In the editing section of this chapter, you will work on some of the things you studied in earlier chapters: you will edit to improve sentence structure and to avoid verb tense problems. You will also study the present perfect tense.

The following editing section includes three steps: (1) editing for verb tenses; (2) editing for sentence structure problems; and (3) editing for sentence variety. If time permits, you may choose to work through all three of these editing steps. If any one of these problems has not appeared in your earlier paragraphs, then you may choose to skip the section on the problem. If your time is limited, focus on the one or two types of problems that have appeared most frequently in your previous paragraphs.

1. EDITING FOR VERB TENSES AND STUDYING THE PRESENT PERFECT TENSE

Choosing to Center Your Paragraph in the "World of the Past" or the "World of the Present"

A writer sometimes chooses a verb tense for one sentence, such as choosing the past tense to describe a past event. More often, however, a writer must choose tenses for a group of sentences that work together logically. In this case, the writer must first decide whether to center the group of sentences or the paragraph in what we can think of as the "world of the present" or the "world of the past." This decision is important because each of these worlds has a particular group of verb tenses that work together within the world. As you learned in Chapter 1, a writer may choose to center a group of sentences or a paragraph in the "world of the past" to describe events that took place completely in the past—events that are no longer happening now. To describe events that are still happening now, a writer will center a group of sentences or a paragraph in the "world of the present." After choosing either the "world of the present" or the "world of the past," the writer will then be able to choose from the particular set of verb tenses that can be used in the "world" chosen.

Think for a moment about whether you want to center your paragraph about a custom in the "world of the present" (for a custom that is still practiced today) or in the "world of the past" (for a custom that is no longer practiced by your people).

A Paragraph Centered in the "World of the Present"

If you choose to center your paragraph largely in the "world of the present," you need to be certain that you are correctly using the other tenses that may be used in a paragraph centered in the present. The following activity will help you discover the tenses that can be used in the "world of the present," including the new tense you will learn in this chapter—the present perfect.

❏ *ACTIVITY 4.6:* **IDENTIFYING TENSES USED IN THE "WORLD OF THE PRESENT"**

In the following paragraph, the verb tenses are in italics. For each verb, identify the tense and write it in the margin. If you are not sure about a verb's tense, discuss with your classmates what the tense is called.

In Japan, one of the most important customs of my family *is* the tea ceremony, which *has been* an important custom in Japan for centuries. My mother *has* a tea ceremony teaching certificate that she *earned* at Haoku Academy. My family *has performed* the tea ceremony every year for as long as I *remember*. The tea ceremony *has* as its primary purpose the teaching of gracefulness, inner harmony, and recognition of the human's relation with nature. My mother usually *prepares* a tea kettle designed in a beautiful Japanese style, a mixer made with bamboo, and a tea cup which *is* like a little bowl. While she *is making* all the preparations, there *is* no talking. The aim *is* to achieve complete physical and mental relaxation. When the tea *is* ready, she customarily *bows* to us and *turns* the cup counterclockwise three times to harmonize the cup and the tea. After she *gives* me the cup, I *bow* to her and *turn* the cup clockwise three times. While I *am drinking* the tea, I *appreciate* a quiet, lonely mood, the astringent brew and solitude. In fact, Japanese *think* this appreciation *is* a positive measure of aesthetic joy in Japan. Not only *am* I able to have good relationships with my family, but I *am* also able to brace myself up and start working harder after the tea ceremony. This *is* why the tea ceremony *has been* my favorite Japanese custom for years. I *have* myself *performed* the tea ceremony for four years now, and I *have* never *regretted* the many hours I *spent* learning it. One day, I *will pass* this custom along to my children.

The preceding paragraph is *centered* in the "world of the present." This means that all the events in the paragraph revolve around a centering point that is in present time. Look at the diagram below and imagine that the "world of the present" revolves around an axis that is *centered* in present time.

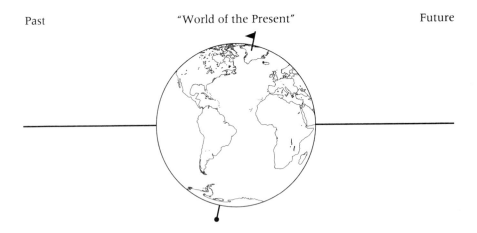

Past   "World of the Present"   Future

As the writer writes, she keeps this centering point uppermost in her mind and chooses verb tenses in relation to this centering point—certain verbs for "time before" the centering point, certain verbs for "same time" as the centering point, and certain verbs for "time after" the centering point.

Verb Tenses for "Time Before" the Present Centering Point. Within a paragraph centered in the "world of the present," a writer uses *past tense* to refer to events that took place at a specific time in the past—in "time before" the present centering point.

> My mother has a tea ceremony teaching certificate that she *earned* at Haoku Academy.

"Time Before and Up To" the Present Centering Point. To describe a state of being or an action occurring in a time period that began in the past (the "time before") and continues to the present, the writer uses the *present perfect tense,* which you will learn more about in the following section.

> This is why the tea ceremony *has been* my favorite Japanese custom for years. . . .

"Same Time" as the Present Centering Point. To describe an action in progress—one occurring at the "same time" as the present centering point—the writer uses the *present tense* (for a state of being or habitual present) or the *present progressive tense* (for an action in progress). The present progressive is formed by the present of *be* and the *-ing* form of the verb.*

> While I *am drinking* the tea, I appreciate a quiet, lonely mood, the astringent brew and solitude.

In an earlier draft, the writer had discovered an error with the present progressive tense and corrected it: She had incorrectly used a stative verb (*think*) in the progressive form. *Stative verbs* are "state of being" verbs; therefore, they cannot be used in the progressive. (See Appendix C for a list of stative verbs.)

> *Incorrect:*
>
> In fact, Japanese *are thinking* that this appreciation is a positive measure of aesthetic joy in Japan.

> *Correct:*
>
> In fact, Japanese *think* that this appreciation is a positive measure of aesthetic joy in Japan.

"Time After" the Present Centering Point. To describe an action that will take place in the future—in "time after" the present centering point—the writer uses verb forms that signal *future* time:

> One day, I *will pass* this custom along to my children.

---

*See Appendix C for a more complete discussion of present and past progressives. The appendix also includes a discussion of stative verbs (which do not usually take the progressive) and other verbs that take either the present or past progressive or the simple present or past tense.

As you can see, you may use a number of verb tenses in a paragraph that is centered in the "world of the present." It is, however, very important to keep the present centering point uppermost in your mind as you choose tenses to refer to the "same time" as the present centering point and the "time before" and "time after" the present centering point.

"World of the Present"

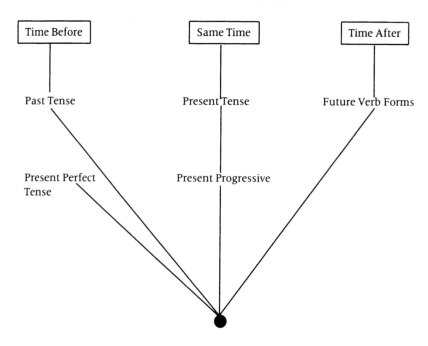

The Present Perfect Tense

In writing about events within the "world of the present," the present perfect tense is very helpful because it allows you to relate past events to the present:

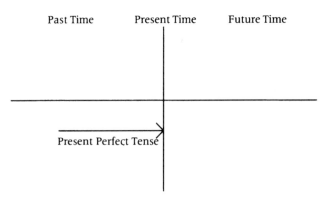

In the following example, note how the present perfect tense bridges the past and present time periods, allowing you to refer to a time period that spans from past time up to and including present time:

My family *has practiced* the tea ceremony for many years.

Formation of the Present Perfect Tense

The present perfect tense of a verb is formed with the present form of *have* and the past participle.* For example:

	Present Form of *Have*	Past Participle	
I	have	learned	the tea ceremony.
My mother	has	taught	the tea ceremony to me.

Uses of the Present Perfect Tense

As you could see from the present perfect verbs you found in the tea ceremony paragraph, you can use the present perfect tense to express several meanings.

State of Being. The present perfect can be used to express a state of being occurring in a time period that leads up to and includes the present time:

The tea ceremony *has been* an important custom in Japan for centuries.

In choosing between the *past tense* and the *present perfect tense,* a writer uses the past tense to indicate a state of being that occurred in the past but that is not now occurring in the present. As you learned earlier, there is a gap in time between the time when the state of being occurred "then" (in past time) and "now" (in present time):

Past Tense:

My mother *was* a student at Haoku Academy.

However, a writer uses the present perfect to indicate a state of being that began in the past and that continues at least up until the present. (It *may* continue into the future also.)

Present Perfect Tense:

My mother *has been* a well-known expert in the tea ceremony for many years.

---

*For regular verbs, the past participle is the same as the past tense verb (*learned* = past tense; *learned* = past participle). See the list of irregular verbs in Appendix B or consult your dictionary for the past participle forms of irregular verbs. (The past participle form is the third dictionary entry for irregular verbs.)

An Event Occurring at an Unspecified Time. The present perfect is also used to describe an event occurring at an unspecified time within a time period leading up to the present:

I *have just learned* the advanced steps of the tea ceremony.

In choosing between the *past* and *present perfect tenses,* a writer uses the past tense when describing an event that occurred at a specified, definite time in the past (see Chapter 1). This specific, definite time in the past may be indicated by a time signal or may be understood:

Past Tense:

My grandmother *learned* the tea ceremony when she was a child.

However, a writer uses the present perfect to indicate that an event occurred at an indefinite time in the past. Here the writer does not have a specific, definite time in the past in mind:

Present Perfect Tense:

I *have* just *watched* a video on the ancient forms of the tea ceremony.

Habitual or Recurring Events. Finally, the present perfect is used to describe a habit or event that has been recurring within a time period leading up to the present:

I *have watched* my mother perform the tea ceremony many times.

In choosing between the *past* or *present perfect tenses,* a writer uses the past tense to describe a past habit or sequence of events that occurred within a time period that is all in the past—that is, a time period that does not come up to present time. (There is a gap between this past time period and present time.)

Past Tense:

My grandmother *used* her tea set for sixty years.

However, a writer chooses the present perfect to indicate a habit or sequence of events occurring in a time period that begins in past time and continues at least into the present time. The present perfect tense may also suggest that the habit or recurring event may continue into the future:

Present Perfect Tense:

I *have performed* the tea ceremony for only four years.

Using Adverbials with the Present Perfect Tense

Duration Adverbs. Adverbs signaling duration often occur with the present perfect tense when used to express a state of being or to describe a habitual or recurrent event.

A *duration adverb* indicates that something occurred over a span of time, from one point in time to another:

Duration Adverbs

for	ever since
since	over
up to now	

I have wanted to have my own tea set *ever since* I was a child.

Frequency Adverbs. A *frequency adverb* may also occur with habits or recurrent events in the present perfect. A frequency adverb describes something that happens a number of times repeatedly.

Frequency Adverbs

often	many times
every day	each afternoon

I have *often* looked at tea sets in shop windows.

Time Adverbs. *Time adverbs* may occur with the present perfect tense when it is used to indicate an event that occurred at an indefinite time in the past. The time adverb indicates that the event occurred in the past, but at an indefinite time, not at a specific time.

Time Adverbs—Indefinite Time

lately	recently	just
already	never	ever
yet	in the past	

I have *recently* started to collect books on the tea ceremony.

Editing Tenses in Your Paragraph Centered in the Present

1. Underline each verb in your paragraph. Check to see that you have used the simple present tense to describe actions that happen each time you practice the custom, since the present tense represents "same time" as the present centering point.

Mother *bows* to us and *turns* the cup counterclockwise.

2. Be certain that you have reserved the past tense only for the occasional description of an event that took place at a specific time in the past and is no longer taking place in the present.

She has a teaching certificate that she *earned* at Haoku Academy.

3. Be certain that you have used the present perfect tense for any of the following examples of "time before and up to" the present centering point:

• A state of being occurring in a time period that leads up to and includes the present time.

The tea ceremony *has been* an important custom in Japan for centuries.

- An event occurring at an unspecified time within a time period leading up to the present.

    Mother uses a tea kettle that she *has polished* earlier.

- A habit or an event recurring within a time period leading up to the present.

    My family *has practiced* the tea ceremony for as long as I can remember.

4. Be certain that you have used the present progressive to describe an action in progress that has some duration (the "same time" as the present centering point):

    While mother *is making* the preparations, the family does not talk.

5. Finally, check to see that you have not used the present progressive for stative verbs. (See Appendix C for a list of stative verbs.)

A Paragraph Centered in the "World of the Past"

If you choose to center your paragraph in the "world of the past," perhaps to describe a custom that was practiced in the past, you need to be certain that you are correctly using the tenses that may be used in a paragraph centered in the past.

In looking at the diagram below, imagine, as you did in Chapter 1, that the "world of the past" is a world of people and events that stands completely in past time—it is all over and has nothing to do with what is happening now in present time. (Notice that there is a gap in time between the "world of the past" and present time.)

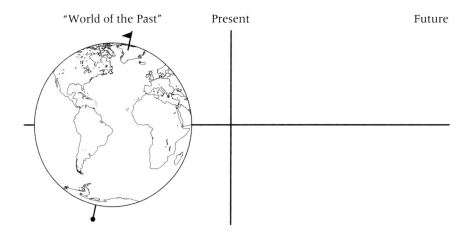

As you see, the centering point—the axis that runs down the middle of the globe—rests on a point in past time. As you write, you need to keep this past centering point uppermost in your mind and choose verb tenses in relation to this centering point. You will need to choose certain verb tenses for "same time" as the past centering point and certain verb tenses for "time after" the past centering point.

"Same Time" as the Past Centering Point. In a paragraph centered in the past, you depend largely on the *past tense,* which represents "same time" as the past centering point. (In Chapter 5 you will learn about using the past perfect tense in the "world of the past" to discuss time before past time. Now, however, you should concentrate on using the past tense.)

> The ceremony of marriage *was* an important custom in China before the revolution of 1949.

> The wedding *lasted* one week.

> The groom *went* to the bride's house to pick her up on the third day.

Occasionally, you may find it necessary to use the *past progressive* to describe an action in progress in the past. The past progressive is most often used to show that one action was in progress (using the past progressive) at a particular time in the past (signaled by the past tense or a specific time in the past):

> *By the time the sun rose,* the bride *was preparing* her dress.

> *While* the bride's mother *was pouring* three little cups of white wine, the bride and groom *knelt* and *faced* a statue of the Buddha. Then the bride's mother *placed* the wine in front of the bride and groom for them to drink.

"Time After" the Past Centering Point. To describe an event that took place at a "time after" the past centering point, you use the *past tense,* not the present or future tenses. That is, within the "world of the past," there is no distinction in tenses between the "same time" as the past centering point and the "time after" the past centering point:

> The bride and groom *married* in an elaborate ceremony.

> Later, they *moved* into the home of the groom's family.

If your paragraph about a custom is centered in the "world of the past," you should check carefully to make sure you have *not* used the present tense, except in a rare case for a "timeless truth" that would sound awkward or unclear in the past tense:*

> The family made many preparations because marriage *is* important to a Chinese family.

*See Chapter 1 for more on "timeless truths" in the present tense and for how to use the present tense for "timeless truths" when you are centering a passage in the past.

Here the present tense refers to a "timeless truth"—the importance of the marriage ceremony in Chinese custom. The sentence could be written in the past tense, but it would sound awkward to the reader:

> The family made many preparations because marriage *was* important to a Chinese family.

As you can see in the accompanying diagram, when you choose to center a group of sentences or a paragraph in the "world of the past," you use past tense and occasionally past progressive to refer to events that occurred at the "same time" as the past centering point. You use past tense (not present tense) to refer to events that occurred at a "time after" the past centering point.

Some Tenses Used in the "World of the Past"

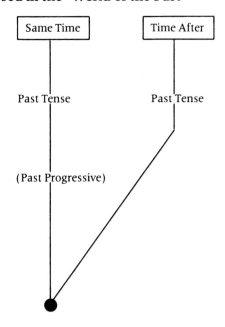

Editing Tenses in Your Paragraph Centered in the Past

1. Underline each verb in your paragraph. Check to see that you have used the past tense to refer to actions that were practiced in the past since the past tense represents "same time" as the past centering point.

> The bride and groom *bowed* three times.

2. Be certain that you have used the past progressive to describe an action in progress in the past or to show that one action was in progress at a particular time in the past, since the past progressive also refers to "same time" as the past centering point.

While the bride and groom *were kneeling,* the mother poured three cups of white wine.

3. Check to see that you have *not* used the past progressive for stative verbs. (See Appendix C for a list of stative verbs.)

4. Be certain that you have reserved the present tense only for the description of a general statement of fact or a "timeless truth" that would sound awkward or unclear if expressed in the past tense:

The marriage ceremony was an important ceremony in China, which *is* a country located in Asia.

2. EDITING FOR SENTENCE STRUCTURE PROBLEMS: FRAGMENTS, RUN-ON SENTENCES, AND COMMA SPLICES

Now edit your draft paragraph for sentence structure problems.

1. Check for *fragments*—Does each sentence have at least one independent clause consisting of a subject and a finite verb that can stand alone? (See Chapter 2.)

2. Check compound sentences for *comma splices* and *run-ons*—two independent clauses joined incorrectly with only a comma or joined incorrectly with no comma and no conjunction. (See Chapter 2.)

❑ *ACTIVITY 4.7:* **IDENTIFYING PROBLEMS IN SENTENCE STRUCTURE**

Identify and correct the fragments, comma splices, and run-on sentences in the following student paragraph.

Most Indonesians are Muslim, and they have one special holiday that they all celebrate called *Idul Fitri,* also known as *Lebaran.* Indonesians celebrate *Idul Fitri* after fasting for one month from all earthly desires. Such as not eating or drinking from 4 A.M. until 6 P.M. They also cannot be angry at anyone at that time. If they fail to fast from all earthly desires, they must repeat the fast after *Lebaran.* Thus, *Lebaran* is a happiness day to celebrate after fasting from all earthly desires. On *Lebaran,* after going to the mosque in the morning, Muslim people visit their elder families to apologize to each other. They then eat foods such as yellow rice and "*ketupat* with *sambal goreng,*" these are special foods made from rice. After eating, they visit another elder family or go to the cemetery to pray for their family members who are dead. *Lebaran* is not only for happiness but also for apologizing to each other it makes the family close.

3. EDITING FOR SENTENCE VARIETY

You will also want to look closely at your draft to see that you have variety in sentence structure, rather than the same type of structure in one sentence after another. The two following activities will help you add sentence variety to your paragraph.

If time permits, you and your classmates can do both of the following sentence variety activities (Activities 4.8 and 4.9). For example, you can join with your classmates or with a partner to practice adding sentence variety to a student paragraph in Activity 4.8. Then you can work with a partner on Activity 4.9, which will help you add sentence variety to your own paragraph. If time is limited, you and your partner can choose to do only Activity 4.9.

❏ *ACTIVITY 4.8:* **EVALUATING A STUDENT'S PARAGRAPH**

Practice improving sentence variety in the following student paragraph. Read one sentence at a time and mark it in the following manner:

1. Underline each simple sentence.
2. Circle each compound sentence.
3. Put brackets around each complex sentence.

Next, join logically related sentences where appropriate. That is, if you find too many simple sentences, join logically related simple sentences with coordinate or subordinate conjunctions. If you find too many compound sentences, change some of them into complex sentences by using subordinate conjunctions.

One of the typical customs of Koreans is the bow to elders (the *Seibai*) on the first day of the lunar new year. On New Year's Day, everyone gets up very early in the morning. They prepare to visit the elders' houses. The children dress up with new jumpers with sleeves of many different colored stripes. The adult man wears a traditional Korean *Hanbok* cloth made of colored silk with large sleeves and big blue-jade buttons, and the adult woman wears a short Korean jacket and a long skirt of beautiful figured silk. When all the family members are ready, the children politely perform a bow just once to their parents for the first time of the day. While the children are bowing and saying "Happy New Year," the elders are sitting on a traditional silk cushion with multicolored figures. The bow is done. The elder person gives a small gift to the youngsters. This might be a coin, a Korean rice cake, or a wheat gluten, which is very popular to the Korean kids because of its sweetness. The children finish bowing. They move to the next house and do the same thing until the day is over. The purpose of the custom of bowing on New Year's Day is to observe the proprieties, promote friendship with close neighbors and other family members, and, most of all, to teach young people to respect their elders.

❏ *ACTIVITY 4.9:* **ADDING VARIETY TO YOUR SENTENCES**

First, read your paragraph aloud to see if it needs more sentence variety. (To review sentence types, see Chapter 2.) Then read one sentence at a time, marking it in the following manner:

1. Underline each simple sentence.
2. Circle each compound sentence.
3. Put brackets around each complex sentence.

If you cannot determine whether a sentence is simple, compound, or complex, ask your partner for help or refer to Chapter 2.

After all of the sentences in your paragraph are marked appropriately, use the following questions to determine how to rework your sentences as needed. Discuss your paragraph and the changes needed with your partner, and then edit your sentences for variety.

DISCUSSION QUESTIONS

1. Does your paragraph have too many simple sentences or spots where one simple sentence follows another?

2. Does your paragraph have too many compound sentences or spots where one compound sentence follows another?

3. Can you join any logically related simple sentences with coordinate or subordinate conjunctions? (See Appendix A for lists of coordinate and subordinate conjunctions.)

4. Can you join any clauses with subordinate conjunctions instead of coordinate conjunctions?

☑ *EDITING CHECKLIST* ─────────────────────

Check off the portions of the following editing checklist that you have completed and turn in a copy of this checklist with your final draft to your instructor.

Checklist for Final Draft

▢ Checked for correct verb tenses _____.

▢ Checked for sentence structure problems: fragments, run-on sentences, and comma splices _____.

▢ Checked for sentence variety _____.

CHAPTER 5

Writing about Choosing a Field of Study

In this chapter, you will write a paragraph about choosing your college major or field of study. Before you begin work on your paragraph, you will read the following selection about why one Cuban American student, Roxana Gonzalez, made her choice. In the reading, from *Southern Living* (September 1994), the author explains how Roxana, while a high school sophomore, began to do research in what became her chosen field—molecular biology and genetics. Reading this selection will help you later as you write your paragraph about choosing a field of study.

▶ *BEFORE YOU READ*

1. In the reading, the author discusses Roxana Gonzalez's research in the field of molecular biology and genetics. Do you know what molecular biologists and geneticists do? If so, share your knowledge with your classmates.

2. Have you known or do you know high school students who have done research in science or prepared projects for science fairs? If so, discuss this research or projects with your classmates.

3. Have you decided on a field of study? Can you remember when you first thought about studying that field? What made you want to study the field?

from *EINSTEINS IN THE MAKING*

MELISSA BIGNER

When Roxana Maria Gonzalez . . . talks about **molecular biology,** everything about her **ignites.** Her words, **tinged** with a Cuban American accent, fly from her like **sparks,** and her dark eyes flash with **irrepressible** energy. Mention **DNA** and she becomes simply electric.

"What can I say?" she says, shaking her head. "I absolutely love **genetics!**" Not something you'd expect to hear from a high school student. But if you listen to the Miami native, you'll hear a tale about an island community **plagued** for centuries by a condition known as Laron **Dwarfism,** and the 300-year-old skeletons that **unraveled** the mystery.

Dr. Jane Day, founder of Research Atlantica, was **honeymooning** in the Bahamas and visited Spanish Wells, an island about 1 mile north of **North Eleuthera.** Several of the islanders there showed the effects of Laron Dwarfism. While the dwarfism doesn't **affect** mental **capabilities,** scientists and carriers alike are interested in finding a treatment.

Miami researchers collected blood samples and **pedigrees** from the Spanish Wells population. In 1991, an **archaeological expedition** on a nearby island turned up six 17th-century skeletons in an **isolated** spot known as Preacher's Cave. The short **stature** of the **skeletons,** as well as their **proximity** to the Spanish Wells, led Dr. Day to believe that they might be the islanders' **ancestors.**

Dr. Lisa Baumbach, a researcher in molecular biology and genetics at the University of Miami's Mailman Center, then came **on board.** Her **task** was to lead a team to find the DNA connection that would prove the skeletons were relatives. Enter Roxana.

A sophomore at the time, Roxana was in the Dade County school system's Laboratory Research Internship program. Her after-school assignment was to find a way to **extract** DNA from the skeletons. They decided to use the teeth.

Nice idea, but the only other person to achieve such a thing used **molars** that were barely 20 years old. **Undaunted,** Dr. Baumbach showed Roxana the lab methods and let her go at it.

After 10 **trial runs,** she was ready for the skeletal teeth. "They were **disgusting,**" she says. "They were brown and had sand and **algae** all over them. Nothing I could do would get them clean." Once she cracked them open, got the **pulp,** and **amplified** it with a PCR (**polymerase chain reaction**) machine, she couldn't find *any* DNA.

"I felt awful, I cried," she says. "After I messed up again on the second tooth, I got so nervous because I was wasting these valuable teeth."

Finally, Roxana realized the problem—**contamination.** She went through another round of alcohol **disinfectants,** acidic solutions, wire brushes, and **ultraviolet light,** and tried once again. Six months later, she got it. The DNA appeared as a faint band on the **electrophoresis gel** picture.

"I screamed so loud that everyone came running in. They all thought I fell off my chair!" she says, "We were laughing and yelling.

'We got it! We got it!' It was unbelievable!" Unbelievable is right—Roxana was the first person to extract DNA from such an old tooth.

Playing with her silver rings, one of which reads *Carpe Diem* ("seize the day"), she laughs again and says earnestly, "I love that you can find something that can help improve a person's life. It's like solving a mystery," she says. "It's so **addictive!**" Sounds like a pretty healthy addiction—for a scientist of any age.

▶ *AFTER YOU READ*

1. What was Roxana's assignment? How would the information she gained be helpful to other researchers studying Laron Dwarfism?

2. Why do you think Roxana succeeded in extracting DNA from the skeletons? Do you think this was an unusual achievement for a high school student? Why or why not?

3. In your opinion, why did Gonzalez choose molecular biology and genetics as her field of study?

Supplemental Reading List—Chapter 5

Berghese, Abraham. *My Own Country: A Doctor's Story of a Town and Its People in the Age of AIDS.* New York: Simon and Schuster, 1994.

Berghese, an immigrant doctor, describes how he chose his field, as well as how he treated AIDS patients and others in his small practice in Tennessee.

Galdikas, Birute M. F. *Reflections on Eden: My Years with the Orangutans of Borneo.* Boston: Little, Brown, 1995.

In this moving book, anthropologist Galdikas tells of her mentors (including Louis Leakey) and how she developed such an interest in orangutans that she spent twenty years living with and studying them in Borneo.

✍ **WRITING ASSIGNMENT:** *Writing about Choosing a Field of Study*

In this chapter, you will first learn about using cause-and-effect logic in your writing and then work through the stages of the writing process to develop your paragraph about choosing a field of study. Before you begin writing, discuss the following question with your classmates. Your response to this question will become the focus of your paragraph.

Question: What field or major have you chosen to study, and why?

If you have not yet chosen one, focus on the possible fields of study that you are considering. Write a paragraph in which you analyze the *one* reason why you chose your field of study or major. Or, write a paragraph about why you are considering one particular major or field of study. Use specific evidence to support your point and use analysis to explain why you chose or are considering the field of study.

Guidelines on Cause-and-Effect Writing

USING CAUSE-AND-EFFECT LOGIC

In your paragraph about choosing a field of study or a major, you will use cause-and-effect logic to show your reader why a cause led to an effect:

Cause: The *one reason* you chose your field of study

Effect: Your decision to study that field or major

In your paragraph, you want to make the cause-and-effect logic clear to your reader. You can do this by announcing in a topic sentence the one reason why you chose (or are considering) your field or major. For example:

Topic Sentence:

The primary reason why I chose to go into architecture is because I have been interested in designing buildings since I was a child.

Next, to support the point of the paragraph, you need to provide specific evidence for this one reason for choosing your field of study:

Specific Evidence:

Specific, concrete details
Specific examples
Specific facts and quotations

USING CAUSE-AND-EFFECT ANALYSIS

In your paragraph, you also need to provide analysis. One common weakness of this type of cause-and-effect paragraph is that writers present evidence for a cause but fail to analyze how the cause led to a particular effect. Thus, in addition to providing a topic sentence and evidence for the cause, you need to explain to the reader how or why the cause led to the effect:

Topic Sentence:

Cause: The one reason you chose your field or major
       Specific evidence

Effect: Your decision to study that particular major or field

In analyzing (explaining how/why the cause led to the effect), you might consider answering one or more of the following types of questions:

- What is the connection between the field or major and the reason you chose it?
- What is it about the field of study that relates to your past interests, experiences, or desires (described in your evidence)?
- What do you want to accomplish in this field that is tied to your past interests, experiences, or desires?

❏ *ACTIVITY 5.1:* **EVALUATING TWO STUDENTS'
       PARAGRAPHS**

Read student paragraph A and then discuss it in terms of the following questions. Repeat the same procedure for paragraph B.

DISCUSSION QUESTIONS

1. *Topic Sentence:* Does the writer make the cause-and-effect logic clear in the topic sentence—the one reason for choosing the field of study?

2. *Evidence:* Does the writer present enough specific and concrete evidence for the reason?

3. *Analysis:* Does the writer clearly explain the cause-and-effect connection between the reason and the particular field of study chosen? Or, does the writer need to explain more about how this field of study or major relates to the writer's past experiences, interests, or desires?

4. Which student paragraph—A or B—do you think is the stronger piece of writing? Why?

PARAGRAPH A

The major I chose is fiber and polymer science, which is in the field of textiles. I chose this major because when I was young, I had a skin allergy that was caused by the carpet in my apartment. Although the carpet was new, I got the allergy because of carpet bacteria. Before I had the allergy, I already had other allergies that were caused by chemically combined fibers in carpet. Therefore, I will study as hard as I can in fiber and polymer science.

PARAGRAPH B

The primary reason why I chose civil engineering as my major was because I have always been curious about how buildings, bridges, and highways are built. When I was young, I used to build small houses and bridges; I spent all day decorating and arranging them into a small village. I also went to the construction areas in our town to help the workers with some chores and learn a few facts about construction. As I moved the wood around and passed nails to the workers, I noticed every step that they did. When I went back home, I tried to make a small house by joining together pieces of the spare wood that I brought back with me from the construction area. With the dream of becoming a constructionist, I chose civil engineering as a field of study where I can expand my knowledge and improve my skills about construction. As a civil engineer, I will contribute my knowledge to my home country of Vietnam by building Vietnam into the most beautiful country in the world. I will also come back to my village and reconstruct a new village, which I have had in mind since I was young.

Prewriting: Generating Ideas

Before you begin writing your paragraph, take a few minutes to generate some ideas on your topic, using the prewriting technique of *brainstorming*.

Plan to spend ten to fifteen minutes on brainstorming. Write at the top of a blank piece of paper the question you chose for your paragraph:

Why did I choose my field of study or major?

or

Why am I now considering this one particular field of study or major?

Then write down everything you can think of in response to the question—words, phrases, more complete thoughts, anything. List your thoughts and ideas as they come to mind. Do not worry about whether an idea seems unconnected to the event—write it down anyway. Also, don't worry about spelling or grammar. Your goal during brainstorming is to get down on paper as many ideas as you can, as quickly as possible.

As the following example shows, brainstorming is different from freewriting. In freewriting, you write sentences across the page, line after line, much like a paragraph. In brainstorming, however, you make a list of words and phrases *down* the page. The result looks something like a grocery list. The following example was done by a student who was gathering ideas about why she chose her major. Note that, as this student brainstormed, she did not try to write her thoughts in complete sentences or to use correct grammar. Instead, she tried to get on paper all the ideas she could think of about choosing her major.

Brainstorming Example:

Why did I choose to major in environmental science?

like science
interested in outdoors
river rafting
water sources
lakes
animals
agriculture
like problem solving
computer modeling
like computers
toxins
Vietnam—environmental problems in rivers
dioxin in rivers/women's blood
affects babies/people
hard to clean up

FOCUSING AND ORGANIZING YOUR IDEAS

After generating ideas for your paragraph, you are ready to begin focusing and organizing them. Look through your brainstormed list and decide which ideas you want to get rid of, which you think belong together, and which you want to emphasize in your paragraph.

Note in the following example how the student who created the preceding brainstormed list went about organizing her ideas. As you can see in her organized brainstorming, she grouped the ideas that came out in brainstorming and then labeled them in terms of reasons why she chose her major. She can then choose one of these reasons for her paragraph.

Organized Brainstorming:

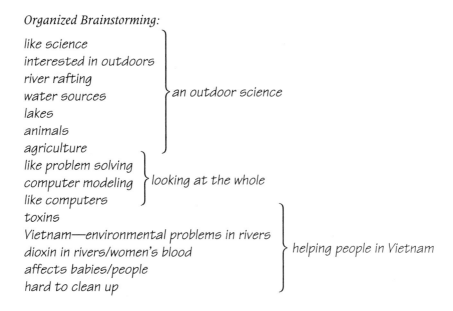

like science
interested in outdoors
river rafting
water sources   } *an outdoor science*
lakes
animals
agriculture
like problem solving
computer modeling   } *looking at the whole*
like computers
toxins
Vietnam—environmental problems in rivers
dioxin in rivers/women's blood   } *helping people in Vietnam*
affects babies/people
hard to clean up

PLANNING

After generating some ideas about your topic, jot down a few notes about how you plan to develop your paragraph. This plan might include, for example, your topic sentence and ideas for developing your evidence, as well as analysis.

Planning is an important step in the writing process. Successful writers take the time to plan their paragraphs and essays. Remember, though, that your plan is a rough guide; you will probably change it as you draft and then revise your paragraph. The purpose of planning at this point is to help you form an image in your mind of how you will develop your paragraph.

Drafting

With your prewriting and rough plan completed, you are now ready to begin drafting your paragraph about your field of study. Try to complete the draft in one sitting. Also, remember to focus on getting your ideas down on paper. Do not be concerned about sentence problems or other matters that you will correct later when you revise and edit.

Revising

Before sharing your draft paragraph with your writing group, practice evaluating the cause-and-effect paragraph that follows in Activity 5.2.

❏   *ACTIVITY 5.2:*   **EVALUATING A STUDENT'S PARAGRAPH**

In evaluating the following student paragraph, you want to determine if it has (1) a clearly focused point, (2) enough specific evidence, and (3) sufficient analysis to prove the point.

After one class member reads the paragraph aloud, discuss the questions that follow it.

The primary reason why I chose food science as my major was because I realized that food is very important to the human body. For example, before I came to the United States, I was living with my grandmother in Brazil. Because she was eighty years old, I helped her with the housework. Usually, my work included the cooking. One day my grandmother became sick because of a heart attack. I was so anxious about her health that I asked the doctor what I should do for her. He said that I should be careful not to make high cholesterol foods for her. After that, I began to learn about nutrition, and I tried to make food that was not only full of nutrition but also low in cholesterol and delicious for her. As a result, my grandmother began to recover; therefore, I was really thankful for the food. Now I think food science is a very good major for me because I can not only learn about technical nutrition but also make good food for my grandmother. In addition, I hope that I can help a lot of people's health with good food.

DISCUSSION QUESTIONS

1. *Central Point:* Does the writer convey the point of the paragraph in a clearly focused topic sentence that announces both the cause and the effect?

2. *Evidence:* Does the writer include enough specific evidence about why she chose food science as a major? Is the evidence specific enough to build a vivid picture in your mind?

3. *Analysis:* Does the writer analyze the evidence, explaining why the cause led to the effect? That is, does the writer show the connection between the cause (the reason why she chose food science as a major) and the effect (the choice of this particular major)?

❏ *ACTIVITY 5.3:* **PEER RESPONSE**

Now share your draft paragraph with your writing group. Use the following procedure:

1. One group member should begin by reading aloud his or her draft. The group should then discuss the paragraph in terms of the questions listed on the Peer Response Sheet for Activity 5.3 on page 344. Another member should record the group's comments on the sheet.

2. After you are finished filling out the sheet, give it to the writer so that he or she can consider the comments when revising the draft.

3. Repeat the procedure for each group member.

4. Then revise your own draft paragraph, keeping in mind the suggestions of your writing group.

Editing: The Past Perfect Tense

In writing about why you chose your field or major, your paragraph will probably be centered in the "world of the past" because of the past interests and experiences that led you to choose that major. When you wrote about the "world of the past" in earlier chapters, you depended on the past tense and occasionally on the past progressive. In this chapter, you will learn how to use another tense associated with the "world of the past"—the *past perfect tense*. This tense is most helpful when you need to distinguish between the time of two events that occurred one after another in the past. The following activity will help you see how past tense, past progressive, and past perfect tense work together in the "world of the past."

❏ *ACTIVITY 5.4:* **IDENTIFYING TENSES USED
IN THE "WORLD OF THE PAST"**

The following reading is about Carl Sagan, an astronomer at Cornell University in Ithaca, New York. In this reading (first published in *Time* in 1980 and then in *Reader's Digest* in 1990), the author, Frederic Golden, explains how Sagan chose his field of study—astronomy, which is the scientific study of the universe beyond the earth.

As you read the passage, notice that it is centered in the "world of the past." After reading the passage, underline all the verbs in the past tense and the past progressive. Next, see if you can find and then circle a verb form that refers to an event that occurred in "time before" the past centering point of the paragraph.

from *THE COSMIC EXPLAINER*

FREDERIC GOLDEN

As a child growing up in Brooklyn, astronomer Carl Sagan was already thinking of the heavens. "I remember asking my friends what the stars were," he recalls. "They told me they were lights in the sky." Unsatisfied with this answer, Sagan found a book that told him that the stars were enormously distant suns. "I got my first sense of the immensity of space," he says. "Until then my universe had been my neighborhood. I was hooked."

The hook worked its way in deeper when Sagan read the Martian tales of Edgar Rice Burroughs, who wrote about a man who miraculously transported himself to the Red Planet simply by gazing at it and longing for it. The dark-eyed young Sagan, looking up at the sky, tried vainly to follow his hero into space.

It was a dream the astronomer has never forgotten.

In the space provided, write the sentence that has a verb referring to an event that occurred in "time before" the past centering point of the paragraph.

_____

_____

In the preceding paragraph, the writer describes events that took place within the "world of the past." As you see from the globe diagram below, this "world of the past" took place entirely in the past—it has nothing to do with present time.

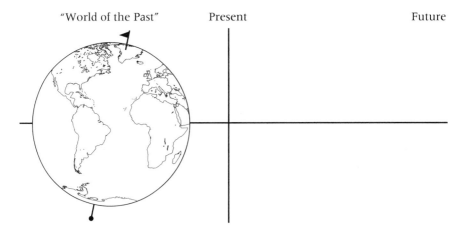

"World of the Past"   Present   Future

As you see from the line diagram on page 107, a writer chooses verb tenses within the "world of the past" in relation to the past centering point of this world:

- past tense for "same time" as the past centering point
- past perfect tense for "time before" the past centering point
- past tense for "time after" the past centering point

Past Tense for "Same Time" as the Past Centering Point:

Sagan *found* a book that *told* him that the stars were enormously distant suns. "I *got* my first sense of the immensity of space," he says.

Past Perfect Tense for "Time Before" the Past Centering Point:

"Until then my universe *had been* my neighborhood."

Past Tense for "Time After" the Past Centering Point:

Sagan *got* a book from the library about the stars. He *became* hooked on astronomy.

The past perfect tense is used exclusively within the "world of the past"; that is, it is always oriented or positioned relative to a point in past time—the centering point of this world. Past perfect time, then, is established not by itself but in relation to another point in past time. This "orienting" point in past time may be either expressed or understood.

"World of the Past"

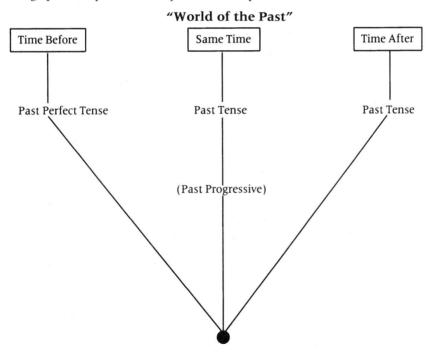

| Time Before | Same Time | Time After |

Past Perfect Tense   Past Tense   Past Tense

(Past Progressive)

Often the relationship between the two time references—"same time" as the past centering point and "time before"—is set up between two clauses:

SAME TIME
Until Sagan *found* a book on the stars,

TIME BEFORE

his universe *had been* his neighborhood.

This relationship between the two time references may also be set up between the past perfect tense ("time before") and a time reference to past time ("same time").

SAME TIME

Before *his twelfth birthday* (1946),

TIME BEFORE

Sagan *had thought* of his neighborhood as his "universe."

FORMATION OF THE PAST PERFECT

First look carefully at the past perfect verbs in the following two sentences:

Sagan *had* already *read* books on the stars when he read Edgar Rice Burroughs's tales about Mars.

Because a character in the Burroughs books *had transported* himself to Mars by gazing at it, Sagan decided to gaze at the sky in order to send himself into space also.

Now determine how the past perfect tense (for example, *had read, had transported*) is formed:

Past Perfect Tense =

_____ + _____
   AUXILIARY VERB   VERB FORM

USING LOGICAL CONNECTORS AND ADVERBS WITH THE PAST PERFECT

Several logical connectors, including subordinate conjunctions and transitions, are commonly used with the past perfect tense:

Subordinate Conjunctions		Transitions
before	until	subsequently
after	because	thereafter
by the time that	since	
when	although	
as soon as	even though	

Examples:

Even though Sagan's friends had given him one explanation of the stars, he searched for a more satisfactory explanation in books.

As a child, Sagan had thought about the heavens; *subsequently,* he read books about the stars and was hooked on the study of astronomy.

A number of adverbs are also often found with the past perfect tense: *just, already, ever, never.*

Example:

Sagan had *never* been satisfied by explanations of the stars until he read a book that described the stars as enormously distant suns.

The Subordinate Conjunctions *Before* and *After*

With the logical connectors *before* and *after,* you can often use the past tense to convey both the "same time" as the past centering point and the "time before" because these subordinate conjunctions tell the reader precisely which event happened first. Thus, when you use the subordinate conjunctions *before* and *after,* you often do not need the past perfect tense. Notice how in the following example sentences, *before* and *after* tell the reader the precise sequence of events. In each sentence, which event occurred first and which occurred second?

Examples:

After Sagan *finished* his graduate work, he *went* to Cornell University to teach astronomy.

Before Sagan *co-produced* the television series "Cosmos," he *wrote* several books, such as *The Dragons of Eden: Speculation on the Evolution of Human Intelligence* and *Broca's Brain.*

❏ *ACTIVITY 5.5:* **PRACTICING THE PAST PERFECT TENSE**

The following sentences describe the time the former prime minister of Pakistan, Benazir Bhutto, spent at Radcliffe College in Boston and the years immediately thereafter.*

Look carefully at the two sentences in each pair and decide which refers to the "same time" as the past centering point of the group of sentences and which refers to the "time before" the centering point. Then combine the two sentences, using the past tense and the past perfect tense as necessary. Also use the logical connector or adverb in the parentheses. In some sentences, you may have to remove or change words.

---

*Information in the sentences in this activity is from *Daughter of Destiny* (1989), by Benazir Bhutto.

1. (*because*)

Bhutto's mother stayed with her in her first few weeks at Radcliffe College. Bhutto was not homesick during her first term.

_____

_____

_____

2. (*after*)

Her mother left.

Benazir shed the *shalwa khameez* (long tops over loose pants) and reemerged in jeans and a sweatshirt.

_____

_____

_____

3. (*by the time*)

The first term ended.

During the first term, Benazir drank gallons of apple cider and ate hundreds of peppermint-stick ice-cream cones.

_____

_____

_____

4. (*as soon as*)

Benazir graduated from Radcliffe.

She flew to England to study at Oxford University.

_____

_____

_____

❏   *ACTIVITY 5.6:*   **EDITING VERB TENSES**

If time permits, practice editing verb tenses in the following paragraph. Find and correct errors in verb tense. In some cases, more than one answer may be correct.

The major reason I chose pre-med as my major is because I have always wanted to help people who don't speak English, especially Hispanic newcomers. About four years ago, my sister needed emergency treatment because she accidentally break one of her fingers in school while playing volleyball. Although my brother drive her to the hospital immediately, she waited for one hour before her surgery began because there isn't enough staff who could speak Spanish. Because of that incident, I had recently decided that I want to major in pre-med because I believe that as a bilingual I can be very helpful to new immigrants who need medical care. I enjoy science, and I had been interested in medicine for many years. I believe that in medicine I can combine my interest in helping people with my interest in working with people of different races and cultures.

 EDITING CHECKLIST ——————————————————————

As you edit the sentences in the latest draft version of your paragraph, check carefully for the following:

- ☐ Check for correct use of the *past* and *past perfect* tenses. When you are writing about the "world of the past," be sure to use the past perfect for "time before" the past centering point of your paragraph.
- ☐ Check that you have *not* used the present tense to describe the "world of the past," except for rare cases. (See Chapter 1.)
- ☐ Check that you have clearly *signaled a shift* from the "world of the past" to the "world of the present." This might be a time signal or a transition.

Example:

When I was young, I liked to play with blocks on my kitchen floor and build tall buildings. *Recently,* I have decided that the field of architecture fits my interest in building and my talents.

- ☐ Check for correct use of *verb tenses* if you are writing about the "world of the present." (See Chapter 4.)
- ☐ Check for *sentence structure problems:* fragments, run-on sentences, comma splices.
- ☐ Check for *sentence variety.*

CHAPTER 6

Writing about a Family or Cultural Value

In this chapter, you will write a paragraph about a value of your family or culture that you either accept or reject. Before you begin work on the paragraph, you will read the following selection about a Chinese value that cellist Yo-Yo Ma decided to reject. The reading will help you understand what the concept *value* means and how difficult it can be deciding whether to accept or reject the values of one's first culture. The reading will also give you ideas for your own paragraph about a family or cultural value.

The excerpt that follows is from "A Process Larger Than Oneself," by David Blum (*The New Yorker*, May 1, 1989). It is about the life of Yo-Yo Ma, a world-famous Chinese American cellist. Ma was born in Paris to Chinese parents; the family later immigrated to the United States. In the selection, Blum tells of Ma's life as a child and as a teenager in New York. He also describes one Chinese value—unquestioning obedience to and complete identification with one's parents—and how Ma eventually came to reject this value.

▶ *BEFORE YOU READ*

1. What is a cellist? What does a cello look like?

2. What is a family value? A cultural value? How is a value different from a custom?

3. List some of the values of your family or culture. Do most people from your culture keep their cultural values when they immigrate to the United States or when they come to the United States to study?

from *A PROCESS LARGER THAN ONESELF*

DAVID BLUM

If the move to America opened new horizons for the Ma family, it posed problems as well. "America was my father's third culture, and it

112

Cellist Yo-Yo Ma (Drawing by Kelwynn Alder; © 1989 The New Yorker Magazine, Inc. All rights reserved.)

was hard for him to **adjust,**" Ma said. "One of the duties of an Oriental child is unquestioning obedience to the parents; this is supposed to continue throughout one's life. It goes beyond obedience; the parents **identify** completely with the child. When I got into trouble, it was not considered my fault; it was somebody else's fault. I couldn't have **deliberately** done anything wrong, because I was, after all, an **extension** of my parents. As soon as we moved to America I had to deal with two **contradictory** worlds. At home, I was to **submerge** my **identity.** You can't talk back to your parents—period. At school, I was expected to answer back, to reveal my **individuality.** At home, we spoke only Chinese; we were taken to Chinese movies to remind us of our traditional values. But I was also American, growing up with American values. I became aware that if I was to be a cellist playing **concertos** I would have to have ideas of my own; that's one of the great things about being a musician. My **conflict** was **apparent** to **Pablo Casals,** to whom I was presented when I was seven. I don't remember what he said about my cello playing, but he did suggest that I should be given more time to go out and play in the street.

"My home life was totally structured. Because I couldn't **rebel** there, I did so at school. In the fifth grade, I began to cut classes, and I continued doing so through high school. I spent a lot of time wandering through the streets, mainly because I just wanted to be alone." Eventually, in 1968, Ma entered the Professional Children's School, in

New York, but he missed so many classes that his teachers **concluded** that he was bored and would be better off in an **accelerated** program. That program **enabled** him to graduate from high school when he was fifteen. He spent the following summer at Ivan Galamian's camp for string players, at Meadowmount, in the **Adirondacks.** It was his first experience on his own, away from home.

"Suddenly, I was free," Ma told me. "I had always kept my emotions bottled up, but at Meadowmount I just ran wild, as if I'd been let out of a **ghetto.** The whole structure of **discipline** collapsed. I exploded into bad taste at every level. Mr. Galamian [American violinist and teacher at the Juilliard School of Music in New York] was concerned that the boys and girls maintained a certain **decorum.** He would say, 'They shouldn't go into the bushes together.' I took some white paint and decorated the stone walls with **graffiti** on the subject. When Galamian found out, he was **horrified.** I knew I had gone too far, and spent a whole day washing the walls. I would leave my cello outside, not worrying if it might rain, and run off to play Ping-Pong. That summer, I played the Schubert Arpeggione Sonata and the Franck Sonata with **uninhibited** freedom—just letting go, in a way that had never happened before." Lynn Chang, who was then also studying at Meadowmount, remembers these performances as *"appassionato,* full of **abandon,** tremendously impressive." Ma's playing leapt startlingly into another dimension, bursting not only with **virtuosity** but with imagination, **irritating** those who admire **restraint** in youth, and **gratifying** those who share **Blake's** view that "**Exuberance** is Beauty."

▶ *AFTER YOU READ*

1. In your own words, what would you say is the Chinese value that Ma rejected?

2. Why do you think Ma rejected this value? As a cellist and a musician, why did Ma insist on having "ideas of [his] own"?

3. Do you think it was a good idea for Ma to reject this value? Why or why not?

4. Reread the last sentence in the selection. What is the meaning of this sentence?

Supplemental Reading List—Chapter 6

Mahfouz, Najib. *Palace Walk.* New York: Doubleday, 1990.

Mahfouz, Najib. *Palace of Desire.* New York: Doubleday, 1991.

Mahfouz, Najib. *Sugar Street.* New York: Doubleday, 1992.

> The three volumes above (called The Cairo Trilogy) by Nobel-prize-winning author Mahfouz will help you discover the values of traditional Egyptian culture.

✍ **WRITING ASSIGNMENT:** *Writing about a Family or Cultural Value*

In this chapter, you will first learn more about values and how to write about abstract concepts. Then you will work through the stages of the writing process to develop your own paragraph about a value. Before you begin writing, discuss the following question with your classmates. Your answer to this question will become the focus of your paragraph.

Question: What cultural or family value do you accept or reject as important, and why?

Write a paragraph about a value that you either accept or reject. Be sure to include specific evidence for this value and to analyze the value by explaining why you accept or reject it.

Guidelines on Writing about Abstract Concepts

In earlier chapters, your paragraphs focused on concrete topics, such as possessions, hobbies, and customs. The writing assignment in this chapter, however, asks you to write about an *abstract concept*—a value. You will probably find that writing about an abstract concept will demand more of your skills as a writer, both in understanding what the concept means and in getting your ideas down on paper. Therefore, before you begin working on your paragraph, you need to think about what a value is and why a person might decide to accept or reject it.

WHAT IS A VALUE?

To understand what a value is, it is helpful to distinguish it from a custom. In Chapter 4, you wrote about a *custom*—a practice that is common to a particular group of people. A custom is something that people do outwardly, something that can be observed or seen by others.

A *value*, however, differs from a custom in that it is more inward; it is a belief in a certain abstract principle that a group of people considers important. For example, one common value of American culture is independence. Because many Americans believe in the importance of independence, they raise their children to become independent adults. People of other cultures, however, regard dependence in children of all ages as an important value.

Some cultural values have developed because of a group's environment—the natural conditions of the area in which they live. Certain desert-dwelling tribes value cooperation, for instance, because the unpleasant conditions of desert life require people to cooperate with each other in order to survive. Other values are based on a group's religion or philosophies. The great value placed on education by the Chinese, for example, comes from Confucian philosophy, which holds that education is of central importance in a society. The value of purity, which is very important to many Indians, comes from the Hindu religion. Still other values are brought into a culture by outsiders—missionaries (people from foreign countries sent in to teach religion), immigrants from other countries, or invaders who come in and gain power over the native people.

❑ *ACTIVITY 6.1:* **BRAINSTORMING VALUES**

Working with your classmates, brainstorm a list of values. One class member should record the list on the board as the class brainstorms all the values that they can think of. Then discuss the items listed on the board. Are some of them actually customs? Which are true values? How can you tell the difference?

EVIDENCE

In your paragraph, you want to make certain that your reader understands the value you are writing about. You can accomplish this by providing a definition of the value (if needed) as well as by presenting evidence for the value.

In order to define the value in a meaningful way, you need to think carefully about the knowledge of your readers. For example, if you are writing about the Bedouin value of courage, you can assume that your readers will know what the word *courage* means; however, they probably will not know exactly what it means in Bedouin culture. (Bedouin are nomadic Arabs who live in the deserts of Arabia, Syria, and North Africa.)

In describing the Bedouin value of courage in *The Saudis: Inside the Desert Kingdom* (1988), writer Sandra Mackey carefully defines the word for the reader in terms of what it means to the Bedouin people:

Courage can best be defined by the ability to endure deprivation, withstand physical pain, or suffer emotional stress, without showing signs of suffering. In other words, it is stoicism.

In presenting your evidence for your value, you want to include specific details—facts, examples, and quotations. Remember that only with specific, concrete details and examples will your reader be able to form a clear, sharp picture of the value.

ANALYSIS

In your analysis, you need to explain to the reader why you accept or reject the value. This is something you will want to think carefully about.

There is much to be said for a people who hold onto their culture's customs and values. This argument is presented in the following passage from *East Africa* (The Editors of Time-Life Books, Time-Life Books B.V., 1986), in which the writer explains why the people of East Africa need to hold onto some of their old customs and values in the face of the great changes that have come with independence.

from *EAST AFRICA*

The Editors of Time-Life Books

Since the first years of the Independence struggle, writers and artists have warned that the customs and beliefs of the past could not be **abandoned** without cost. Although they had **evolved** in the countryside, and were not easily **adapted** to life in the towns, they alone provided the individual with a clear moral outlook, as well as a sense of belonging to a wider community. **Imported ideologies** could never fill the **gap,** whether they were taken from the West or the East; there had to be an African **solution,** and this would mean building on the wisdom of the past.

For East Africans in the 1980s, this is proving a forbidding **task.** The European **invasion,** and the **disparagement** of tribal ways by both missionaries and teachers, seriously **undermined** their **traditional** way of life. Children may no longer be taught their **ancestral myths,** nor be instructed in the complex **etiquette** that many communities had developed; few **undergo** the training in moral **conduct** that used to **accompany initiation.** Consequently, much of the old knowledge has been lost forever, since most communities had no means of preserving their culture; they had no written language and few artistic traditions strong enough to survive in an **era** of change.

There can, of course, also be appropriate reasons for abandoning the values of one's culture, as Yo-Yo Ma did. Sometimes this is a purely personal choice; other times it is an unavoidable choice, such as when keeping a certain cultural value is impossible in a new situation. For example, in order to survive in a different culture, immigrants may have to abandon certain values of their own culture.

All cultures change, and the customs and values of a culture must also change to a certain extent in order to adapt to a changing world. Yet with too much change comes loss—and sometimes the loss of the customs and values of a culture.

You want to think about these issues carefully as you explain to the reader why you reject or accept the value you are writing about.

Prewriting: Generating Ideas

Before you begin writing your first draft, take a few minutes to generate some ideas about your topic. Use one of the prewriting techniques you learned in earlier chapters: clustering (pages 10–11), freewriting (pages 31–32), tree diagraming (page 54), or brainstorming (pages 101–103).

Set aside ten to twenty minutes to work on the prewriting activity. Write this controlling question at the top of your page before you begin:

Controlling Question:

What cultural or family value do I accept or reject, and why?

After generating some ideas about your topic, look more carefully at the items in your prewriting. Identify the material you want to include in your paragraph, such as examples or ideas that explain why you accept or reject the value.

Drafting

With your prewriting completed, you are ready to begin drafting your paragraph. Think about how you want to organize or plan your paragraph. For example, consider what you want your topic sentence to convey, how you can best define the value, what kind of evidence you need to present, and how you should explain why you reject or accept the value. Write down a few notes about your plan or create a plan in your mind.

When drafting your paragraph, try to complete it in one sitting. Also, remember to concentrate on the ideas you are developing, not on sentence or grammatical problems.

Revising

If time permits, practice analyzing the strengths and weaknesses of the following student paragraphs in Activity 6.2 before sharing your draft paragraph with your writing group.

❏ *ACTIVITY 6.2:* **EVALUATING TWO STUDENTS'**
    PARAGRAPHS

After one class member reads paragraph A aloud, discuss it in terms of the following questions. Repeat the same procedure for paragraph B.

DISCUSSION QUESTIONS

1. *Definition:* Does the writer give the reader a clear idea of the value being discussed? If not, how can the writer define the value further?

2. *Evidence:* Does the writer present enough specific evidence to give the reader a clear, sharp picture of the value? Or, does the writer need to use more specific details in the evidence? If needed, what specific evidence could the writer add?

3. *Analysis:* Does the writer analyze the value, explaining clearly and thoroughly why he or she rejects or accepts it?

PARAGRAPH A

One value of the Taiwanese culture that I do not accept is the Taiwanese belief that boys are more important than girls. In Taiwanese families, this value shows itself in the way boys receive more attention from parents and grandparents, more education, and more privileges. Boys have the priority to dominate the great things in the world in Taiwan. Taiwanese people value boys more because in centuries of old, the position of the king was dominated by males. Also, after boys get married, they have to take care of their parents. Therefore, the parents think that the boy is more important than his sister. Yet I do not believe in this value of my culture because I feel that boys and girls should have the same level in society. They should both have the same opportunity to show their abilities in terms of education and to show their responsibility by the privileges they have. If men and women have equal rights, then our Taiwanese society will have more excellent and intelligent people in different jobs and schools. Therefore, Taiwan will have rapid improvement and a successful future.

PARAGRAPH B

One value of Korean culture that I thoroughly accept is the Korean people's belief in the importance of the extended family. In an extended family, several generations live together in a big house or in several small living units around a courtyard. The past origin of the extended family was for the family's protection from animals in the prehistoric age. Now, Koreans have kept the extended family in order to keep good relationships among relatives. For example, three or four generations usually live together in a house and create a rural village with just the same relatives (same last name). Therefore, when they work on their farm, they work easily and effectively by helping each other. I like this value very much because in the extended family there is intimacy between father and son in terms of love and obedience. Also, because of the extended family, Koreans do not have problems caring for old people, or with suicide, loneliness, or starving. Old people keep their position of authority within the extended family, and they are able to give good advice because of their plentiful experience. They also enjoy taking care of their grandsons and granddaughters. I believe that all these things are benefits of the extended family.

❏ *ACTIVITY 6.3:* **PEER RESPONSE**

Now share your draft paragraph with your writing group. Use the following procedure:

1. One group member should begin by reading aloud his or her draft. The group should then discuss the paragraph in terms of the questions listed on the Peer Response Sheet for Activity 6.3 on page 345. Another group member should record the group's suggestions on the sheet.

2. After you are finished filling out the sheet, give it to the writer so that he or she can consider the comments when revising.

3. Repeat the procedure for each group member.

4. Then revise your own draft paragraph, keeping in mind the suggestions of your writing group.

Editing: Coherence

In earlier chapters, you have had considerable practice in writing paragraphs. Now, as you take on the more challenging task of writing about an abstract concept, you are ready to turn your attention to one of the more difficult principles of good writing—coherence. Studying coherence in this and the following chapter will help you to strengthen your writing.

WHAT IS COHERENCE?

The term *coherence* in written English means that a paragraph or group of sentences has a smoothly developing train of thought—that is, one idea follows from the previous idea and leads to the next idea. In other words, as the ideas advance, there is an emerging train of reasoning or thought being developed:

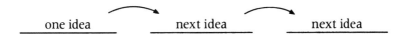

one idea   next idea   next idea

Read paragraph B again on page 120. As you read, notice how the ideas advance smoothly from one sentence to the next. The ideas seem to develop or emerge logically, with one idea leading to the next idea. After reading this paragraph, you can say, "Yes, I see what the writer means by 'the extended family in Korean culture.'" When writing has good coherence, the reader can say, "Oh, yes. I understand what the writer means."

If writing does not have good coherence, the reader becomes confused. As you read the following paragraph, consider how poor coherence affects you as a reader. Can you understand what the writer is trying to say?

One very important value of Pakistani culture that I have accepted is respect between parents and children and also between other members of the family. Family development does not occur all alone. Culture and history also influence the development of the children in the family. These influences have continued from many generations until now and will continue in the future. Pakistani children or teenagers must be very cautious when they talk to or behave with others who are older or younger than themselves. They are not allowed to show their anger by yelling or breaking the peace. Youths in Pakistani culture are totally under the control of parents. Youths in Pakistani families play an important role in the family. This is why I accept this value. Parents in Pakistani culture spoil their children. Children are cherished by their parents.

In the paragraph, one idea does not logically follow the previous idea nor lead to the next idea. Instead, the paragraph contains a "jumble" of mixed-up ideas. This jumble makes it difficult for the reader to understand the point the writer is trying to make about one of the values of Pakistani culture.

PROVIDING COHERENCE

In order to make certain that your paragraphs have coherence, you need to know what makes a paragraph coherent. Three major factors work together to make a paragraph coherent. You will study the first two factors in this chapter and the third one in Chapter 7.

1. Continuity in the developing train of ideas
2. Continuity revealed by surface signals
3. More surface signals—logical connectors

Continuity in the Developing Train of Ideas
The most important factor leading to coherence is continuity in the developing train of thought. As noted earlier, one idea follows from the previous idea and leads to the next idea in a coherent paragraph.

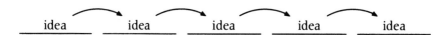

idea   idea   idea   idea   idea

The writer advances the point of the paragraph in a logical way so that one idea smoothly emerges or develops from the previous idea and then leads to the next idea.

In the following paragraph, note how one idea emerges from the previous idea and leads to the next. Also note the continuity in the way the ideas of the paragraph advance in a smooth, logical way.

One value of Salvadoran culture that I do not accept is the value of purity in women. A Salvadoran woman must be absolutely pure, or else she is considered worthless. For an unmarried woman, purity means virginity, while purity for a married woman means that she has only had sexual relations with her husband. Yet I believe female purity is an unrealistic value in Salvadoran culture because I think that women who do not remain "pure" are too harshly punished; they are considered an "outcast" or "dirty" if they have sexual relations before marriage or outside of marriage. This standard is too high and the punishment is too harsh because women, after all, are human beings and should not have their lives ruined by making one mistake in judgment. I think the standards for sexual behavior should be more realistic and should be applied to both men and women.

How can you make certain that a paragraph has coherence—that one idea smoothly leads to another? One way involves using the principle of "something old/something new" in writing your sentences. *"Something old/something new"* means that in creating a sentence, you pick up "something old" from the previous sentence or from an earlier sentence in the paragraph and add to it "something new." Picking up "something old" from a previous sentence bridges the gap between sentences, while the "something new" advances the idea being developed. The "something old" often goes at the beginning of the sentence, and the "something new" follows in the middle or near the end of the new sentence.

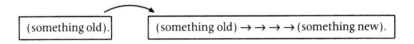

The "something old" that the writer picks up may be an idea from a previous sentence or an earlier part of the paragraph. Or, it may be a word from a previous sentence.

In the second of the following two sentences, underline the "something old" that is being picked up from the first sentence, as well as the "something new" that has been added.

One important value in Brazilian culture is hospitality. Hospitality to a Brazilian means essentially that your "door" is always open to friends, relatives, and guests.

❏ *ACTIVITY 6.4:* IDENTIFYING "SOMETHING OLD" AND "SOMETHING NEW"

Reread the paragraph about the value of female purity in Salvadoran culture on page 122. This time, though, for each sentence except for the first, identify the "something old" that the writer has picked up from a previous sentence. Draw an arrow from the word or idea in the previous sentence to the word or idea in the following sentence. Then underline the "something new" in each sentence.

Continuity Revealed by Surface Signals

Although continuity in the developing train of thought is the most important factor leading to coherence in writing, at times you will need to bridge gaps between ideas presented in two clauses or between sentences with *surface signals*. These signals tell the reader—in a direct, "surface" way—the logical connection between one idea and the next.

There are several types of surface signals that can help you use the principle of "something old/something new." (In Chapter 7, you will study other surface signals, including logical connectors.) Some of the surface signals that link "something old" and "something new" are the following:

- Repetition and synonyms:

    One of the values of Saudi Arabian culture is *modesty* in *women*. *Women* show their *modesty* by covering themselves with a veil.
- Demonstrative adjectives and pronouns (*this, that, these, those, such*):

    This veil covers the woman's head and often much of her face.
- Pronouns (*he, she, it, they, you*):

    She may also choose to wear a mask that shows only her eyes.

❏ *ACTIVITY 6.5:* **IDENTIFYING SURFACE SIGNALS**

In the following paragraph, circle each surface signal that you find. Then draw an arrow between the "something old" in the previous sentence and the surface signal. The first two examples are done for you. Discuss your results with your classmates.

One important value in Brazilian culture that I accept is hospitality. To a Brazilian, hospitality means that your "door" is always open to friends, relatives, and guests. Hospitality is very important in my family's home in Brazil; acquaintances and relatives are always welcome to drop in on us. They can appear at the doorstep and know that they will be invited in to share a meal or to join the family for an evening of conversation. Acquaintances and relatives know that when they travel to Sao Paulo, there is a bed in my parents' home for them, whether for a day or for several months. This Brazilian value of hospitality is important to me because I believe sharing your home and food with others is important. You not only help others by sharing extra food and space, but you also make your own life richer by getting to know other people and hearing their ideas about the world.

Pronouns as Surface Signals

As noted earlier, *pronouns* are among the *surface signals* that give coherence to your writing by connecting an idea in one sentence to an idea in the next:

> Many Japanese believe in the importance of teamwork. *They* teach *their* children to think of the group first, rather than *their* own individual needs.

In using pronouns as surface signals, you will want to be careful with pronoun reference and agreement. Problems in pronoun reference and agreement confuse the reader and cause a breakdown in coherence.

❑ *ACTIVITY 6.6:* **LOOKING FOR PRONOUN REFERENCE/AGREEMENT PROBLEMS**

Underline problems in pronoun reference and agreement in the following passage and then discuss with your classmates why these problems confuse the reader and cause a breakdown in coherence.

> An important value of people in my culture is generosity. They are expected to share their goods and wealth with others, especially needy people. He may not have as much as you do, or your children may be hungry. This is important to people in my culture.

The following brief section on pronoun agreement and reference will help you as you edit your draft for coherence.

Pronoun Agreement. A pronoun commonly takes the place of a noun preceding it. The preceding noun is called the pronoun's *antecedent*. A pronoun should agree with its antecedent in *person, number,* and *gender.*

Personal Pronouns		
	Number	
Person	*Singular*	*Plural*
1st	I, me, my	we, us, our
2nd	you, your	you, your
3rd	he, she, it; him, her, it his, her, its	they, them, their

Person:

3RD PERSON

People in my culture will share *their* goods and wealth with a poor widow's family.

Number:

PLURAL

Widows do not have to worry about *their* children starving.

Gender:

FEMININE

People in the village will give a *widow* all the help *she* needs.

A **demonstrative pronoun** (*this, that, these, those*) also refers back to a noun preceding it (its *antecedent*). A demonstrative pronoun must agree with its antecedent in number:

PLURAL

In a poor country, *generosity* and *sharing* of one's wealth are essential. *These* are especially important values when a country has few government services for the poor.

Pronoun Reference. In editing, you will want to make certain that each personal pronoun or demonstrative pronoun clearly refers to its antecedent:

Clear Reference:

When a *father* is gravely ill, *he* knows that others in the village will care for his family.

If two nouns come before a *personal pronoun*, be sure the reader can see clearly which noun the pronoun refers to:

Ambiguous Reference:

The family members will not be embarrassed by their neighbors' generosity. *They* will be understanding.

Clear Reference:

The family members will not be embarrassed by their neighbors' generosity. *They* will be understanding of their neighbors' eagerness to help.

Ideally, a *demonstrative pronoun* should refer back to a specific antecedent.

A neighbor may appear at the door with a pot of stew. *This* is just the first of many gifts of food.

In editing, you will want to make certain that a demonstrative pronoun's reference is not ambiguous or vague:

Ambiguous Reference:

A farmer may lose his crops in a drought, or they may be washed away in a flood. *This* means his family may need a great deal of help.

Clear Reference:

A farmer may lose his crops in a drought, or they may be washed away in a flood. *This* loss of crops means his family may need a great deal of help.

Vague Reference:

Neighbors may bring the farmer seeds for a new crop after the weather has ruined his current crop. *This* pleases him.

Clear Reference:

Neighbors may bring the farmer seeds for a new crop after the weather has ruined his current crop. *This* kind of generosity pleases him.

The same problem with vague reference may occur with the personal pronoun *it:*

Vague "It" Reference:

The neighbors themselves may have suffered crop damage. *It* does not matter to them. They will still share their few seeds with a neighbor who has lost everything.

Clear Reference:

The neighbors themselves may have suffered crop damage. *This loss of crops* does not matter to them. They will still share their few seeds with a neighbor who has lost everything.

❑   *ACTIVITY 6.7:*   **IDENTIFYING PRONOUN REFERENCE/AGREEMENT PROBLEMS**

Underline each pronoun (personal or demonstrative) in the following passage. Draw an arrow back to what you think is its antecedent, as is done in the first example. Next, identify, correct, and discuss with your classmates any problems you find in pronoun reference or agreement.

One highly prized value among Arabs is family honor. They see honor as a family having a good reputation in the community. They are each held in high regard because of the family's honor. In the same sense, the behavior of any one family member will reflect upon their honor. If a son steals money from a shopkeeper, this will make the whole family less honorable in the eyes of his neighbors. If a young woman has a baby out of wedlock, they will lose family honor. All family members—father, mother, brothers, sisters, aunts, and uncles—will lose honor because of those.

 **EDITING CHECKLIST**

After revising your paragraph about a value and considering the suggestions of your writing group, you are ready to edit. Take the time to check the following:

☐ Check for *coherence problems* in your paragraph. Ask a classmate or friend to read your draft aloud to you. As he or she reads it, listen for breaks in coherence, where one sentence does not logically follow another. If you notice breaks in coherence, ask yourself the following questions:

• Can I use the principle of "something old/something new" to improve coherence? Try picking up "something old" from a previous sentence and adding to it "something new."

• Can I use a surface signal—repetition or synonyms, demonstrative adjectives or pronouns, or pronouns—to link one sentence to the next?

If time permits, also check your draft for the following:

☐ Check for any problems in *pronoun reference* or *agreement.*

☐ Check for correct *verb tense.*

☐ Check for *sentence structure problems:* fragments, run-on sentences, and comma splices.

☐ Check for *sentence variety.*

CHAPTER 7

Writing about a Decision

In Chapters 1–6, you learned how to write paragraphs. In this chapter and those that follow, you will write essays. An *essay* is a longer piece of writing that includes several paragraphs. In this chapter, you will write an essay about a decision—one that you or your family made—and the causes or effects of this decision. Before you begin work on your essay, you will read the following selection, which is longer than some of the selections in previous chapters. Reading this longer selection will not only help you improve your reading skills but will also give you ideas for your essay about a decision.

The reading is from *My Life* (1975), the autobiography of Golda Meir, former prime minister of Israel. After Meir's family immigrated to the United States from Ukraine (in southeastern Europe), she spent her childhood in Milwaukee, Wisconsin. She later became a teacher, taught in the United States, and then immigrated to Palestine. She was one of the founders of Israel and served from 1969 to 1974 as prime minister.

In the reading, Meir tells of a decision she had to make when she was fifteen—whether to become independent from her parents. She mentions Sheyna (her sister), Shamai (Sheyna's husband-to-be), Clara (her other sister), and Regina and Sarah (her girlfriends). Sheyna had earlier come down with tuberculosis (a lung disease) and was hospitalized in a sanatorium (a medical clinic for tuberculosis patients).

▶ *BEFORE YOU READ*

1. Do you know where Israel is? Can you locate it on the map that appears in the front of this book?

2. Have you ever disagreed with your parents about something that was important in your life? Did you decide to go along with your parents' decision? Why or why not?

from *MY LIFE*

GOLDA MEIR

When I was fourteen, I finished elementary school. My marks were good, and I was chosen to be class **valedictorian.** The future seemed very bright and clear to me. **Obviously** I would go on to high school and then, perhaps, even become a teacher, which is what I most wanted to be. I thought—and still think today—that teaching is the noblest and the most satisfying **profession** of all. A good teacher opens up the whole world for children, makes it possible for them to learn to use their minds and in many ways **equips** them for life. I knew I could teach well, once I was **sufficiently** educated myself, and I wanted that kind of responsibility. Regina, Sarah and I talked endlessly about what we would do when we grew up. I remember on those summer evenings how we sat for hours on the steps of my house and discussed our futures. Like teenage girls everywhere, we thought these were the most important decisions we would ever have to make—other than marriage, and that certainly seemed much too **remote** to be worth our talking about.

My parents, however—as I ought to have understood but did not—had other plans for me. I think my father would have liked me to be educated, and at my Fourth Street graduation ceremony his eyes were **moist.** He understood, I believe, what was **involved;** but in a way his own life had defeated him, and he was unable to be of much help to me. My mother, as usual and despite her **disastrous** relationship with Sheyna, knew exactly what I should do. Now that I had finished elementary school, spoke English well and without an accent and had developed into what the neighbors said was a *dervaksene shein meydl* (a fine, **upstanding** girl), I could work in the shop full time and sooner or later—but better sooner—start thinking seriously about getting married, which she reminded me, was forbidden to women teachers by state [Wisconsin] law.

If I insisted on **acquiring** a profession, she said, I could go to secretarial school and learn to become a **shorthand** typist. At least, I wouldn't remain an **old maid** that way. My father nodded his head. "It doesn't pay to be too clever," he warned. "Men don't like smart girls." As Sheyna had done before me, I tried in every way I knew to change my parents' mind. In tears, I explained that nowadays an education was important, even for a married woman, and argued that in any case I had no intention whatsoever of getting married for a very long time. Besides, I **sobbed,** I would rather die than spend my life—or even part of it—**hunched over** a typewriter in some **dingy** office.

But neither my arguments nor my tears were of any **avail.** My parents were convinced that high school, for me at least, was an **un-**

warranted luxury—not only unnecessary, but undesirable. From the distance of Denver, Sheyna (now convalescent and out of the **sanatorium**) encouraged me in my **campaign,** and so did Shamai, who had joined her there. As they wrote to me often, sending their letters to Regina's house so my parents wouldn't find out about the **correspondence,** I knew that Shamai had first washed dishes in the sanatorium and had then been taken on to work in a small dry-cleaning plant that served one of the big Denver hotels. In his spare time he was studying **bookkeeping,** and most important of all, in the face of repeated warnings from Sheyna's doctor, they were going to be married. "Better we should live less," Shamai had decided, "but live together." It was to be one of the happiest marriages I ever knew, and despite the doctor's grim **prediction,** it lasted forty-three years and resulted in three children.

My parents were very upset at first, especially my mother. "Another **lunatic** with grand ideas and not a cent in his pocket," she **sniffed.** *That* was a husband for Sheyna? That was a man who could support and take care of her? But Shamai not only loved Sheyna, but understood her. He never argued with her. When he was sure that he was right about something, he went ahead and did it, and Sheyna always knew when she was beaten. But when she wanted something and it was really important to her, Shamai never stood in her way. To me, the news of their marriage meant that Sheyna now had what she most needed and wanted—and that I at last had a brother.

In my secret letter to Denver I wrote in detail about the continuing fights over school that were making my life at home almost **intolerable** and were leading me to decide to become independent as soon as possible. That autumn, the autumn of 1912, I **defiantly** began my first term at Milwaukee's North Division High School and in the afternoons and on weekends worked at a variety of odd jobs, determined never again to ask my parents for money. But none of this helped; the **disputes** at home went on and on.

The **last straw** was my mother's attempt to find me a husband. She didn't want me to get married at once, of course, but she very much wanted to be sure not only that I would get married at what she considered a reasonable age, but that, unlike Sheyna, *I* at least would marry somebody **substantial.** Not rich—that was out of the question—but at least solid. In actual fact, she was already **discreetly negotiating** with a Mr. Goodstein, a pleasant, friendly, relatively **well-to-do** man in his early thirties, whom I knew because he used to come into the store now and then to chat for a while. Mr. Goodstein! But he was an old man! Twice my age! I sent a **furious** letter to poor Sheyna. The reply came from Denver by return mail. "No, you shouldn't stop school. You are too young to work; you have good chances to become something," Shamai wrote. And with perfect generosity: "My advice is that you should get ready and come to us. We are not rich either, but you will have good chances here to study, and we will do all we can for you." At the bottom of his letter, Sheyna wrote her own warming invitation: "You must come to us immediately." There would be enough of everything for all of us, she **assured** me. All together, we would manage. "First, you'll have all the opportunities to study; second, you'll have plenty to eat; third, you'll have the necessary clothes that a person ought to have."

I was very touched then by their letter, but reading it today, I am even more moved by the readiness of those young people, still so far from being established themselves, to take me in and share whatever they had with me. That letter, written from Denver in November, 1912, was a turning point in my life because it was in Denver that my real education began and that I started to grow up. I suppose that if Sheyna and Shamai had not come to my rescue, I would have gone on fighting with my parents, crying at night and still somehow going to high school. I can't imagine that I would have agreed under any **circumstances** to stop studying and marry the probably much-**maligned** Mr. Goodstein; but Sheyna and Shamai's offer was like a **lifeline,** and I grabbed at it.

In the years that have passed since that November, I have also often thought of Sheyna's last letter to me before I joined her in Denver. "The main thing," she wrote, "is never to be excited. Always be calm and act coolly. This way of action will always bring you good results. Be brave." That was advice about running away from home, but I never forgot it, and it stood me in good stead within a few years when I came to what was to be my real home, the land in which I was prepared to fight to the death in order to stay.

Getting to Denver was not easy. I couldn't possibly expect my parents to agree to my leaving home and going to live with Sheyna. They would never have permitted it. The only **solution** was not to tell them anything at all, simply to leave. It might not be the bravest course, but it would certainly be the most **efficient.** Sheyna and Shamai sent me some money for a railway ticket, and Regina and I planned my flight down to the last detail. The first problem to be solved was how to get together enough money to pay for the rest of my ticket. I borrowed some of it from Sarah (which was certainly a very "cool" action considering that I had no idea how I would ever pay it back), and Regina and I persuaded a number of new immigrants on the street into taking English lessons from us for ten cents an hour. When we had collected enough money, we set about **plotting** the details of my **departure.**

Regina was a **marvelously devoted ally.** Not only was she absolutely trustworthy and could be **relied on** not to tell either my parents or her own anything about my plans, but she was also very imaginative—although now that I write about it, I have an idea that she must have mixed up my escape with an **elopement.** What she **proposed**—and what I very gladly accepted—was that since we lived above the store then, I should make a **bundle** of my clothes (just as well that it wouldn't be a very large bundle) and lower it the evening before my departure to Regina, who would **spirit it away** to the baggage department of the railway station. Then, in the morning, instead of going to school, I could go right to the train.

When the fateful evening arrived, I sat in the kitchen with my parents as though it were just any ordinary night, but my heart was very heavy. While they drank tea and talked, I **scribbled** a note for them to read the next day. It was only a few words and not very well-chosen ones at that. "I am going to live with Sheyna, so that I can study," I wrote, adding that there was nothing for them to worry about and that I would write from Denver. It must have hurt them terribly to read that note the next morning, and if I were to write it today, I would do so only after much thought and with very great care. But I was under extreme pressure then and only fifteen. Before I went to sleep that night, I went over to Clara's bed and looked at her for a minute. I felt very guilty about leaving her without even saying good-bye, and I wondered what would happen to her now that both Sheyna and I were out of the house, as I thought, for good. Clara was growing up to be the most "American" of us all, a quiet, shy, undemanding little girl, whom everyone liked but to whom I had never paid much attention and whom I didn't really know very well. Now that I was going to leave her, I remember feeling a sudden sense of responsibility. It turned out, though I couldn't have known it then, that being the only child at home was actually to make her life easier. My parents were far more **lenient** with Clara than they had ever been with Sheyna or with me, and my mother even spoiled her sometimes. We weren't a **demonstrative** family, but that night I stroked her face and kissed her, although she slept through my **farewell.**

Very early the next morning, I left home as planned and went to the station to board the train for Denver. I had never traveled alone before, and the idea that trains run according to a timetable had never occurred either to me or to my fellow **conspirator,** so I was still sitting nervously, with a pounding heart, on a bench in the station when my parents opened and read the note I had written for them at home. But as the **Yiddish** saying goes, I had considerably more luck than brains, and somehow or other, in the confusion, no one looked for me until the train had left and I was on my way to Sheyna, knowing that I had done something that deeply wounded my mother and father, but that was truly **essential** for me. In the two years that I was to spend in Denver, my father, unforgiving, wrote to me only once. But from time to time my mother and I exchanged letters, and by the time I came back I no longer had to battle for the right to do as I wanted.

▶ *AFTER YOU READ*

1. Why did fifteen-year-old Meir decide to become independent from her parents? That is, what was the cause of her decision?

2. Do you think Meir made the right decision? Why or why not?

3. Think of one important decision that you or your family made in the past. Why did you make this decision? In other words, what was the cause of the decision?

Supplemental Reading List—Chapter 7

Danticat, Edwidge. *Breath, Eyes, Memory.* New York: Vintage Books, 1994.

Danticat, Edwidge. *Krik? Krak!* New York: Soho Press, 1995.

In these two works of fiction, the young Haitian American author Danticat tells moving, unforgettable stories of the lives of Haitians, both in their native country and in the United States.

✐ WRITING ASSIGNMENT: *Writing about a Decision*

In this chapter, you will first learn about writing cause-and-effect essays. Then you will work through the stages of the writing process to develop your own essay about a decision. Before you begin writing, discuss the following question with your classmates. Your answer to this question will become the focus of your essay.

Question: What important decision did you or your family make in the past, and what were its causes or effects?

Perhaps you made the decision to immigrate to the United States or to come to the United States to study. Or, maybe you made a personal decision to change something in your life—to stop smoking, to stop procrastinating (putting off doing things), or to start exercising and eating healthy foods. Whatever decision you choose as your topic, make certain that it is significant enough to allow you to write an entire essay about it.

After choosing your topic, select *one* of the following options for your essay:

1. Write an essay in which you analyze the most significant *causes* for the decision that you or your family made.

2. Write an essay in which you analyze the most significant *effects* of the decision that you or your family made.

Be sure to present in your essay specific evidence for the causes or effects of the decision and to analyze your evidence by explaining to the reader the cause-and-effect logic of the decision.

Guidelines on Essay Writing

WHAT IS AN ESSAY?

In the paragraphs you wrote in earlier chapters, you developed one point about a topic. In an essay, you state your views about a topic and then break down your ideas about it into *subpoints*.

An academic essay usually consists of three parts:

1. Introductory paragraph
2. Body paragraphs
3. Concluding paragraph

Introductory Paragraph

In the *introductory paragraph* (also called the *opening paragraph*), you want to introduce your topic to readers and draw readers into the essay by gaining their attention. The introduction also includes a thesis statement that conveys to readers the overall idea of your essay.

Body Paragraphs

In the *body paragraphs* (also called *middle paragraphs*), you develop the main idea of the essay by breaking it down into several subpoints. You then develop each subpoint in one or more body paragraphs. As in paragraph writing, the subpoints of an essay are developed through specific evidence and analysis.

Concluding Paragraph

In the *concluding paragraph,* you bring the essay to a close by reemphasizing the overall main idea of your essay. In addition, you broaden the subject somewhat by suggesting what the overall idea of the essay means to the reader. At times, you may want to include in the conclusion some specific statement directed at the reader, such as a call for action, a quotation, or a question.

In this chapter, you will focus on the body paragraphs of an essay, as well as on developing a thesis statement, outline, and subpoints. You will learn how to write the introductory paragraph in Chapter 8 and the concluding paragraph in Chapter 9. In this chapter, you will still write a brief introduction and conclusion for your essay, but you will concentrate on writing the thesis and body paragraphs.

ESSAYS AND THE WRITING PROCESS

For the paragraphs you wrote in earlier chapters, you moved through the stages of the writing process—prewriting, drafting, revising, and editing. Essay writing also requires you to work through these stages, but each stage will take longer to complete for an essay. Planning, drafting, revising, and editing will each consume more of your time. In addition, you may find yourself moving back and forth between stages more often. For instance, while you are revising your essay, you may find that you need to generate more ideas about your topic or that you need to draw up a new plan or outline.

Prewriting: Generating Ideas and Developing Subpoints, Thesis Statement, and Outline

GENERATING IDEAS

Before you begin planning and drafting your essay about a decision, take a few minutes to generate some ideas about your topic. First, write at the top of a blank sheet of paper the controlling question you are answering:

What were the causes of the decision made by me or my family?

or

What have been the effects of the decision made by me or my family?

Then use one of the prewriting techniques you learned in earlier chapters— clustering (pages 10–11), freewriting (pages 31–32), tree diagraming (page 54), or brainstorming (pages 101–102)—to generate ideas about your topic.

FOCUSING AND ORDERING SUBPOINTS

After gathering ideas on your subject, you are ready to focus and order those ideas. *Focusing* and *ordering* mean that you focus the overall main idea of your essay and form a rough idea of its subpoints. For your essay about a decision, your subpoints will be either the causes or the effects of that decision:

Main idea of your essay
    Subpoint 1
    Subpoint 2
    Subpoint 3

You also need to *focus the subpoints* of your essay. In the space provided here, write a short phrase that describes each of your subpoints (that is, each cause or effect):

1. _____

2. _____

3. _____

Then think about how you want to *order the subpoints*. You might consider *emphatic order*, which means that you give "emphasis" or more force to one point by presenting it last in the order of subpoints. This subpoint should be your strongest, and the one you have the most to say about.

PLANNING

Now take some time to draw up a rough plan for your essay. The object of *planning* is to get an idea of the organizational structure of the essay before you begin writing. At the very least, your plan should include the overall main idea and subpoints of your essay. Remember, though, that this is only a preliminary plan; you may decide to change your plan later on while drafting or revising.

DEVELOPING A THESIS STATEMENT AND OUTLINE

Unlike paragraph writing, essay writing often involves more in-depth planning, perhaps in the form of an *outline*. For your essay about a decision, you will want to prepare an outline that includes your *thesis statement* (which conveys the overall main idea of your essay to the reader) and your *topic sentences* (which announce the subpoints of your body paragraphs).

The thesis statement, which is placed near the end of the introductory paragraph, should directly answer your controlling question. If you wish, you may also include in your thesis the subpoints of your essay. Here are some examples:

Sample Controlling Question:
What caused me to decide to immigrate to the United States?

Sample Thesis Statement (with Subpoints):
The most important reasons why I decided to immigrate to the United States were to have a better quality education and to escape the terrible political situation in Ethiopia.

Sample Thesis Statement (without Subpoints):

Five years ago, my father decided to bring our family out of Vietnam and to immigrate to another country. There were several reasons for his decision.

You may find it helpful to write the topic sentences for your body paragraphs and include them in your outline. Just as you use a topic sentence to announce the point of a single paragraph, the topic sentences in an essay announce the points of the body paragraphs. Each paragraph should have a topic sentence. In your essay about a decision, the topic sentences should announce the one cause or effect of the decision.

The sample outline below contains a thesis statement and topic sentences for three body paragraphs. Note, too, that the second and third topic sentences contain transitions (*also, nevertheless*), which help to connect the body paragraphs. (You will learn more about transitional words in the Editing section later in the chapter.)

When drawing up an outline for your essay about a decision, you may choose to include only your thesis statement and topic sentences. Or, you may also include some rough ideas about how you will develop the sub-

Sample Outline with Thesis and Topic Sentences

Thesis Statement:
Some good effects of my family's immigration to the United States include having a better educational system and better job opportunities; however, we are also facing the problem of separation from relatives and friends as a result of our immigration.

Topic Sentence 1:
One good effect of my family's immigration to the United States is that my brothers and I are getting a better education than we would have had in Peru.

Topic Sentence 2:
Each member of my family *also* has better job opportunities as a result of our immigration to the United States.

Topic Sentence 3:
Nevertheless, immigrating to the United States has not only brought good effects to my family; we *also* have problems as a result of immigration because we are now separated from our dear relatives and friends in Peru.

points in each body paragraph. The sample outline on page 140 includes some notes about the subpoints as well as a thesis and topic sentences.

Drafting the First Body Paragraph

With your prewriting and outlining completed, you are ready to begin drafting your essay about a decision. Remember that, in this chapter, you will focus on writing the body paragraphs of an essay. Although you will still write a short introduction and conclusion, you will concentrate on these types of paragraphs in Chapters 8 and 9.

Think about the steps you will take in drafting your essay. You may now choose whether to write your short introductory paragraph first or later, after completing the thesis statement and body paragraphs of your essay. Thus, you may either write a short introductory paragraph and include your thesis at the end, or simply write your thesis statement at the top of the page and save the introduction for later. Next, set aside twenty to thirty minutes to draft your first body paragraph. The guidelines that follow will help you in drafting your first body paragraph.

ANALYZING CAUSES OR EFFECTS IN THE BODY PARAGRAPHS

In this essay, you will be analyzing either the causes or the effects of a decision. If you are analyzing the causes, you need to convey what led to the decision—that is, the reasons why you or your family made the decision. As you can see in the diagram on page 141, the causes lead to the decision.

If you are writing about the effects, you need to analyze what happened as a direct result of the decision. As you can see in the diagram on page 142 the decision leads to the effects.

When drafting your body paragraphs, keep in mind the principles of cause-and-effect logic that you learned in earlier chapters. Look back at the paragraph you wrote about choosing a field of study (in Chapter 5). Much of what you learned in that chapter about cause-and-effect analysis will be useful in writing your essay.

Analyzing Causes

In your first body paragraph, announce in a topic sentence the cause to be discussed. Then analyze the cause, explaining to the reader why this particular cause led to the decision.

Sample Outline with Thesis, Topic Sentences, and Notes on Subpoints

---

Thesis Statement:
I decided to accept a scholarship to study in the United States for several reasons: I wanted to experience American society, to learn English, and to get a good education.

Topic Sentence 1:
One reason that pushed me to accept the scholarship to study here was my desire to have the opportunity to learn about American society.
  Knew something about American society from television, newspapers, and magazines
  Knew that American society had many advantages
  Wanted to see the society and its people—could do that in the four years in school here

Topic Sentence 2:
Another important reason that influenced me to accept the scholarship was my long-held wish to learn English.
  Had studied English for five years in Costa Rica
  Knew I had to live in an English-speaking country to become completely fluent
  Fluency in English would help me in my future profession

Topic Sentence 3:
Most important, the scholarship would allow me to get better educational training than I would have had in my home country of Costa Rica.
  Educational level in Costa Rica is high, but not much technology available in my field—agronomy
  Learning about that would help me benefit my home country later

---

To determine what you need to explain, you should try to anticipate your reader's questions. For example, Golda Meir might state the following as one of the reasons for her decision to become independent from her parents:

One reason I decided to become independent from my parents was in order to become a teacher.

In anticipating the reader's questions about this reason, the writer might predict that the reader would ask the following:

Analyzing Causes

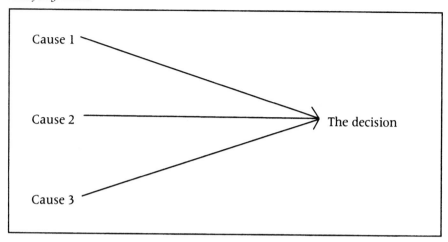

> Why did this reason (wanting to become a teacher) lead to your decision (to become independent from your parents)? In other words, why did you have to become independent from your parents in order to become a teacher?

The writer would then know that in her analysis she would need to explain the cause-and-effect logic—why she had to become independent from her parents in order to become a teacher.

Analyzing Effects

In analyzing effects, you also need to anticipate the reader's questions. For example, Meir might state the following as one effect of her decision:

> As a result of my decision to become independent from my family, I became a stronger person.

Then the writer might anticipate that the reader would question how the cause led to the effect:

> How did becoming independent from your parents make you a stronger person?

The writer would then realize that she needs to make the cause-and-effect connection clear to the reader by explaining how becoming independent made her a stronger person.

As you can see, whether you are writing about causes or effects, you need to develop each point thoroughly by bringing in specific evidence to support the cause or the effect. In addition, you need to provide enough analysis to make the cause-and-effect logic of each paragraph clear to the reader.

Analyzing Effects

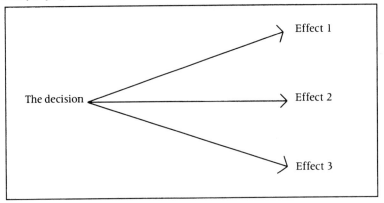

Revising the First Body Paragraph

Now that you have completed at least your thesis, outline, and first body paragraph, you are ready to share your work with your writing group. First, though, if time permits, practice evaluating the thesis statements and body paragraphs in Activity 7.1.

❏ *ACTIVITY 7.1:* **EVALUATING THESIS STATEMENTS AND BODY PARAGRAPHS**

Step 1: Read these thesis statements and then discuss the questions that follow them:

Thesis Statement A:

As a result of immigrating to the United States, my family has been re-united with relatives and has improved economically. However, the young people in the family have lost touch with their Peruvian heritage because of this immigration.

Thesis Statement B:

In 1985, my family decided to leave Shanghai for America. The reasons for this difficult decision were to have better educational opportunity for me and to have a better standard of living for our family.

DISCUSSION QUESTIONS

1. Does each thesis statement state the overall main idea of the essay? That is, does it answer the controlling question?

2. Are the subpoints of the essay (as announced in each thesis statement) made clear? What suggestions for improvement can you offer?

Step 2: In the following example, the student chose to create a more general thesis statement and then announce the subpoints of the essay in topic sentences. After reading the thesis and the subpoints in the plan, discuss the questions that follow.

Thesis Statement and Plan:

My family decided to immigrate from Malaysia to the United States for several reasons.

1. Depression
2. Discrimination against Chinese in Malaysia
3. Education

DISCUSSION QUESTIONS

1. Does the thesis statement convey the essay's main idea?
2. Are the subpoints in the writer's plan clear?
3. What suggestions for improvement can you offer?

Step 3: As you read the two body paragraphs that follow, look at the two writers' use of cause-and-effect logic. Also determine if the writers "stay on track" in explaining the logic of the cause-and-effect relationship. Then discuss the questions that follow the paragraphs.

SECOND BODY PARAGRAPH A

One important reason why my parents immigrated to the United States was that they wanted me to have better educational opportunities. Although there are some very good universities in China, a population of ten billion people makes it hard for a high school student to get into college. In fact, the ratio of Chinese students who enter college is one out of ten. I doubt that I would have made it to a college if I had stayed in China. I think my parents knew this too. However, my parents knew that in the United States there were fewer people and more colleges and universities than in China. They also had heard from our relatives in California that there were many junior colleges in the United States where students could start out. Thus, because my parents could see that there would be a better opportunity for me to advance my knowledge, they decided to immigrate to the United States.

SECOND BODY PARAGRAPH B

Looking forward to having a decent life-style was one reason my family immigrated to America five years ago. After the Communists took over Vietnam, the economic bonding between the United States and Vietnam was cut. Without the support and trade from the United States, our country slowly became very poor. The condition is so bad now that the government is paying its workers with cheap food instead of money. My uncles and aunts, for instance, have been teaching high school in Vietnam for the past ten years now. They often write letters to us in America asking my parents to send money and goods home for them. They explain to us that the Communist government is paying them a few pounds of rice as a monthly salary, and it is not enough for their family. Also in Vietnam today, many people are so poor that they go to sleep hungry while working overtime for extra money to support their family.

DISCUSSION QUESTIONS

1. *Topic Sentence:* Does each topic sentence clearly announce the subpoint of the paragraph? What suggestions for improvement can you offer?

2. *Evidence and Analysis:* Does each paragraph present enough evidence as well as thorough analysis to convince the reader of the logic of the particular cause-and-effect relationship being proved?

3. Does the writer "stay on track" in proving the cause-and-effect relationship? What suggestions for improvement can you offer?

❏ *ACTIVITY 7.2:* **PEER RESPONSE**

Now share your thesis, plan or outline, and first body paragraph with your writing group. Use the following procedure:

1. One group member should begin by reading aloud his or her thesis, plan or outline, and first body paragraph. The group should then discuss the writer's work in terms of the questions listed on the Peer Response Sheet for Activity 7.2 on page 346. Another group member should record the group's comments on the sheet.

2. When you are finished filling out the sheet, give it to the writer so that he or she can use the group's suggestions when revising.

3. Repeat the procedure for each group member.

4. Then revise your thesis, plan or outline, and first body paragraph, keeping in mind the suggestions of your writing group.

Drafting the Other Body Paragraphs

You are now ready to draft the remaining body paragraphs of your essay. As you draft, keep in mind the suggestions that your writing group made about your first body paragraph.

Revising the Other Body Paragraphs

Before sharing your body paragraphs with your writing group, practice evaluating the strengths and weaknesses of the student paragraphs in Activity 7.3.

❑   *ACTIVITY 7.3:*   **EVALUATING TWO STUDENTS'**
      BODY PARAGRAPHS

After reading paragraph A, discuss the following questions with your classmates. Repeat the procedure for paragraph B.

DISCUSSION QUESTIONS

1. What are the strengths of the paragraph? What makes it memorable or interesting?

2. What are the weaknesses of the paragraph? What does the writer need to do to improve the cause-and-effect logic of the paragraph? Does the writer provide enough evidence and analysis to develop the paragraph's subpoint?

PARAGRAPH A

The most important reason I decided to study at Kilgore College was that it is located in a small town. I had spent most of my life living in large cities such as Hong Kong and New York. Therefore, I realized that I wanted to attend a college that was not located in or near a major city. I made this decision two years ago when I gave my sister a ride back to Kilgore. I was fascinated by the beauty of the campus, the trees, the plants, and Kilgore's isolation from the major cities.

PARAGRAPH B

The reason I decided to study in the United States was I wanted to learn to be an independent person. In my home country of Indonesia, my parents were always ready to help me to do anything, such as applying for a new school, buying new dresses, and cooking meals. For instance, my parents chose and applied to a new high school for me when I was in the last year of junior high; I just knew that I had to take an admission test. Besides, I also never did the housework, such as washing clothes, cleaning the house, and ironing my clothes because my mother did these things. For these reasons, I decided to come to the United States alone. I thought coming to the United States would be a good way of learning to be an independent person because in the United States I would be on my own, far from my parents. In the United States, I would have to do everything by myself, such as cleaning my apartment, cooking, applying for a new school, washing a car, and fixing the table. With doing everything by myself, I would have to be an independent person, and I would then be prepared for my future because I would not be able to depend on my family forever.

❏ *ACTIVITY 7.4:* **MORE PEER RESPONSE**

Now meet with your writing group again to discuss the body paragraphs you just completed. Follow the peer response procedure outlined in Activity 7.2. Use the questions on the Peer Response Sheet for Activity 7.4 on page 348.

Next, complete the rest of your essay. If you have not yet written a short introduction and conclusion, you should do so now. Then revise your body paragraphs, keeping in mind the suggestions of your writing group.

Editing: More on Coherence

If you studied Chapter 6, you learned about the importance of coherence in writing. Here you will learn more about coherence. Strengthening the coherence of your writing will be particularly helpful when you write academic essays because a high degree of coherence is expected in academic essays.

Remember that, in the preceding chapter, you learned about coherence in terms of (1) continuity in the developing train of ideas and (2) continuity revealed by surface signals. In this chapter, you will learn about (3) more surface signals—logical connectors—and how they help make writing coherent.*

*The information in the example sentences and exercises in this grammar section is taken from *My Life* by Golda Meir (1975).

MORE SURFACE SIGNALS—LOGICAL CONNECTORS

Logical connectors are another means of making writing coherent. *Logical connectors* are also "surface signals" that bridge the gap from one clause to another clause, from one sentence to the next sentence, or from one group of sentences to the next group of sentences.

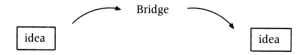

Like the other surface signals—repetition and synonyms, demonstrative pronouns and adjectives, and pronouns—a logical connector tells the reader directly the logical relationship between the first idea and the second idea:

> Meir wanted to be a teacher; *however,* her parents wanted her to get married.

Here, the logical connector *however* tells the reader that the logical relationship between the two ideas is *contrast.*

A logical connector might be a coordinate conjunction, a subordinate conjunction, or a transition. In Chapter 2, you learned how to use *coordinate conjunctions* as logical connectors:

> Meir wanted to become a teacher, *but* her parents wanted her to get married.

In Chapter 3, you learned how to use *subordinate conjunctions* as logical connectors:

> *Although* Meir thought she should continue her education, her parents thought she should work in the shop.

> In this chapter, you will learn how to use *transitions* as logical connectors.

TRANSITIONS AS LOGICAL CONNECTORS

Transitions are connector words that show the logical relationship between two clauses, between two sentences, or between two groups of sentences.

Using a Transition to Join Two Independent Clauses

One way of joining two independent clauses is with a comma and a coordinate conjunction. But you can also join two independent clauses with a transition:

> Independent clause; transition, independent clause.

Meir became successful as a teacher; *furthermore,* she became prime minister of Israel.

What do you notice about the punctuation of this type of coordinated sentence?

Punctuation:

When joining two independent clauses with a transition, a _____ comes before the transition, and a _____ follows it.

Using a Transition to Connect Two Sentences

You can also use a transition to tell the reader the logical relationship between two sentences:

> First sentence. Transition, second sentence.

Meir's parents did not think she should become a teacher. *However,* her sister and brother-in-law gave her the encouragement and support that she needed to achieve her goal.

Punctuation:

When using a transition to show the connection between two sentences, you use a _____ after the transition.

Placement of Transition:

Rather than placing the transition at the beginning of the second sentence, you may place it in the middle of the second sentence.

> First sentence. Second sentence begins, transition, second sentence ends.

Meir's parents did not think she should become a teacher. Her sister and brother-in-law, *however,* gave her the encouragement and support that she needed to achieve her goal.

Punctuation:

When positioning a transition in the middle of the second sentence, a _____ goes before the transition as well as after it.

Using a Transition to Connect Two Groups of Sentences

When writing a paragraph or a larger piece of writing, you can use a transition to show the reader the logical relationship between one group of sentences and another group of sentences. This is particularly useful when you want to let the reader know that you are shifting from one group of sentences (one idea) to another group of sentences (another idea), especially if you have developed each of these ideas with several sentences.

You might begin a paragraph, for example, by stating a point in the topic sentence and then making several general statements about the point. Once you are ready to bring in specific evidence for that point, you might then signal the shift by using a transition:

Sample Paragraph

> Topic sentence
> General statements
> *For example, . . .*
> Specific example

In presenting a contrasting example in the paragraph, you might use a transition that signals contrast:

Sample Paragraph

> Topic sentence
> General statements
> Specific example
> *However, . . .*
> Contrasting example

In each of the preceding cases, you use a transition to *bridge the gap* between two ideas. Without the transition, you are asking too much of the reader, expecting him or her to determine the logical relationship between one group of sentences (one idea) and the next. With the transition, you help the reader bridge this gap by telling him or her exactly what the logical relationship is between one idea and the following idea.

WHAT TRANSITIONS CAN CONVEY

Each transition indicates to the reader a particular logical relationship between two clauses, sentences, or groups of sentences. The accompanying list shows the logical relationships that the various transitions convey. In the following section, you will practice using transitions to join two independent clauses (the result of which is a compound sentence).

Logical Relationship	Transition
Addition	moreover furthermore in addition besides
Contrast	conversely however in contrast nevertheless nonetheless on the contrary on the other hand otherwise
Similarity	likewise similarly
Result	consequently thus therefore accordingly hence as a result
Reinforcement/emphasis	indeed in fact
Time	meanwhile subsequently
Exemplification	for example for instance in particular

Transitions Showing Addition

Logical Relationship	Transition
Addition	moreover furthermore in addition besides

The logical connectors in the preceding diagram signal *addition*. That is, they convey to the reader that you are using the second clause to add an additional idea to the first clause.

Meir's parents wanted her to get a job; *moreover,* they wanted her to get married.

Complete each of the following sentences with a transition that signals addition. Remember to include the correct punctuation before and after the transition.

1. Meir wanted to go on to high school _____ she wanted to become a teacher.

2. Meir knew that teaching would be satisfying for herself _____ she knew that as a teacher she could help children.

❏ *ACTIVITY 7.5:* **USING TRANSITIONS TO SIGNAL ADDITION**

Complete each sentence by adding an appropriate transition of addition and an independent clause. Be sure to add the necessary punctuation as well.

1. Meir was able to complete her education _____ she _____ _____.

2. Meir knew that she could count on the support of her married sister Sheyna _____ she _____.

Transitions Showing Contrast

Logical Relationship	Transition
Contrast	conversely however in contrast nevertheless nonetheless on the contrary on the other hand otherwise

As you read the following sentences, try to determine what each transition means. Can you find differences in meaning among the transitions that signal contrast? That is, do some seem to fit certain situations better than others?

Meir did not want to disobey her parents; *however,* she knew that she needed an education.

Meir believed that a woman needed an education; *in contrast,* her parents believed that a woman only needed to get married.

Meir's parents thought she could be happy with Mr. Goodstein; *on the contrary*, Meir knew she could not be happy with a husband she did not love.

In Meir's time, a woman could have a short career as a typist or a shop clerk; *otherwise*, the focus of her life should be marriage.

You probably noticed in the preceding sentences that transitions signaling contrast have slightly different meanings and uses:

* *However, on the other hand,* and *in contrast* signal *contrast;* each introduces a clause that is the *opposite* of the clause before it. For example:

  Meir did not want to disobey her parents; *however,* she knew that she needed an education.

  Meir believed that a woman needed an education; *in contrast,* her parents believed that a woman only needed to get married.

These are the most general transitions signaling contrast; they apply to many different types of writing situations.

Other transitions, however, have very particular meanings or are used only in certain situations. The following transitions fall into this category:

* *Nevertheless* and *nonetheless,* while also signaling contrast, mean in particular "despite that" ("that" being the idea just mentioned).

  Sheyna and Shamai had very little money; *nevertheless,* they decided to get married.

* *Conversely,* while also showing contrast or opposition, means in particular an opposite point of view. It is most commonly used to show opposition of ideas or opinions.

  Meir's mother thought Meir should become a typist; *conversely,* Meir knew that she would die as a typist hunched over a typewriter in a dingy office.

* *On the contrary* shows strong opposition or complete disagreement with what was said in the previous clause.

  Meir's father believed that a woman should not be too smart; *on the contrary,* Meir believed that a woman should develop her mind.

* *Otherwise* means "other than that" ("that" being the idea just mentioned).

  In Meir's time, a girl could have a short career as a typist or a shop clerk; *otherwise,* the focus of her life should be marriage.

❏ *ACTIVITY 7.6:* **USING TRANSITIONS TO SIGNAL CONTRAST**

Complete each of the following sentences with an independent clause that fits the logical connector of contrast used.

1. Meir dreamed of becoming a teacher; however, _____

_____.

2. Meir thought she would go on to high school after elementary school; on the contrary, _____

_____.

3. Meir believed that education was important even for a married woman; conversely, _____

_____.

4. Meir wanted to please her parents; nevertheless, _____

_____.

5. Meir primarily objected to Mr. Goodstein as a husband; otherwise,

_____.

Transitions Showing Similarity

Logical Relationship	Transition
Similarity	likewise similarly

The logical connectors in the preceding box signal *similarity*—the idea in the second clause is similar to that in the first. For example:

Meir dreamed of her future as a teacher; *likewise,* Regina and Sarah talked endlessly about what they would do when they grew up.

Regina supported Meir's decision to become independent; *similarly,* Sheyna and Shamai wrote of their approval in letters from Denver.

❏ *ACTIVITY 7.7:* **USING TRANSITIONS TO SIGNAL SIMILARITY**

Complete each sentence by adding a clause that logically fits the first clause as well as the transition given.

1. Shamai advised Meir to come to Denver; likewise, Sheyna _____

_____.

2. Sheyna helped by sending money for a train ticket; similarly, _____

_____.

Transitions Showing Result

Logical Relationship	Transition
Result	consequently thus therefore accordingly hence as a result

The logical connectors in the preceding box signal *result*—telling the reader that the first clause gives the *cause* and the second (introduced by the transition) gives the *result:*

> Clause signaling cause; *transition,* clause signaling result.

Meir's parents thought she should marry someone "substantial"; *therefore,* they chose for her the well-to-do Mr. Goodstein.

Meir's parents began arranging her marriage with Mr. Goodstein; *consequently,* she decided to become independent from her parents.

❑ *ACTIVITY 7.8:* **USING TRANSITIONS TO SIGNAL RESULT**

Complete each sentence by adding the appropriate result clause.

1. Meir's parents knew Mr. Goodstein had a comfortable income; thus,

_____.

2. Meir didn't love Mr. Goodstein; hence, _____

_____.

3. Meir decided never again to ask her parents for money; as a result,

_____.

Transitions Showing Reinforcement or Emphasis

Logical Relationship	Transition
Reinforcement/emphasis	indeed in fact

The logical connectors in the preceding box signal *emphasis* or *reinforcement*—the second idea adds emphasis or reinforcement to the first. In the following sentences, in what way does the second idea emphasize or reinforce the first idea?

Meir was pleased by Sheyna and Shamai's invitation to come to Denver; *indeed,* their offer was to her a lifeline that she grabbed.

Meir didn't want to marry Mr. Goodstein; *in fact,* she didn't want to marry anyone for a long time.

❑ *ACTIVITY 7.9:* **USING TRANSITIONS TO SIGNAL REINFORCEMENT OR EMPHASIS**

Complete each sentence by adding a clause that fits the other clause in the sentence, as well as the logical connector given.

1. Meir knew her parents would never agree to her leaving; in fact, _____

_____.

2. _____;

indeed, leaving home was the turning point in Meir's life.

Transitions Showing Time

Logical Relationship	Transition
Time (same time as)	meanwhile
Time (afterward)	subsequently

What is the meaning of each transition in the following sentences?

Meir sat at the kitchen table planning her escape; *meanwhile,* her parents drank tea and talked.

Meir arrived at the train station at 5 A.M.; *subsequently,* she found out that the Denver train didn't leave until 7 A.M.

Meanwhile means that two events or actions are occurring at the same time or simultaneously.

> Meir sat at the kitchen table planning her escape; *meanwhile,* her parents drank tea and talked.

Subsequently means that one event occurred and then another occurred after the first one.

> Meir arrived at the train station at 5 A.M.; *subsequently,* she found out that the Denver train didn't leave until 7 A.M.

❏   *ACTIVITY 7.10:*   **USING TRANSITIONS TO SIGNAL TIME**

Complete each sentence by adding the appropriate transition—*meanwhile* or *subsequently.*

1. Meir and Regina planned Meir's escape from home; _____,

Sheyna and Shamai prepared for her arrival in Denver.

2. Meir completed her education in Denver, _____,

she became a teacher and later prime minister of Israel.

Transitions Showing Exemplification

Logical Relationship	Transition
Exemplification	for example for instance in particular

In the following sentence, which of the two clauses is the more general statement? Which is the more specific statement? Which clause does the transition introduce?

> Meir's life at home became intolerable; *for example,* she and her parents had many arguments.

What would you say the transitions *for example, for instance,* and *in particular* mean?

❏   *ACTIVITY 7.11:*   **USING TRANSITIONS
     TO SIGNAL EXEMPLIFICATION**

Complete each sentence by adding a clause that logically fits the first clause as well as the transition given.

1. Meir did not agree with the decisions her parents made about her life; for example, _____.

2. Meir didn't want to get married; in particular, _____

_____.

❏   *ACTIVITY 7.12:*   **USING TRANSITIONS CORRECTLY**

Complete each of the following sentences by adding the appropriate transition. Refer to the list of transitions on page 150 as needed.

1. Lucas had always wanted to know more about American society; _____, he decided to apply to a university in the United States.

2. Lucas wanted to know more about the American people; _____, he wanted to improve his English.

3. Lucas had studied English for five years in school in Costa Rica; _____, he still had difficulty communicating in English.

4. Lucas's sister Mercedes had improved her English by studying in the United States; _____, his cousin Enrico had become fluent in English after four years of college in the United States.

5. Lucas sent for applications to several U.S. universities; _____, he discussed his decision with his parents.

6. Lucas knew his parents did not have a great deal of money for his education; _____, he did not give up his dream since he knew he could apply for a scholarship.

7. Lucas knew that there were several good programs in his field of food science in the United States; _____, he had heard that Cornell University had an excellent food science program.

8. Lucas received positive results from the applications he sent out; _____, he was admitted to five of the six schools he had applied to.

✓ *EDITING CHECKLIST*

After revising your draft essay for content, you are ready to focus on editing it. Concentrate on eliminating any problems you find with coherence and sentence problems. Check for the following:

☐ Check for *coherence problems* in your essay. Ask a classmate or friend to read your draft aloud to you. As he or she reads, listen for breaks in coherence where one sentence does not seem to follow another. If you notice breaks in coherence, use the following questions to help you solve the problem.

- Can I use the principle of "something old/something new"? That is, to solve a break in coherence, should I pick up "something old" from a previous sentence and add to it "something new"?

- Can I use a surface signal to link one sentence to the next—repetition or synonyms, demonstrative pronouns or adjectives, pronouns, or transitions?

☐ Check for possible problems with *transitions:* Are there spots where transitions are needed? Does each transition used signal the appropriate logical connection between sentences or clauses?

☐ Check for correct *verb tense.*

☐ Check for *sentence structure problems:* fragments, run-ons, comma splices.

☐ Check for *sentence variety.*

CHAPTER 8

Writing about the Value of an Ethnic Studies Course

In many colleges and universities today, students are required to take one ethnic studies course about a culture other than their own. A student might, for example, take a course about African American culture, Chinese culture, Arab culture, or Latin American culture. In this chapter, you will write an essay about what students can learn by taking an ethnic studies class about your culture.

Ethnic studies classes are offered by many colleges and universities today because the United States has become a very diverse culture. In the past, many immigrants came to the United States from Europe. Today, however, immigrants come to the United States from all parts of the world—from Africa, the Middle East, Latin America, South America, Asia, and elsewhere. As a result, the United States today is a multiracial, multi-ethnic society.

Ethnic and racial diversity, however, can lead to conflict and even violence when people from different groups do not understand one another. Yet experts suggest that people of very different backgrounds can live together harmoniously if they learn to understand each other and respect each other's differences.

The following interview is from *Bill Moyers: A World of Ideas* (1989). In the interview with Bill Moyers, Nigerian author Chinua Achebe explains a proverb (a wise saying) of the Ibo people of Nigeria (a West African country). This proverb focuses on the principle of respect for other people's differences.

from "Chinua Achebe," in *BILL MOYERS: A WORLD OF IDEAS*

MOYERS: There's a proverb in your tradition that says, "Wherever something stands, something else will stand beside it." How do you interpret that?

159

Nigerian author Chinua Achebe
(© 1989 Rose Marston, photographer)

ACHEBE: It means that there is no one way to anything. The Ibo people who made that proverb are very insistent on this—there is no absolute anything. They are against excess—their world is a world of dualities. It is good to be brave, they say, but also remember that the coward survives.

MOYERS: So if you have your God, that's all right because there must be another God, too.

ACHEBE: Yes, if there is one God, fine. There will be others as well. If there is one point of view, fine. There will be a second point of view.

MOYERS: Has this had any particular meaning for you, living as you do between two worlds?

ACHEBE: Yes, I think it is one of the central themes of my life and work. This is where the first conflict with the missionaries who came to improve us developed. The missionaries came with the idea of one way, one truth, one life. "I am the way, the truth, and the life." My people would consider this so extreme, so fanatical, that they would recoil from it.

MOYERS: And yet your father became a Christian, and you were raised by a Christian family.

ACHEBE: Yes, completely—but there were other ways in which the traditional society failed to satisfy everybody in it. Those people who found themselves out of things embraced the new way, because it promised them an easy escape from whatever constraints they were suffering under.

MOYERS: So one of the reasons missionaries, colonial administrators, and other Westerners seldom penetrated the reality of the African society was that the African could embrace the Christian God while still holding on to the traditional gods.

ACHEBE: Yes. But it was not necessary to throw overboard so much that was thrown overboard in the name of Christianity and civilization. It was not necessary. I think of the damage, not only to the material culture, but to the mind of the people. We were taught our thoughts were evil and our religions were not really religions.

One way to bring about the kind of understanding and respect for other people's cultural and ethnic differences that Achebe describes is to have college students take an ethnic studies class. In these classes, students study another culture's values, customs, religions, and ways of thinking. For example, a student taking an Arab studies class might learn about the culture of the Bedouins, who are nomadic Arabs living in the deserts of Arabia, Syria, and North Africa. (Nomads are groups of people who move from place to place rather than having permanent homes.)

Before you begin work on your essay describing an ethnic studies class about your culture, read the following selection. Imagine that you are reading this selection for an Arab studies class. Think about what you could learn about the Bedouins by taking an Arab cultures course. This will help you write your essay about what students can learn from an ethnic studies course about your culture.

The reading, from *The Arabian Peninsula* by the Editors of Time-Life Books (1986), describes a Bedouin named Ali ibn Salim al-Kurbi, who is a seventy-year-old elder in the Al Kurbi branch of the Al Munrrah tribe. Members of this Bedouin tribe migrate over much of the Saudi Arabian peninsula.

▶ *BEFORE YOU READ*

1. Can you locate Saudi Arabia on the map that appears in the front of this book?

2. What do you know about the Bedouin tribespeople who migrate throughout the Saudi Arabian peninsula? Share what you know about the Bedouins with your classmates.

3. Do you imagine that Bedouins would be generous or not-so-generous people? That is, would they share their food and other supplies with travelers and visitors? Why or why not?

from *THE ARABIAN PENINSULA*

THE EDITORS OF TIME-LIFE BOOKS

Such an **environment** [as the desert] might have made the Bedouin self-pitying, **stingy,** and mean, but quite the opposite is true. There are few people on earth as **lavishly hospitable** as they. Should a visitor—even a stranger—arrive at a nomad's tent, the owner will give him a warm welcome and offer to **slaughter** a sheep or a young camel—no matter how **scarce** meat may be. If the host has nothing on hand but coffee and a few dates, he will serve them to his guest nonetheless, even if it means that he himself must go hungry.

When the guest is a fellow tribesman, the sense of occasion can be overwhelming. Once Ali, returning from **Mecca** with a party that included other members of the Al Kurbi and an American friend, happened upon the camp of a **kinsman** whom he had not seen for months. The kinsman's 20-year-old son Hurran, the first to spot the travelers as they approached the **encampment,** came rushing out of his tent to bid them a tearful welcome. "He kissed the old man Ali and the Al Kurbi and all of us one by one," the American recorded.

"By **Allah,** you will eat meat," Hurran said between **sobs,** and he turned to run into the desert to fetch a camel. Ali, thinking to let common sense **prevail** over tradition at a camp where the herd was small, stopped him. "By Allah, Hurran, we will not," he said.

"It's been half a year and we've been in the desert and we haven't seen anyone. By Allah you must eat," the young herdsman **rejoined.**

"Listen, my son," Ali insisted. "We are all one; your house and my house are one and our herds are one."

Because of the old man's insistence, Hurran **acceded.** But his **impulsive** generosity was typical of a **sentiment** that is **instilled** in the soul of every Bedouin from babyhood.

In a sense, generosity is an **adaptive** response to an extraordinarily difficult environment. Particularly in times past, a traveler in the sandy wastes needed all the cooperation he could get, or else he would **perish.** His host was honor-bound to feed and clothe him and—if he had been robbed of his camels or in some other way been victim of **foul play**—to defend him to the death against further attack. And should the **wayfarer** lose any goods or **chattel** during his stay, the host would be **obliged** to replace them. After three days, the host would see the traveler safely on his way with presents of clothing and food to sustain him.

Many **rituals** of desert hospitality have **persisted** unchanged for centuries. When a guest arrives, he is seated on a rug and the coffee fire is lit. A boy generally takes charge of **brewing** and serving. While the water boils, he roasts the beans lightly in a long-handled **skillet** and then **pulverizes** them in a heavy brass **mortar.** He pours the powder into a long-beaked brass or copper coffee pot along with boiling water from the kettle, and sets the pot on the fire to boil up again.

The brewer then calls to one of the women for **cardamom** seeds, which he **grinds** in the mortar and adds to the coffee. A **platter** of dates is handed across the tent divider for the boy to pass around, first to the guest and then to everyone else according to age. Then he serves the coffee, having tested it first for flavor.

With the pot in his left hand and a stack of tiny **porcelain** cups in his right, he moves around the group, filling each cup about one quarter full and **proffering** it to one person after another. He circles again to pour refills until each drinker **wiggles** his cup to **indicate** he has had enough. If the family is well-to-do or the visitor a special one, a dish of **incense** or smoking sandalwood is usually passed round after the coffee cups have been collected. Everyone takes a **bracing whiff**—an agreeable custom that chases away the odors of the tent. If the visitor has come to do business, the men deal with it when the coffee and incense are finished.

Bedouin women seldom stay as **secluded** as their urban **counterparts,** and if the visitor is a kinsman or known by everybody, they will drift back and forth between the men's and the women's section of the tent. Should a visitor arrive when all the men are absent, a woman will serve the coffee and entertain him.

The nomad's **compulsive** hospitality, while **enhancing** his honor and **status,** tends to keep him poor. One of the most respected tribesmen in southern Arabia in the 1950s was an elder of the Bayt Imani tribe. In his **prime** he had been rich in camels, but over the years he had slaughtered his entire herd to feed the guests that came his way. In ancient times such a man would simply have replaced the animals by **raiding** another tribe's herd. That being no longer possible, the elder was broken by his own generosity, and he ended up a **rheumy-eyed** old man in a **tattered** loincloth.

To a true Bedouin, such **poverty** hardly matters. Wealth—in the form of money, camels or other possessions—is most of all a **medium** for expressing **largess,** something to be shared with companions of any description and with kinsmen in particular. As such it serves as part of a tribal **welfare** system.

▶ *AFTER YOU READ*

1. What did you learn about the Bedouin tribespeople from the reading?

2. In what ways might your new knowledge of the Bedouins and of Arab culture be of value to you and other students?

Supplemental Reading List—Chapter 8

Stark, Freya. *Baghdad Sketches.* London: J. Murray, 1937.

   In this volume, explorer Dame Freya Stark—winner of the Royal Geographical Society's Gold Medal—tells of her travels from Damascus, through Iraq, to Kuwait. You will enjoy reading her vivid descriptions of the people and places she saw as she traveled through the Middle East.

🖊 **WRITING ASSIGNMENT:** *Writing about the Value of an Ethnic Studies Course*

   In this chapter, you will work through the stages of the writing process to develop an essay about the benefits to students of taking an ethnic studies course about your culture. Before you begin writing, discuss the following question with your classmates. Your answer to this question will become the focus of your essay.

Question: What could other students learn in an ethnic studies course on your culture?

   For your essay, imagine that your college is considering adding a requirement that would make it necessary for students to take one ethnic studies course about a culture other than their own. A student might, for example, choose a Chicano studies class, a Vietnamese studies class, an African studies class, or one of many other ethnic studies courses about cultures from around the world. Also imagine that your college is considering an ethnic studies course on your culture.

   Write an essay in which you analyze what college students can learn by taking an ethnic studies course about your culture. In the opening paragraph, announce the name of the ethnic studies course. In the body paragraphs, include specific evidence about what students can learn from the course. In addition, analyze the topic by explaining how students' new knowledge of your culture will be of value to them.

Guidelines on Choosing Verb Forms for Your Essay about an Ethnic Studies Course

   In this chapter, after you have generated ideas about your topic and created a plan, you will learn about how to write an opening paragraph for your essay. Then, when you are ready to draft your first body paragraphs, you will think once again about how to use specific evidence and thorough analysis to support the subpoints of your essay.

As you write this essay, you may want to try to avoid conditional verb forms since you probably have not yet studied how to use the conditional. Here is an example of conditional verbs:

Conditional:

If students *took* an ethnic studies course about Persian culture, they *would learn* about . . .

Instead, consider using some of the following verb forms and tenses for this essay:

Simple Present:

A student who *takes* an ethnic studies course about Chinese culture . . .

Modals:

A student who takes an ethnic studies course about Chinese culture *may learn* (*can learn, might learn*) about . . .

Future Verb Forms:

A student who takes an ethnic studies course about Chinese culture *will learn* about . . .

Prewriting: Generating Ideas for Your Essay

First, decide on a name for the ethnic studies class about your culture. In some cases, this decision will be simple. If you or your family is from Japan, for instance, you can write about a Japanese studies course. However, if your family is from Saudi Arabia, you might write about a Saudi Arabian studies course or a more broad Arab studies course.

Next, develop your controlling question—the one-sentence question you will answer in your essay. Include in it the course name you have chosen. Here are two examples:

Sample Controlling Questions:

What can students learn by taking a Brazilian studies class?

What can students learn by taking a Central American studies class?

Then use one of the prewriting techniques you learned in earlier chapters—clustering (pages 10–11), freewriting (pages 31–32), tree diagraming (page 54), or brainstorming (pages 101–102)—to develop some ideas about your topic.

FURTHER OPTIONAL PREWRITING: INTERVIEWING

In order to gather more ideas about your topic, you might try conducting interviews. By interviewing friends or family members, you can get their ideas about your culture.

Before you actually begin an interview, you need to list the questions that you will ask each person. These questions, of course, will serve only as a guide; your interview is likely to take a direction of its own as it progresses.

In addition, decide whether you want to take notes during the interview or tape-record the conversation. If you decide on note-taking, you should rewrite your notes immediately after the interview has ended. If you choose instead to tape-record the interview, you need to get permission to do so from the person being interviewed. If you would like to include in your essay some direct quotations from the people you have interviewed, then you will want to be as accurate as possible in writing down these quotes or in writing down quotes from your tape recording.

FOCUSING, ORDERING, AND PLANNING

After you have generated ideas through prewriting and interviewing, you are ready to focus and order these ideas. Begin by looking over the material you have generated and/or the notes you have made from your interview. Then choose the subpoints you want to discuss in the essay—those that focus on what students can learn by taking an ethnic studies course about your culture.

Next, develop a rough thesis statement as well as a preliminary plan for your essay. Remember that the thesis statement should directly answer your controlling question. The thesis may also include the subpoints of your essay. (See Chapter 7 for more on the thesis statement.) Write your controlling question and thesis statement here:

Your Controlling Question:

_____

_____

Your Thesis Statement:

_____

_____

The preliminary plan for your essay might be an outline (like the one you created in Chapter 7) or a box diagram. In Chapter 3, you learned that a box diagram is a visual sketch of each paragraph. It contains notes on how each paragraph in an essay will be developed.

As you can see in the sample box diagram on page 168, the student jotted down some notes for each paragraph of an essay—the opening paragraph, the subpoints of the body paragraphs, and the concluding paragraph.

Whether you use a box diagram or an outline to write out your plan, remember that it is only a preliminary plan of what you *think* you want to say in your essay. As you draft and then revise the essay with the suggestions of your writing group in mind, you may decide to change your plan. At that point, you can draw up a new plan for the essay or make changes to your original plan.

Drafting the Opening and First Body Paragraphs

In Chapter 7, you focused on writing the thesis statement and body paragraphs of an essay. In this chapter, you will learn about the opening and first body paragraphs of an essay. (In Chapter 9, you will learn about the concluding paragraph.)

THE OPENING PARAGRAPH

The opening paragraph of an essay usually performs three main functions:

1. It catches the reader's attention.
2. It introduces the subject.
3. It announces the essay's focus.

Catch the Reader's Attention

The opening paragraph of your essay should catch the reader's attention or interest in some way. For example, you might tell a brief but dramatic story, pose an interesting question, present a quotation, or use an analogy.

Drama. A brief dramatic story or specific example can be used to catch the reader's attention in the opening paragraph. As you read the following paragraph, consider how it catches your attention:

> When I was studying at Northeast High in Miami, I made a lot of American friends in my physical education class. They would ask me questions about my home country, such as "Where is Chile?" "Is it

Sample Box Diagram

Opening Paragraph
Draw the reader's attention with a vivid example — Tiananmen Square
Introduce my subject – a Chinese studies course
Thesis
Taking a Chinese studies course can help students better understand Chinese history, the Chinese economic situation, and the formation of the Chinese government.

Body Paragraphs
Subpoint 1
Students can learn a lot about Chinese history by taking a Chinese studies class.
Wars; new dynasties after the wars
Famous people in the wars— Wu Zhe Tien, a woman emperor, why she's important, and what can be learned from her

Subpoint 2
In addition to learning about Chinese history, students may find out about the economic situation in China by taking a Chinese studies course.
Chinese proverb — poor versus rich
standard of living— compare to Taiwan
How this affects immigration

Subpoint 3
Most importantly, students taking a Chinese studies course can become acquainted with the formation of the Chinese government.
Government formed by 90 percent elder persons (how they love to be treated like emperors)
Why they don't want Chinese people to have freedom of speech or economic freedom (fear of Western influence)
Who elects these leaders — are they representative?
Why they like to keep their power

Concluding Paragraph
China is thousands of years old
Importance of understanding China
How students can then know what led to Tiananmen Square
Will also know what China is really like

---

near Cuba?" "Isn't Chile just like Mexico?" Sometimes I felt like I had come from "Mars" since my new friends knew so little about my homeland. If my high school friends and other American students have the opportunity to take a college course on Chilean culture, they will learn much about the culture of Chile and its unique features.

DISCUSSION QUESTIONS

1. In what ways does this opening catch the reader's attention?

2. On the scale of general to specific, how specific is this example?

Question. Another way to catch the reader's attention in the opening paragraph is with a question. The more unexpected or startling the question is, the more likely it will grab the reader's attention. As you read the following opening paragraph, note how the question works to capture your attention:

> Do you know which African country was settled three thousand years ago? Do you know that this same country was the home of the biblical figures, the Queen of Sheba and King Solomon? Do you know that this same country, which is twice the size of Texas, was once known as Abyssinia? If you take an ethnic studies class about this country, you will find out that it is Ethiopia. Along with other students in an Ethiopian studies class, you will learn about Ethiopian culture—its history, its religions, and its arts.

DISCUSSION QUESTIONS

1. Do you think the opening paragraph catches the reader's attention? If so, how?

2. How specific are these questions on the scale of general to specific? Would more general questions work just as well?

Quotation. A quotation is also useful in gaining the reader's attention, especially if it is very specific or startling. The following opening paragraph about an Arab studies class begins with a quotation that describes Arabs as "bogeymen," which are scary, monsterlike figures. As you read the paragraph, note how the quotation gets you interested in what the writer has to say:

> As writer Jack G. Shaheen says in "The Media's Image of Arabs," "America's bogeyman is the Arab. . . . Arabs [are] either billionaires or bombers." It's true that when you say the word *Arab* to an American, he or she thinks of either a billionaire Kuwaiti sheik or an Arab terrorist. Yet most Arabs are just normal people, like everyone else, who

have an ancient and interesting culture of their own. Students who take an Arab studies course will learn much about Arab culture: ancient Arab history, the Arabian colonial past, and Arabians' development of modern cities in the barren desert.

DISCUSSION QUESTIONS

1. Does the quotation in the above opening paragraph catch your attention? Why or why not?

2. What specifics make this opening vivid?

Analogy. Another method of drawing the reader into your essay involves using an analogy. In an *analogy,* you compare one thing to another thing that is seemingly unlike the first. The analogy helps explain the first thing or make it clear to the reader.

For example, if you were trying to explain your roommate's personality to a friend, you might say that your roommate is "like an angel." Of course, you don't mean that your roommate is an actual angel; rather, by calling upon the well-known characteristics of angels, you make clear to your friend the personality of your roommate.

In the following opening paragraph about a Japanese studies class, note how the writer uses an analogy to visualize Westerners' image of Japan today. After you read the paragraph, discuss the questions that follow with your classmates.

In the past, Japan was known as the "Land of the Rising Sun." Today, however, many Westerners think of Japan as a sparkling pot of gold at the end of a rainbow that stretches across the Pacific Ocean. This is because of the many economic opportunities in Japan today. In fact, many American students have become interested in Japan because it is a great economic power and because there are jobs in Japan for American college graduates. If these students take a Japanese culture class in order to prepare for jobs in Japan, they will learn much about the living conditions, the customs, and the ways of thinking of the Japanese.

DISCUSSION QUESTIONS

1. What is the analogy in this opening? That is, what two things is the writer comparing?

2. Do you think the analogy catches the reader's attention in this opening paragraph? If so, why?

Introduce the Subject

After capturing the reader's attention, the introductory paragraph should introduce the subject of the essay. For your essay on an ethnic studies course, you should name the course you've chosen to write about. You also need to determine whether your reader has some knowledge of your subject or whether you should explain the topic further. For example, if you are writing about Micronesia, you will need to explain to the reader where the island groups known as Micronesia are located and which islands make up Micronesia. However, a familiar topic like China or Japan would not require in-depth explanation for the reader to identify the subject.

If you are not sure about how much information your reader will need to identify your subject, consult with your writing group.

Announce the Essay's Focus

Finally, the opening paragraph should announce the main idea or focus of the essay. This is done in the thesis statement, usually the last sentence of the opening paragraph. As noted earlier, the thesis may also include the subpoints of the essay.

TYING TOGETHER THE THREE PARTS OF THE OPENING PARAGRAPH

To avoid having three disconnected parts in your opening paragraph, you want to make certain that these parts flow smoothly one into another—that is, that they are coherent. (See Chapters 6 and 7 for ways to improve coherence.)

In some cases, you may tie one of the parts of the opening into the next with a transition such as *however, on the other hand,* or *therefore.* In other cases, you need to "build a bridge" from one part of the opening into the next. This "bridge" might be one or more sentences. Or, you might make use of the principle of "something old/something new" or of surface signals such as repetition and synonyms, demonstrative pronouns and adjectives, and pronouns (see Chapter 6).

❑ *ACTIVITY 8.1:* "BUILDING BRIDGES" IN THE OPENING PARAGRAPH

Working with your writing group, have one class member read the following opening paragraph aloud. Underline and then discuss the words, phrases, and sentences in the paragraph that "build bridges" or tie the parts of the opening together.

On June 4, 1989, the eyes of the world were focused on Tiananmen Square where thousands of Chinese students gathered to stage a hunger strike against the Chinese Communist government. Those watching, especially young people, were shocked to see that the elderly government leaders chose to stop the young protesters by shooting hundreds in the crowd with machine guns and running over others with tanks. College students in the West found it especially hard to believe that the Chinese leaders would kill the young protesters. Yet if these same college students choose to take a Chinese culture class, they will learn about the formation of the Chinese Communist government, as well as about China's rising democracy movement, which led to the events in Tiananmen Square.

As you draft your opening paragraph, keep in mind the guidelines listed in the accompanying box.

Guidelines for the Opening Paragraph

- Catch the reader's attention with a dramatic story or example, a question, a quotation, or an analogy.
- Tell your reader the subject of your essay and provide as much background on the subject as is needed.
- Announce the focus of your essay in a thesis statement.
- Make certain that the three parts of your opening flow smoothly and are coherent.

THE FIRST BODY PARAGRAPH

Next, draft the first body paragraph of your essay. As you do so, make certain that you make the subpoint clear to the reader—that is, what students can learn by taking the course on your culture. In addition, include enough specific evidence (specific, concrete details, facts, examples, or quotations) for the subpoint. Then, in your analysis of the subpoint, explain to the reader *how* or *why* the knowledge students gain from the ethnic studies course will be valuable to them. For example, what would be the benefit of learning about the Indian value of purity or about the Bedouin values of sharing, generosity, or cooperation?

Revising the Opening and First Body Paragraphs

Now that you have drafted your opening paragraph and your first body paragraph, you are ready to share your work with your writing group. First, though, practice analyzing the strengths and weaknesses of the opening and first body paragraphs in Activity 8.2, if time permits.

❑ *ACTIVITY 8.2:* **EVALUATING STUDENTS' PARAGRAPHS**

After one class member reads aloud the opening paragraph, discuss the questions that follow it. Repeat the procedure for the sample first body paragraph, which is written by another student about another ethnic studies class.

Controlling Question:
What can students learn by taking an ethnic studies course about India?

STUDENT SAMPLE A: OPENING PARAGRAPH

Everywhere around us in America today, we see people who trace their roots to other parts of the world—a physician from India who lives next door, an Iranian refugee engineer, a Brazilian computer scientist, a Vietnamese ophthalmologist. Rather than seeing this great diversity as a problem, we can instead look upon it as a strength—as a source of cultural richness for America. One way of helping Americans learn about the positive side of the many cultures now in the country is to encourage college students to take an ethnic studies course about a culture other than their own. If students take an ethnic studies course about my culture, India, they will learn about the customs, the religion, and the achievements of Indians.

DISCUSSION QUESTIONS

1. How does the paragraph capture the reader's attention?

2. Does the opening paragraph let the reader know the subject of the essay?

3. Does the thesis announce the essay's focus?

4. What suggestions for improvement can you offer?

STUDENT SAMPLE B: A BODY PARAGRAPH

Students can learn a great deal about Chinese history by taking a Chinese studies class. They will learn about the wars that have happened in Chinese history. There are so many wars in Chinese history; almost every new dynasty came after a war, and there was always at least one person who became famous because of the war. For instance, Wu Zhe Tien was the only woman emperor in Chinese history. If a person takes a Chinese studies class, he or she will know how hard it was for a woman to become emperor. Wu Zhe Tien had to go against Chinese culture because a woman was not even allowed to be a head of a family; she also had to go against society because men didn't want a woman as emperor.

DISCUSSION QUESTIONS

1. Is the overall point of the paragraph focused and clear?

2. Does the writer present enough specific evidence (specific, concrete details, facts, examples, and so on) to support the point of the paragraph? What suggestions for improvement can you offer?

3. Does the writer analyze the evidence? That is, does the writer explain why learning about Chinese history will be valuable to students taking the course? What suggestions for improvement can you offer?

❏ *ACTIVITY 8.3:* **PEER RESPONSE**

Now share your draft opening and first body paragraphs with your writing group. Use the following procedure:

1. One group member should begin by reading aloud his or her opening and first body paragraphs. The group should then discuss the writer's work in terms of the questions listed on the Peer Response Sheet for Activity 8.3 on page 350. Another group member should record the group's suggestions on the sheet.

2. When you are finished filling out the sheet, give it to the writer so that he or she can refer to the group's comments when revising.

3. Repeat the procedure for each group member.

4. Then revise your opening and first body paragraphs, keeping in mind the suggestions of your writing group.

Drafting the Other Body Paragraphs and Conclusion

You are now ready to draft the remaining body paragraphs, as well as the conclusion for your essay. However, since you will study how to write the concluding paragraph in the next chapter, you may choose at this time to write only a short conclusion for your essay on an ethnic studies course.

Revising the Other Body Paragraphs and Conclusion

Now that you've drafted your entire essay, you can share it with your writing group. First, though, practice evaluating the two student body paragraphs in Activity 8.4, if time permits.

❏ *ACTIVITY 8.4:* **EVALUATING TWO STUDENTS' BODY PARAGRAPHS**

After reading paragraph A and thinking about its focus, evidence, and analysis, discuss the following questions with your classmates. Repeat the procedure for paragraph B.

DISCUSSION QUESTIONS

1. Is the overall point of the paragraph focused and clear? That is, does the paragraph focus on one subpoint?

2. Does the writer present specific evidence for the subpoint?

3. Does the writer analyze the evidence, explaining how students' new knowledge of the culture will be of value to them?

4. After reading both paragraphs, which do you think is the stronger one? What makes it more effective than the other paragraph?

BODY PARAGRAPH A

Students taking a Vietnamese studies class can learn about the food and the traditional celebrations of Vietnam. They can also learn about the Vietnamese language and the history of the country. Learning about the language and history of Vietnam can help students understand Vietnamese culture better. For example, they may discover that many Vietnamese customs are similar to Chinese customs.

BODY PARAGRAPH B

By taking an Ethiopian culture class, students can learn that Ethiopian people have many reasons to be proud of their history. Ethiopia and Liberia were the only countries in Africa that were not colonized by an outside country. Students can also learn that in the past Ethiopia had a very strong government and that the Ethiopian people were very patriotic. In addition, Ethiopia has one of the oldest cultures in the world; it has some old buildings that were built before Christ (B.C.) and had great leaders. The Queen of Sheba and King Solomon are examples of ancient Ethiopian political leaders. Ethiopians are proud of their country because Ethiopia is one of the originators of civilization. This may be surprising to some students because Ethiopia today is among the poorest countries in the world, and some students may not know that Ethiopia has had this kind of history. Students can also learn that Ethiopia used to be one of the strongest and most powerful countries in the Mideast because Ethiopia colonized Saudi Arabia, Yemen, and other Arab countries; therefore, Ethiopian people have a lot of pride and self-confidence. For most students, this story is new to them because they have never heard of Ethiopia's history. After learning more about Ethiopia's history, students will know that Ethiopia, although a poor country today, is the home of an ancient and well-respected civilization.

❏ *ACTIVITY 8.5:* **MORE PEER RESPONSE**

Now share your other body paragraphs and conclusion with your writing group. Using the Peer Response Sheet for Activity 8.5 on page 352, follow the peer response procedure outlined in Activity 8.3. Then revise your essay, taking into consideration the suggestions of your writing group.

Editing: Adjective Clauses

THE FUNCTION OF ADJECTIVE CLAUSES

When you need to give extra descriptive information about a noun, you can add modifiers such as adjectives, prepositional phrases, and noun modifiers:*

---

*Information in the example sentences and exercises in this grammar section is taken from *The Arabian Peninsula* by the Editors of Time-Life Books (1986).

the pot

the *brass coffee* pot

the *brass coffee* pot *on the fire*

As a modifier, you can also use an *adjective clause,* which is a dependent clause that begins with a *relative pronoun* (such as *who, whom, whose, which,* or *that*). An adjective clause gives extra information to describe, define, or identify a noun:

• Ali returned from Mecca with a party.

Who was in the party?

Ali returned from Mecca with a party *that included other members of the Al Kurbi tribe and an American friend.*

• Hurran's generosity was typical of a sentiment.

What kind of sentiment?

Hurran's generosity was typical of a sentiment *that is instilled in the soul of every Bedouin from babyhood.*

In writing your essay about an ethnic studies course on your culture, you will find adjective clauses helpful. Such clauses add specific, vivid information that can enrich the reader's knowledge about your culture. With adjective clauses, you can also improve the coherence of your writing. Adjective clauses allow you to provide very close links between your ideas and give you an additional range of sentence variety.

THE FORM AND USE OF ADJECTIVE CLAUSES

An adjective clause is a dependent clause that begins with a relative pronoun and functions like an adjective (in that it describes and modifies a noun). The selection about the Bedouins that you read earlier in the chapter contains many adjective clauses, as you will see in the following sentences adapted from the reading.

The Bedouin have kept the traditions *that came from their nomadic past.*

The generosity *that they show to friends and strangers* is an important Bedouin tradition.

Bedouins believe in preserving the bonds *which link them with their kinsmen.*

Note that the relative pronouns *who, whom,* and *whose* are used to refer to people, whereas *which* and *that* are used to refer to things or objects.

The Position of Adjective Clauses

An adjective clause is placed immediately after the noun it modifies:

NOUN   ADJECTIVE CLAUSE

The generosity | *that they show to friends and strangers* | is an important Bedouin tradition.

RESTRICTIVE AND NONRESTRICTIVE ADJECTIVE CLAUSES

Adjective clauses can be either restrictive or nonrestrictive. A *restrictive adjective clause* gives essential information about the noun it modifies; that is, the information is necessary for the reader to identify the noun. Without this information, the reader does not know which noun, of all the possible nouns in a group, the writer is referring to. For example:

RESTRICTIVE

A meal | *that often includes goat meat, rice, and dates* | will be served to anyone visiting the Bedouin camp.

If we remove the adjective clause in this case, will we know which meal the writer is referring to? Does this adjective clause, therefore, give us essential information?

A *nonrestrictive adjective clause* adds extra, nonessential information about the noun it modifies. The reader does not need this information to identify the noun being referred to:

NONRESTRICTIVE

Camel milk, | *which is a staple of the Bedouin diet,* | is offered to the guest as part of Bedouin hospitality.

If we remove this adjective clause, will we know what milk the sentence is referring to? Why?

PUNCTUATION OF ADJECTIVE CLAUSES

Restrictive and nonrestrictive adjective clauses are punctuated differently. The restrictive clause requires no punctuation before or after it because the clause is essential to the sentence. For example:

RESTRICTIVE

A meal | *that often includes goat meat, rice, and dates* | will be served to anyone visiting the Bedouin camp.

However, because a nonrestrictive adjective clause adds nonessential information to a sentence, it requires a comma both before and after it. The commas indicate that the clause can be removed from the sentence without affecting the meaning of the sentence. For example:

NONRESTRICTIVE

Camel milk, ⌐*which is a staple of the Bedouin diet,*⌐ is offered to the guest as part of Bedouin hospitality.

Compare the two preceding example sentences. If you take the adjective clause out of the restrictive clause example, does that affect the meaning of the sentence? Will the reader know which "meal" the sentence refers to? Is the same true for the nonrestrictive example?

On the following pages, you will study restrictive adjective clauses. The discussion of restrictive adjective clauses is divided according to the grammatical function of the relative pronoun in each type of adjective clause. For example, in some adjective clauses, the relative pronoun serves as the subject of the clause, but in other adjective clauses it serves as the object, as the object of a preposition, or as a possessive. You need to understand the internal structure of the adjective clause in order to choose the correct relative pronoun (*who, whom, whose, which, that*), to choose the right word order in the adjective clause, and to know how to reduce adjective clauses.

TYPES OF RESTRICTIVE ADJECTIVE CLAUSES

Relative Pronoun as Subject (*Who, Which, That*)

Each of the following sentences contains an adjective clause. First, draw a box around the adjective clause. Next, label the elements of the adjective clause—subject, verb, object, prepositional phrase, complement. The first sentence is done for you.

SUBJECT VERB COMPLEMENT

A young man ⌐*who is a Bedouin*⌐ is intensely loyal to his tribe.

He will defend other tribesmen who are his brothers and cousins.

The loyalty that resides in the Bedouin heart will lead him to defend his tribesmen even under dangerous conditions.

Note that in each sentence the relative pronoun (*who* or *that*) functions as the subject of the adjective clause. As shown in the accompanying diagrams, this type of adjective clause—in which the relative pronoun serves as the subject—may modify any one of the nouns in an independent clause (the subject, object, or object of a preposition).

Reduction of Adjective Clauses When the Relative Pronoun Is the Subject. When the relative pronoun in an adjective clause serves as the subject, can you delete or remove the relative pronoun to reduce the clause? What

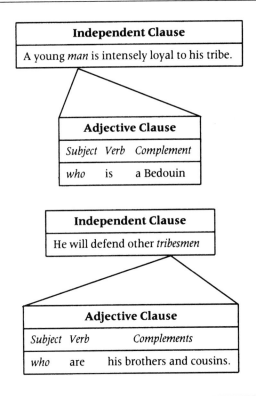

Independent Clause

A young *man* is intensely loyal to his tribe.

Adjective Clause

Subject	Verb	Complement
who	is	a Bedouin

Independent Clause

He will defend other *tribesmen*

Adjective Clause

Subject	Verb	Complements
who	are	his brothers and cousins.

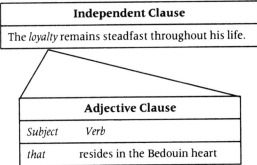

Independent Clause

The *loyalty* remains steadfast throughout his life.

Adjective Clause

Subject	Verb
that	resides in the Bedouin heart

happens when the relative pronoun is removed from the following sentence?

Some Bedouin *who have moved to the city* still try to maintain their traditional customs.

Now circle the correct answer in the parentheses:

When the relative pronoun serves as the subject within the adjective clause, you (*can* or *cannot*) delete the relative pronoun.

❏ *ACTIVITY 8.6:* **WORKING WITH RELATIVE PRONOUNS
    AS SUBJECTS**—*WHO, WHICH,* **AND** *THAT*

Combine each sentence pair into one sentence. The new sentence
should have both an independent clause and an adjective clause in which
the relative pronoun is the subject.

1. A herd belongs to Ali. It consists of sixty camels.

_____

_____

2. Ali's family also owns a goat-hair tent. It is forty feet long.

_____

_____

3. A curtain within the tent divides the men from the women. The
women live on one side of the tent.

_____

_____

4. The tent is made of nylon. Ali just bought it.

_____

_____

Relative Pronoun as Object (*Whom, Which, That*)

In each of the following sentences, draw a box around the adjective
clause (including the relative pronoun) and label the subject, verb, and object within the adjective clause:

The drink *that* Bedouins most love is coffee.

They eagerly watch the person *whom* they have chosen to prepare the
evening's coffee.

As you can see, the relative pronoun in each sentence serves as the object
within the adjective clause.

However, if you look at the accompanying diagrams, you will see that
adjective clauses may modify any noun in the independent clause—the
subject, object, object of a preposition, and others.

The most important thing to remember here is that, within the adjective clause, the relative pronoun functions as the object.

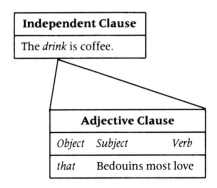

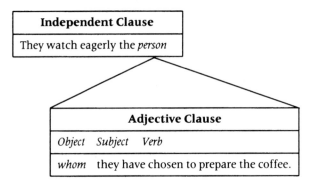

Word Order. The word order in a clause is usually (1) subject, (2) verb, and (3) object:

<pre>
   SUBJECT   VERB   OBJECT
. . . Bedouins most love [coffee]
</pre>

<pre>
   SUBJECT   VERB   OBJECT
. . . they have chosen [the person].
</pre>

However, in an adjective clause, when you change the object to a relative pronoun, the relative pronoun always moves to the front of the clause (this is called "fronting" the relative pronoun):

ADJECTIVE CLAUSE

The drink *that* Bedouins most love (that) is coffee.

ADJECTIVE CLAUSE

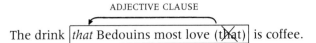

They watch eagerly the person *whom* they have chosen (whom) to prepare the evening's coffee.

Note that in this type of adjective clause (where the relative pronoun serves as the object) you use *whom,* not *who:*

OBJECT

The young woman | *whom* you met | is Ali's daughter.

You use *who* when the relative pronoun in the adjective clause serves as the subject:

SUBJECT

The young man | *who* is milking the camel | is his son.

Reduction of Adjective Clauses When the Relative Pronoun Is the Object. When the relative pronoun serves as the object in an adjective clause, can you delete the relative pronoun? Try deleting the relative pronoun in the following sentence:

The young woman *whom* you met is Ali's daughter.

Now, circle the correct answer in the parentheses:

When the relative pronoun serves as the object within the adjective clause, you (*can* or *cannot*) delete the relative pronoun.

Choosing Who *or* Whom. In each of the following sentences, draw a box around the adjective clause and label the subject, verb, and object within the adjective clause. Then choose the appropriate relative pronoun, *who* or *whom.*

Example:

OBJECT   SUBJECT   VERB

The king | ~~who~~/whom you saw on television last night | is descended from a Bedouin tribe.

Our company has just hired a young engineer *who/whom* is from Kuwait.

The petroleum engineer *who/whom* we hired last year is from Yemen.

❏ *ACTIVITY 8.7:* **WORKING WITH RELATIVE PRONOUNS AS OBJECTS—*WHOM, WHICH,* AND *THAT***

For each of the following sentence pairs, combine the two sentences into one sentence. The new sentence should have both an independent clause and an adjective clause in which the relative pronoun serves as the object. Then, for each new sentence, decide whether you can delete the relative pronoun.

1. Fahd drives a new pickup truck. His father bought it for him.

_____

_____

2. The truck just broke down. Fahd bought it last week.

_____

_____

3. The mechanic is an expert at fixing trucks. Fahd hired him.

_____

_____

4. Fahd usually hires a certain man to fix his vehicles. This man just moved to Riyadh.

_____

_____

Relative Pronoun as Object of a Preposition (*Whom, Which, That*)

For each of the sentences that follow, draw a box around the adjective clause and label elements within the clause—subject, verb, object, adverb, preposition, or object of a preposition.

In each sentence, what is the function of the relative pronoun within the adjective clause?

The animal *that* I rode on yesterday is a camel.

The camel *that* Josef warned us about bites people.

The camel about *which* Josef warned us bites people.

The man *whom* you have just heard about owns seventy-five camels.

The man about *whom* you have just heard owns seventy-five camels.

As you can see in the accompanying diagrams, within the adjective clauses, the relative pronoun (*which*, *whom*, or *that*) serves as the object of a preposition.

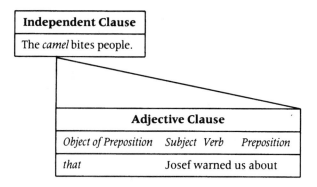

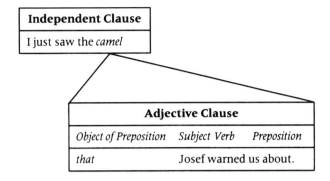

Independent Clause

I just saw the *camel*

Adjective Clause

Object of Preposition	Subject Verb	Preposition
that	Josef warned us	about.

Word Order. Look again at this sentence:

The camel │*that* Josef warned us *about*│ bites people.

In this case, you are embedding one sentence within another or putting one sentence within the other.

The camel bites people.

Josef warned us about the camel.

Usually, the prepositional phrase comes after the subject and verb in a clause, as it does in this sentence:

SUBJECT VERB   PREPOSITION
Josef warned us *about* the camel.

However, when you embed the second sentence into the first one and then change the noun *camel* to the relative pronoun *that,* you must move *that* to the front of the adjective clause since the relative pronoun is always "fronted"—that is, it always moves to the "front" of the adjective clause.

⎨————————————— that
The camel [Josef warned us about t̶h̶e̶ c̶a̶m̶e̶l̶] bites people.

The camel *that* Josef warned us about bites people.

Now look at this sentence:

The camel │*about which* Josef warned us│ bites people.

Here, in addition to moving the relative pronoun to the front of the adjective clause, you may also choose to "front" the preposition by moving it to the front of the adjective clause (before the relative pronoun). Look at the difference between the two versions:

⎨————————————— which
The camel [Josef warned us about t̶h̶e̶ c̶a̶m̶e̶l̶] bites people.

The camel *which* Josef warned us about bites people.

which

The camel [Josef warned us about the camel] bites people.

The camel *about which* Josef warned us bites people.

The second version, with the preposition moved to the front of the adjective clause along with the relative pronoun, is a more formal sentence
that would not be appropriate in informal spoken English. This version is
more appropriate in formal written English. The first version is appropriate
in spoken informal English.

Informal:

The camel which Josef warned us about bites people.

Formal:

The camel about which Josef warned us bites people.

Which *and* That *as Objects of Prepositions.* As noted earlier, the relative pronouns *which* and *that* are used to refer to animals, things, and sometimes to people when they serve as objects of prepositions.

Hazi lovingly polishes the pot *that* he will later make coffee in.

Hazi lovingly polishes the pot *which* he will later make coffee in.

However, if you choose to "front" the preposition (move it to the front
of the adjective clause along with the relative pronoun), then you must use
which, not *that*.

Incorrect:

Hazi lovingly polishes the pot *in that* he will later make coffee.

Correct:

Hazi lovingly polishes the pot *in which* he will later make coffee.

Whom *as Object of a Preposition.* When you are choosing a relative
pronoun to refer to people (when the relative pronoun is the object of a
preposition), you must use *whom*, not *who*.

Incorrect:

Hazi welcomes the guests *who* he can serve cardamom coffee to.

Correct:

Hazi welcomes the guests *whom* he can serve cardamom coffee to.

***Reduction of Adjective Clauses When the Relative Pronoun Is the Object
of a Preposition.*** Can you delete the relative pronoun in an adjective clause
when it serves as the object of a preposition? Try deleting the relative pronoun in the following sentence:

The coffee which Hazi takes pride in is served from a long-beaked brass coffee pot.

Now, circle the correct answer in the parentheses:

When the relative pronoun serves as the object of the preposition within the adjective clause, you (*can* or *cannot*) delete the relative pronoun.

As you can see, when the relative pronoun serves as the object of a preposition in the adjective clause, you can delete the relative pronoun.

If, however, you also move the preposition to the front of the adjective clause ("front" it), you cannot follow the same rule. Look at the two following sentences. In which case can you delete the relative pronoun?

The cup *which* you just drank your coffee from belonged to Hazi's grandfather.

The cup from *which* you just drank your coffee belonged to Hazi's grandfather.

As you see, if you front the preposition (move it to the front of the clause along with the relative pronoun), you cannot delete the relative pronoun. In this case, you must keep the relative pronoun. Note what happens to the sentence if you delete the relative pronoun:

Incorrect:

The person to whom Hazi's wife is now serving dates is an American anthropologist.

Correct:

The person to whom Hazi's wife is now serving dates is an American anthropologist.

❑ *ACTIVITY 8.8:* **WORKING WITH RELATIVE PRONOUNS AS OBJECTS OF PREPOSITIONS—*WHOM, WHICH,* AND *THAT***

Step 1: Combine each sentence pair into one sentence. The new sentence should have an independent clause, as well as an adjective clause in which the relative pronoun is the object of the preposition.

1. I love the dates. You just complained about them.

_____

_____

2. The young woman is a cousin. You just offered your thanks to her.

_____

_____

3. The man is the patriarch of the tribe. You are sitting by him.

_____

_____

4. You just passed the dates to a man. He is the keeper of the goats.

_____

_____

Step 2: Discuss the new sentences with your classmates. Answer these questions:

1. In which sentences can you move the preposition to the front of the adjective clause?

2. In which sentences can you not move the preposition to the front of the relative clause? Why not?

3. From which of the new sentences can you delete the relative pronoun?

Relative Pronoun as a Possessive (*Whose*)

A relative pronoun in an adjective clause may also serve as a possessive. For example:

POSSESSIVE
The doctor |*whose* book you just read| is a Saudi woman.

Here the relative pronoun *whose* replaces a possessive word (such as *my, your, his, her, its, their,* and words ending in *'s*). *Possessives* are adjectives or pronouns that show possession (as in *the boy's hat* or *his hat*).

The doctor is a Saudi woman.

POSSESSIVE
You just read *her* book.

whose
The doctor [you just read h̸e̸r book] is a Saudi woman.

In this case, you must front the relative pronoun *whose* by moving it to the front of the adjective clause. Then, in order for the sentence to be clear, you must also move the noun that the possessive modifies (*book*) to the front of the clause:

———————— whose
The doctor [you just read h̸e̸r book] is a Saudi woman.

———————— whose
The doctor [you just read h̸e̸r book] is a Saudi woman.

The doctor *whose book* you just read is a Saudi woman.

Reduction of Adjective Clauses When the Relative Pronoun Is a Possessive. When the relative pronoun serves as a possessive in an adjective clause, can you delete the relative pronoun? Try deleting the relative pronoun from this sentence. What happens?

The doctor *whose* book you just read is a Saudi woman.

Now, circle the correct answer in the parentheses:

When the relative pronoun serves as a possessive within the adjective clause, you (*can* or *cannot*) delete the relative pronoun.

❏ *ACTIVITY 8.9:* **WORKING WITH RELATIVE PRONOUNS AS POSSESSIVES—*WHOSE***

Step 1: Combine each pair of sentences into one sentence. The new sentence should have an independent clause, as well as an adjective clause in which the relative pronoun is a possessive.

Step 2: If possible, delete the relative pronoun in the new sentence.

1. I do not know the name of the young Kuwaiti woman. Her painting just received a prize.

_____

_____

2. The young Saudi woman has been admitted to medical school. Her scores were the highest on the medical school exam.

_____

_____

3. The banker is a woman from Kuwait City. You just read about her business in the newspaper.

_____

_____

4. The store is owned by a Bedouin woman. You just admired the rugs in the store.

_____

_____

❏ *ACTIVITY 8.10:*   **MORE PRACTICE WITH ADJECTIVE CLAUSES**

Combine each sentence pair into one sentence. The new sentence should have an independent clause and an adjective clause. Use each of the following relative pronouns at least once in the new sentences: *who, whom, whose, which,* and *that.* Finally, check the punctuation in your new sentences.

1. Dr. Ad-Dulaimi is a famous author. He wrote the leading textbook on petroleum geology.

_____

_____

2. Dr. Ad-Dulaimi is a professor. His classes are popular at the University of Petroleum and Minerals.

_____

_____

3. Dr. Ad-Dulaimi is an authority. Other scientists call upon him frequently for consultation.

_____

_____

4. My friend recently scored 95 on a petroleum geology exam. Many other students did not pass the exam.

_____

_____

5. Saudi Arabia is a country in the Middle East. The greatest concentration of Mideast oil is in Saudi Arabia.

_____

_____

6. Max Steineke was a geologist. Historians identify him as responsible for completing Saudi Arabia's first oil well in 1938.

_____

_____

_____

In the Editing Checklist on page 192, you will be checking your draft for sentence variety. If time permits, first practice looking for sentence variety and choppiness in the student paragraphs in Activities 8.11 and 8.12.

❑ *ACTIVITY 8.11:* **EDITING FOR SENTENCE VARIETY**

Look carefully at sentence variety in the following student paragraph. Identify each sentence as simple, compound, or complex.

> Students taking a Laotian culture class can learn about Laotian customs, such as marriage customs. A Laotian couple who wants to become engaged has to have their families' approval. In addition, the man has to pay a dowry in an amount which is determined by the woman's parents. For instance, four months ago when my friend Noy was married, the dowry which she received was $5,000, plus $2,000 worth of twenty-four-karat gold. The man gives a dowry to the woman's family to thank them for raising their daughter so well. If the dowry is not paid, the woman and her family will have a bad reputation because people will think the woman is so bad that the man would give her nothing. Taking a Laotian culture class can thus help students understand many details of the Laotian marriage process. They can learn something about the meaning of Laotian traditions and perhaps even see some similarities to American weddings.

DISCUSSION QUESTIONS

1. In the complex sentences, does the writer use a variety of dependent clauses (for example, adverbial and adjective clauses)?

2. Does sentence variety help to make the paragraph coherent? Why or why not?

❑ *ACTIVITY 8.12:* **EDITING TO ELIMINATE CHOPPY SENTENCES**

Identify the choppy areas in the following draft paragraph (that is, spots where too many simple sentences follow one another). Then edit the paragraph by combining logically related simple sentences with adjective or adverbial clauses wherever possible.

> By taking a Vietnamese studies class, a student can learn about Vietnamese customs, such as festivals and special days. The most important festival is the New Year. A day before the New Year, the kitchen God is supposed to return to heaven to report the conduct of the members of the family since the last anniversary. This is signaled by burning the image of the god, perhaps by smearing his lips

with molasses to ensure that the deity carries with him a final good impression of the household. On the last day of the old year, he is welcomed back, and a fresh picture of him is pasted above the kitchen stove. The day itself and several days following are then devoted to feasting and visiting. Honors are paid to ancestors, and there are family reunions. Children make their obeisances to their parents, pupils pay their respects to their teachers, and friends call on one another to exchange good wishes. In addition, Vietnamese celebrate the New Year by shooting firecrackers and wearing new clothes. Though every country has a New Year's Day and they all celebrate them differently, a student who takes a Vietnamese culture class can discover how the Vietnamese people celebrate their New Year. Moreover, students can learn that the Vietnamese New Year is not simply a holiday, but a chance for all Vietnamese to thank their ancestors, parents, teachers, and friends who have taught them the right things, who have cared for them, and who have been generous to them.

 ### EDITING CHECKLIST

After revising your essay for content, you are ready to edit it. Check for the following:

- □ Check for *sentence variety.* Mark each sentence in your essay as simple, compound, or complex. Then ask these questions:
  - Does each paragraph have sentence variety—a good mixture of simple, compound, and complex sentences?
  - Do I have too many simple or compound sentences?
  - Can I combine some logically related simple sentences with adjective or adverbial clauses?

If time permits, also check your draft for the following:

- □ Check for *correct verb tense.*
- □ Check for *sentence structure problems:* fragments, run-on sentences, and comma splices.
- □ Check for *coherence problems.* Read your essay aloud. If you find breaks in coherence, ask yourself the following questions:
  - Can I use the principle of "something old/something new"—picking up "something old" from a previous sentence and adding to it "something new"?
  - Can I use a surface signal to link one sentence to the next—repetition and a synonym, a demonstrative pronoun or adjective, a pronoun, or a transition?

CHAPTER 9

Writing about Overcoming the Odds

In this chapter, you will write an essay about a time when you overcame the odds that were against you in order to do or achieve something important. "Odds" are probabilities that something will or will not happen. When someone must overcome the odds to achieve something, the probabilities are against his or her success; that is, other people would not expect that person to be successful. In your essay, you will write about a time when you had to overcome the odds and how you did so to do or achieve something important to you.

The two readings that follow will help you better understand the abstract concept of "overcoming the odds"; they will also give you ideas for your own essay.

The first reading, written by C. Gerald Fraser and published in *The New York Times* (June 2, 1990), tells how Nigerian author Buchi Emecheta overcame great odds to become a successful author and the owner of her own publishing house. (Note that, because the article is from a newspaper, it is written in journalistic, not academic, style. The paragraphs are short and the style is narrative.)

▶ *BEFORE YOU READ*

1. Where is Nigeria? Can you locate it on the map that appears in the front of this book?

2. What do you know about Nigeria? Share your knowledge of the country with your classmates.

3. Think about what it means for a person to have to overcome the odds in order to do or achieve something that other people would not expect that person to be able to do. For example, do you think others would expect an African female born in a village in Nigeria in 1945 to become a

193

successful, internationally known writer and the owner of her own publishing company? Do you think the odds would be against her—that it would not be probable for her to become a successful author and publisher? Why or why not?

4. When did you have to overcome the odds to do or achieve something? What did you do to overcome the odds?

from *A WRITER WHO SEEKS TO RECONCILE TWO WORLDS*

C. Gerald Fraser

For as long as she can remember, ever since she was growing up in Nigeria, Buchi Emecheta has wanted to write.

Along the way, her husband angrily burned the **manuscript** of one of her novels because he didn't want her to write. To do **research** for another, Mrs. Emecheta took a job as a cleaning woman at Sandhurst, the Royal Military Academy in Britain, only to have her British publisher **delete** a chapter based on that research without telling her. She decided at that point to set up her own publishing company.

On a recent visit to the United States to **promote** her 16th book, a novel titled *The Family,* Mrs. Emecheta (her name is pronounced BOO-chee EM-uh-chet-uh) talked about a body of work that includes children's books and **teleplays** in addition to her novels.

Most of Mrs. Emecheta's early books are set in her homeland and deal with the **impact** of Nigerian customs and folkways on the nation's people. Later novels are about her experiences in London as a Nigerian immigrant and working mother.

"I came to England in 1962 as a very young bride, in my teens, hoping just to stay two years and go back," the 45-year-old Mrs. Emecheta recalled in an interview in the offices of her American publisher, George Braziller. She spoke five languages—Ibo, Yoruba, Efik, Hausa, and Urhobo—before she spoke English. She took jobs scrubbing floors to support herself and children while she **nurtured** the dream of becoming a writer. She **eventually** enrolled in the University of London and earned a degree with honors in sociology.

Her first books, *In the Ditch* (1972) and *Second Class Citizen* (1975), were autobiographical and reflected Mrs. Emecheta's journey with two children to join her husband in England and the struggle of an immigrant woman to assert her **individuality.**

The Bride Price (1976), *The Slave Girl* (1977), and *Joys of Motherhood* (1979), her next three books, focused on the **challenges confronting** Ibo women in Nigeria's male-dominated society. The Hausa, the Yoruba and the Ibo are Nigeria's three largest **ethnic** groups. Mrs. Emecheta is Ibo.

Nigerian author Buchi Emecheta
(Valerie Wilmer/George Braziller, Inc.)

It was for her sixth book, a novel about the **secession** of Biafra from Nigeria and the country's **ensuing** 30-month civil war, that Mrs. Emecheta took a job as a cleaning woman at Sandhurst. She said she felt certain that the authorities would refuse any official request to do research there, and she needed it for the book.

When *Destination Biafra* was finally published in 1982, Mrs. Emecheta was visiting Nigeria and received a copy from her British publisher. Looking it over, she said, she noticed that an 86-page chapter based largely on her Sandhurst research had been **omitted**. Neither her publisher nor her agent had discussed this **deletion**. She was **aghast**. She said the publisher had later told her that the chapter was lost. She dismissed her agent and decided to set up her own publishing concern, the Ogwugwu Afor Company.

Publishing has meant on-the-job training. "I just started with my son and we learned by experience," said Mrs. Emecheta, who divorced her husband several years ago. "As soon as I finish a book, I sell the paperback rights to different publishers and that's where I **recoup** my money."

Fortunately her publishing **venture** had an **auspicious** start. *Double Yoke*, a story of a student couple in Nigeria, was her company's first book, and helped by favorable reviews, including one by John

Updike in the *New Yorker*, it remained on the best-seller lists in London for several weeks. Mrs. Emecheta gives a large measure of credit to her children, who spent their school vacations working as sales representatives to place the book on dealers' shelves across Britain.

▶ *AFTER YOU READ*

1. What were the odds facing Buchi Emecheta; that is, what made it unlikely for Emecheta to become a successful writer and publisher?

2. In what ways did Emecheta overcome the odds?

3. If you were writing about Emecheta, what adjectives would you use to describe her? Think about what helped Emecheta overcome the great difficulties she faced. Then, working with your classmates, list the adjectives on the board.

The second reading, "Destined to Fly," written by Lawrence D. Maloney and published in *Design News* (February 22, 1993), tells how American Bonnie J. Dunbar overcame the odds to achieve her dream of becoming an astronaut. At the time of this article, Astronaut Dunbar, a materials science engineer specializing in ceramics, had flown on three NASA space flights in 1985, 1990, and 1992. In 1995, she flew on the space shuttle *Atlantis*, with a crew of five Americans and two Russians, on a mission that docked with the Russian *Mir* space station.

▶ *BEFORE YOU READ*

1. Dunbar, who grew up on a farm in Washington State, first began dreaming of space travel in 1957 when she watched the first *Sputnik* satellite. Later, she began cementing her plans to become an astronaut while a high school student in the late 1960s. How likely do you think it would be that a young woman at that time could become an astronaut? Why? How difficult is it now to become an astronaut?

2. Dunbar entered engineering school in the late 1960s. What do you think was the situation for women in engineering (and science) at that time? Has the situation changed for women in science and engineering today?

3. As you will learn from the reading, Dunbar did not always receive encouragement from her teachers. Have you ever had a teacher or counselor discourage you about your ability to achieve your academic goals?

from *DESTINED TO FLY*

Lawrence D. Maloney

Houston—On a starry October night in 1957, a third-grade girl by the name of Bonnie Dunbar watched in **awe** as the Sputnik 1 satellite

streaked across the sky above her family's farm in Washington's Yakima Valley.

On another October night 28 years later, Dunbar enjoyed a **dramatically** different view of space—this time riding the space shuttle Columbia on her first flight as a NASA astronaut.

From that breathtaking **vantage point** 175 miles above the earth, she couldn't help but think of what it had taken to reach her life's dream—the years of hard work, the **frustrations** and disappointments, and the people who had given her a helping hand.

Still, the **saga** of how a farm girl cracked one of the world's most **elite** groups is really one of **unswerving grit** and determination. "When Bonnie was an engineering student at the University of Washington, she talked to me about wanting to be an astronaut," recalls John Buckley, an engineer with Langley Research Center who at that time **monitored** NASA-funded **ceramics research** at the school. "All you had to do was look in her eyes, and you knew she was going to do it."

And so she has, but not without a struggle. Not only was Bonnie the first of her family to attend college, she also chose a field—engineering—that was **overwhelmingly dominated** by men. And that decision has brought with it a measure of **subtle** and not-so-subtle **discrimination** over the years. Add to this family tragedies and **nagging** money worries, which would have **sidetracked** many people.

Career milestones. Yet none of these obstacles blocked Dunbar from building an impressive **array** of accomplishments—

- The 1978 Rockwell International "Engineer of the Year" award for her **pioneering** work on the ceramic tile **heat shield** for the space shuttle.

- Key guidance and flight control duties as a NASA employee at Houston's Johnson Space Center (JSA) for the Skylab reentry mission in 1979.

- Three space shuttle flights as a mission specialist, with duties ranging from **ground-breaking materials science** in **microgravity** to **retrieval** of the vital Long **Duration** Exposure Facility satellite. Dunbar has now **logged** 761 hours in space—more than any woman astronaut, and most male astronauts as well.

- Key **liaison** work as chief of the Astronaut Office's Science Support Group, which advises researchers on the design and operation of **hardware** for a wide variety of space experiments. Of particular importance: the human interface with space experiments. These **investigations** include the growth of **crystals** that could be the building blocks for better drugs, **electronic components**, and structures. . . .

Indeed, some NASA insiders describe her as the single most **dedicated** astronaut when it comes to making space a productive new center for science and industry. "I've never seen anyone as **devoted** as her to the goal of opening up **opportunities** for science during space flight," notes Robert Blount, the former manger of **payload** safety at JSC. "She's the most involved astronaut in the field of materials research, with contacts all over the world."

Adds fellow astronaut David Leestma, director of Flight Crew Operations at JSC: "Bonnie goes the extra mile to help researchers get the most from their experiments, and she **rallies** the astronaut office to support **interactive** science in orbit."

Research marathon. With such a **commitment,** it's not surprising that Dr. Dunbar was named payload commander for the June 1992 space shuttle Columbia flight (STS 50), the first one dedicated to the United States Microgravity Laboratory. Laying important groundwork for Space Station Freedom science operations, this mission featured 32 experiments in **fluid dynamics, combustion science,** and **biotechnology.**

Dreams of space. To be the **catalyst** for such a flight—one of the most closely watched research events of the decade—might seem to be an unlikely role for someone whose roots are far from the technical centers that **spawned** the spacelab's high-tech experiments. The oldest of four children, Bonnie had her first home on a farm in Outlook, WA, in an L-shaped structure made from "two cookhouses pushed together." Her parents raised cattle and grew crops, and Bonnie worked right along with them—driving a tractor at age 10, rounding up **stock** on horseback, packing vegetables, repairing fences, and all the other **chores** that come with a family farm.

Yet along with the **traditional** activities of rural life, such as 4-H projects, she became very interested in science and math. "If I wanted to escape," she recalls, "I would go to my math book. I couldn't wait to do the problems and then see if I was correct by looking at the back of the book for the answers."

Neither of her parents had gone beyond high school, yet they provided valuable lessons in **resourcefulness.** "In a lot of ways, my dad is a self-taught engineer," says Dunbar. "When I was growing up, he designed equipment, did his own **welding** and machine repair, as well as **veterinary** work."

The Dunbars also encouraged their daughter's **budding fascination** with space. It was the beginning of the space race, with the U.S. and Soviet Union in heated competition on everything from satellite **launches** to the first manned flights into space. "John Glenn was my **role model,**" remembers Dunbar.

At Sunnyside High School, reached by an hour-long bus ride, Bonnie was an all-around student: cheerleader, athlete, debater. She also

gobbled up all the science and math courses. "I loved geometry and was one of two girls in my class who took physics." She also became **absorbed** with the idea of being an astronaut. Her interest in science and math was encouraged by Donald Anderson, a physics and chemistry teacher "who loved those subjects and made the courses fun." Anderson also suggested engineering as the best path for her talents.

By the time she graduated from high school in 1967, finishing in the top 10% of her class of about 150, Bonnie had applied to several colleges, including the nation's top technology schools. Cal Tech turned her down because it wasn't accepting women at the time. And she could not begin to afford MIT. In fact, it took National Defense loans and summer jobs to pay her way to the University of Washington.

The wider world. For a young woman from a rural area on the eastern side of the Cascade range, Seattle and the **sprawling** University of Washington had to be a bit of a **culture shock.** "I think I had gone to maybe two movie theaters before I went to college," she **recalls.** She was also pleasantly surprised by all the modern lab equipment **at her disposal.** "All we had in chemistry class at Sunnyside was a **Bunsen burner.**"

Yet there were some **disturbing revelations,** too—like finding that she was one of only six women in an engineering class of 2,000. Nor was she prepared for the **discrimination** she faced. "Mr. Anderson never told me that I would have professors who would come right out and tell me that I wouldn't last in engineering school," she remembers. "Another **informed** me that there were no women's **lavatories** in the engineering building." Still another professor, noting that engineering was no place for a woman, put Dunbar in the back of the room "so I wouldn't **distract** the other students."

Her defense against such treatment? "It was like a **red flag** to me—a challenge to get an 'A.' There was no way I was going to quit. Besides, I truly enjoyed the work. The problem-solving involved in math and science was fun, much like my experiences growing up on the farm where we constantly had to **improvise.** We probably had the biggest pile of **baling wire** in the world."

But Dunbar also could draw on something much deeper. "I guess you could say I have a selective memory," she explains. "I always chose to believe people, such as my parents, who from my earliest years told me I could be whatever I wanted to be. And no matter what anyone else said, that was good enough for me."

Key mentor. Nor was Washington **devoid** of supportive professors. Dunbar originally intended to major in aeronautical engineering, but had second thoughts when Boeing announced big cutbacks. Enter Professor James Mueller, head of the ceramics engineering department. Mueller had a NASA contract to work on **thermal insulation** systems for the space shuttle, a reusable vehicle originally planned for launch by the end of the 1970s. "He was **recruiting** students for his department," recalls Dunbar, "and he pulled out an artist's **concept** of the shuttle reentering the **atmosphere** with the bottom tiles **aglow** from heat. I was hooked."

Mueller, like Anderson before him, was to have a **profound** effect on Bonnie's career, and she shared with him her dream of being an astronaut. His small department not only provided a supportive, almost family atmosphere in a huge school, but the ceramics research **fueled** the young engineering student's goal of getting into the space program.

Under "Doc" Mueller's guidance, Dunbar as an undergraduate assisted in important **vitrification** studies on **silica fibers** for the space shuttle's heat shield. . . .

Graduating cum laude in 1971 with a degree in ceramics engineering, Dunbar accepted an opportunity to **pursue** a master's degree in bioengineering at the University of Illinois. But after a few months, she returned to Washington where she joined Boeing as a systems analyst, learning valuable computer skills. She also joined the Boeing Sea Horses to learn **scuba diving,** a skill she knew would be needed in astronaut training. "I was deathly afraid of water," she **confesses.**

But Boeing could not find an opening in materials engineering, her first love. Then came a call in 1973 from Professor Mueller, who suggested that she come back for a master's degree. He had another NASA grant, this one for **ionic diffusion** materials for **sodium beta alumina batteries** to be used in space. So Dunbar returned to school, earning her master's degree in ceramic engineering in 1975. Then it was off to England for a short research **stint** as a visiting scientist at Harwell Laboratories.

Besides material research on **turbine blades,** the **sojourn** in England gave Bonnie experience in another skill useful for astronaut training—**parachute** jumping—and with none other than the Royal paratroopers.

Springboard to NASA. Returning to the U.S. in late 1976, Dunbar joined Rockwell International's Space Division—the **prime** contractor for the space shuttle—in Downey, CA. There her responsibilities included developing equipment and processes for the manufacture of the space shuttle's ceramic-tile heat shield. . . .

"She was deeply involved in this early work to produce tiles for the shuttle," recalls Howard Goldstein, the NASA Ames scientist who developed coating for the tiles. "And the fact that her work won her the Rockwell Engineer of the Year award was very impressive, especially for someone who was only 28 years old." . . .

NASA beckons. Throughout her work at Rockwell, however, Dunbar didn't lose sight of her astronaut goal. And her desire was **fanned** during trips to the Johnson Space Center, where she **briefed** NASA management on the progress of the space tile efforts.

So, along with Rockwell colleague Anita Gale, she applied in 1977 for the 1978 astronaut class—the first one to take women. Recalls Gale: "Bonnie not only had her application in early, but included **endorsements** from a congressman and the Governor of Washington. She showed a tremendous amount of **initiative**."

But NASA turned down both women. Dunbar was disappointed, but by no means **devastated.** "The first thing you learn when you ride a horse is that, if you fall off, you get back on," she says. Furthermore, JSC management was **impressed** enough with her **credentials** to offer her a job as a payload officer/flight controller.

In Houston at last, she **enthusiastically** took on a whole range of jobs: **evaluating** payloads for the shuttle, helping design a kit to repair the heat shield in space, and serving as a guidance and control officer for the reentry of the Skylab in 1979. . . .

Yet this first NASA job was not without its **hard knocks,** particularly for a young woman who had a tendency to sometimes take her job too seriously. "She had to put up with a lot of male **guff,**" recalls Shannon, "and from people who included some of the big decision makers on the Apollo program."

Meanwhile, she had done some checking on why she hadn't been accepted as an astronaut for the '78 class and discovered that most successful **candidates** had earned a Ph.D. in science or engineering. Dunbar's **reaction:** Start a night school doctoral program at the University of Houston, where she used rats to study the effect of a **simulated** microgravity environment on bone mass and strength. . . .

Welcome Ascan. Dunbar's doctoral work, past engineering experience, and solid NASA record at last won her acceptance in 1980 as an astronaut candidate—"Ascan" as they are called at the space center. She was 31 years old, and had weathered not just years of hard work and frustrations but some serious **setbacks,** such as the deaths of two brothers. But at last, she had finally reached her dream—and she was ready. . . .

Bonnie got her first shuttle flight as a mission specialist aboard STS 61-A in October 1985. Called "Deutschland Spacelab Mission," the flight featured some 75 experiments—including several materials science payloads—from **prominent** researchers in Germany and other European countries. . . .

STS 61-A was also the last successful flight of the Challenger shuttle, which exploded just seconds after its launch on January 28, 1986, killing the entire crew. . . .

With all the analysis and redesign work that went on after the Challenger **tragedy,** Dunbar had faith enough in the vehicle to fly again in January 1990, after the program **resumed** operations in September of 1988. This time, she not only performed crystal growth experiments, but was given major responsibility for operating the

remote manipulator system (RMS) to retrieve the Long Duration Exposure Facility (LDEF) satellite, which had been in **orbit** since 1984.

Described as an international research treasure, the LDEF carried 57 experiments, including **vital data** on the effect of the space environment on materials and structures. . . .

Pondering the future. What new **challenges** await someone who, at age 43, has already experienced and **accomplished** more than most of us could even dream about?

"I really feel that I'm in my particular **niche**," says Dunbar. "If there is a course that every individual is destined to take, I feel very lucky to have found mine. I love this job and believe in NASA's goals. It can be totally absorbing." . . .

Aside from the personal fulfillment, Dunbar feels that being an astronaut allows her to serve her country. "I believe you have a duty at some point to pay something back, and my payback is what I can provide technically for the advancement of the country."

▶ *AFTER YOU READ*

1. What have been Dunbar's accomplishments?

2. What would you say were the odds against her making these achievements? That is, what were the obstacles she faced in order to achieve her dreams?

3. What is it about Dunbar, do you think, that has made her successful in achieving her goals?

Supplemental Reading List—Chapter 9

Tien, Chang-Lin, "America's Scapegoats," *Newsweek,* October 31, 1994, p. 19.

In this essay published in *Newsweek*'s "My Turn" section, Chinese American Chang-Lin Tien, now Chancellor of the University of California at Berkeley, tells of the discrimination he has faced as an immigrant and argues that "immigrant-bashing" is hurting both foreign-born and native-born Americans.

✏ WRITING ASSIGNMENT: *Writing about Overcoming the Odds*

In this chapter, you will first learn about focusing a topic and then work through the stages of the writing process to develop an essay about a time when you overcame the odds. Before beginning work on your essay, discuss the following question with your classmates. Your answer to this question will become the focus of your essay.

Question: How did you overcome the odds to do or achieve something important to you?

Write an essay about your experience. Tell your readers about the odds that were against you when you tried to do something or to achieve something.

For this topic, you will design your own approach and controlling question. Many different approaches are possible; for example, you might analyze (1) the ways in which you overcame the odds against you or (2) what enabled you to do so (such as your own character traits or the support you received from others). As you plan and write this essay, you will want to keep in mind that the assignment calls for analysis, not simply narration of what happened when you overcame the odds against you.

Before beginning your draft, be certain that you have clear in your own mind what the "odds" were against you as you tried to do something or to achieve something. Also, you will want to clearly focus your approach to this assignment—the controlling question you will be answering.

Guidelines on Focusing Your Topic and Analyzing

In this chapter, you will write an analysis essay in which you choose your own particular focus on the topic. Once you have chosen your focus, planned your essay, and drafted your body paragraphs, you will learn how to write a conclusion paragraph for an essay.

Before planning your essay, think about what it means to overcome the odds. As noted earlier, when people seek to achieve something in spite of the odds, that means their success is unlikely. Thus, when they overcome the odds, they achieve something that was not expected of them or that others may have thought they were not able to achieve.

The odds that are against people as they try to do things exist for a variety of reasons. The odds might be against a person because of the place where he or she grew up, because of the political situation there, or because of the person's age, sex, education, race, ethnic group, or social status (or caste). For instance, the odds would be against a person from India's *niravista* ("untouchable") caste who wanted to be elected prime minister of India. In addition, someone with weak skills in a certain language may have to face difficult odds in terms of job opportunities. In the hiring process for airline pilots, for example, the odds would be against a pilot who did not speak English because world air-traffic control is carried out in English. The odds might also be against someone with a physical disability (a blind person who wants to be a painter) or someone who has no education but wants to attend college someday.

In the following reading from *East Africa* by the Editors of Time-Life Books (1986), you will see how an African from Kenya, "Dr. Paul," overcame the great odds that were against him in attaining an education and, ultimately, success as a physician. Reading this selection will help you see more about what a person can do to overcome the odds, as well as the qualities and character traits that help a person to do so.

▶ *BEFORE YOU READ*

1. Where is Kenya? Can you locate it on the map that appears in the front of this book?

2. Imagine a young black African male born in what was known as the Kenya Colony in 1939. He lives in a remote village in the central highlands of Kenya with his people, the Kikuyu. In 1952, he comes of age (thirteen) at a time of great danger and political unrest—when the Mau Mau guerrillas are staging an uprising. Twenty thousand Kikuyu are rounded up by the British as suspects and held in detention camps. Many are tortured (caused great physical pain). What do you think the chances were of this young man obtaining an education and becoming a successful physician?

from *EAST AFRICA*

THE EDITORS OF TIME-LIFE BOOKS

A **prosperous** medical practitioner in Nairobi, Kenya, known to his friends as Dr. Paul, has no doubts that life has changed for the better since his childhood in a small Kikuyu village. His wife runs a successful hairdressing salon; two of his four children are at university in England, and the other two are studying at the best boarding school in Kenya. . . .

Now aged 50, Paul was just 13 years old when the first **rumblings** of the Mau Mau rebellion reached his village. Relatives advised him to leave home and seek education in Uganda, well known at the time for the quality of its schools. He set off with no more than the name of a school, some 300 kilometers away, where he had no friends or relatives to support him. Paul occasionally managed to **cadge** lifts from passing **lorries;** once or twice he rode **pillion** on bicycles. The rest of the way he walked; it took him a week.

The school, when he found it, was a miserable, run-down establishment. The straw-thatched roof **leaked** when it rained and smelled like rotting fruit in the sun. But Paul was in luck. The **Ganda** headmaster, who owned the school, was willing to take anyone who came, and although there were **scarcely** any books he and his two teachers managed to **instill** a thirst for knowledge into the hundred or more pupils.

Paul became the headmaster's servant to pay his keep, and was given a bed in an **outhouse.** He would wake up before it was light to go to the well for water, take the goats out to pasture, then weed the vegetable patch or dig some new ground. In the evenings he worked again, digging or weeding. For breakfast he had a cup of milkless tea and a bowl of yam, **plantain** or **manioc,** cooked by the headmaster's wife, and supper was equally simple.

It was a tough **apprenticeship,** but Paul stuck to his purpose. After three years, the headmaster sent him to a bigger secondary school in Toro, 200 kilometers further away from the land of his birth. Paul spent five years here and then won a **scholarship** to study medicine at the University of East Africa at Makerere, just outside Kampala, which attracted the top students from the whole region. By now Paul could speak both the Toro and the Ganda languages as well as English, Swahili and his own Kikuyu. As he **progressed** towards his doctorate in the **cosmopolitan atmosphere** of Makerere, he **forged** friendships with many students from distant parts and different backgrounds. When they met later in Nairobi or Dar es Salaam, or even overseas, these rising stars of the new African **meritocracy** would talk of their days at the campus, or their nights in Suzanna's Club or the White Nile—two famous dance halls of Kampala—drinking beer and dancing with bar girls and nurses to live bands playing the fashionable Congolese jazz.

Kenyatta [the future leader of Kenya] was released from prison the year Paul **qualified,** and when Independence came, the young doctor was a city medical officer in Nairobi. By this time he was married to a girl from his own Kikuyu district. They moved into a **flat** in a rough part of town; these were days when scarcely any blacks could afford to live in the best **residential** areas. After a few years, though, he opened a private practice. . . .

Dr. Paul still gives one evening's **consultation** a week at the public hospital—working alongside **harassed** and poorly paid **colleagues** who have no private patients—but for the most part the **rigours** of poverty are behind him. One afternoon a week he drives to the Limuru Club for a round of golf. Here, in the **elegant** surroundings once reserved for top **colonial** officials, he can relax with other members of Kenya's **elite**—ministers, permanent secretaries, businessmen and lawyers—and with professionals from abroad. Like them, he has become a member of a community which is far more international than truly African.

▶ AFTER YOU READ

1. What were the odds facing Dr. Paul as he set out to pursue an education and a medical degree?

2. How did Dr. Paul manage to overcome these odds?

3. What character traits of Dr. Paul do you think enabled him to overcome such great odds? List the adjectives that you would use to describe the qualities in Dr. Paul that helped him succeed.

USE ANALYSIS, NOT NARRATIVE

As you plan your essay about overcoming the odds, remember that the assignment calls for an analysis essay, not a narrative essay that simply tells a story. Therefore, you need to be sure that your essay has an analytical focus. Rather than simply telling the story of when you overcame the odds, you need to analyze, explain, or interpret this story. Your analysis may take one of many forms, as noted earlier. You might analyze (1) the steps you took to overcome the odds against you, (2) the character traits that enabled you to do so, or (3) the importance of other people's support to your success.

Whatever approach you choose to follow, make certain that your essay has an overall main idea—your viewpoint on the subject—as well as several subpoints. Remember that your reader will ask: "What is the main idea this writer is trying to convey about his or her struggle to overcome the odds in trying to do or achieve something?"

Prewriting: Generating Ideas

After choosing a workable topic, think about how you want to approach it in the essay. Focus this approach in a controlling question, the one you will answer in the essay. Write your one-sentence question on a blank piece of paper before you begin prewriting.

Then take some time to generate ideas about your controlling question. Use one of the prewriting techniques you learned in earlier chapters—clustering (pages 10–11), freewriting (pages 31–32), tree diagraming (page 54), or brainstorming (pages 101–102)—to develop your ideas.

DEVELOPING YOUR THESIS AND PLAN

Now look over the ideas you generated and decide how you can break them down into subpoints. Make a list of the subpoints you want to include in the essay.

Next, develop a preliminary plan for your essay. In the space provided here, write your controlling question and a rough draft of your thesis statement. Your thesis should directly answer the controlling question. In the essay, the thesis statement should perform two functions: it should convey to the reader (1) your approach to the topic and (2) the main idea of the essay.

Your Controlling Question:

_____

_____

Your Thesis Statement:

_____

_____

If your thesis does not include the subpoints of your essay, now is the time to clarify and focus those subpoints. Look back at your list of subpoints and try to focus what you want to say about each one. Ask yourself: "What is the 'gist' or the essential message I want to convey with this subpoint?"

Think of a reader sitting in front of you. You are telling him or her the "gist" or the essential message for each subpoint you have planned: "In this subpoint, what I really want to say is '_____

_____.'"

As you plan the essay and focus the gist of each subpoint, remember that your work at this point is preliminary. Later on, while drafting and then revising, your original plan is likely to change. At this point, though, you need some rough ideas about your subpoints to guide you.

After deciding how many subpoints you want to cover in the essay, write in a sentence the gist of each subpoint (the essential message):

Subpoint 1: _____

_____

Subpoint 2: _____

_____

Subpoint 3: _____

_____

Now, check over your subpoints. Make certain that each subpoint is distinct from the others—that there is no overlapping of subpoints. Also, check to see that your subpoints are emphatically ordered, with the most important appearing last.

Before sharing your thesis and plan with your writing group, practice evaluating the student examples in Activity 9.1, if time permits.

❏   *ACTIVITY 9.1:*   **EVALUATING STUDENTS' THESES AND PLANS**

Read the three student samples (controlling questions, thesis statements, and plan) that follow and then discuss each one in terms of these questions:

DISCUSSION QUESTIONS

1. *Controlling Question:* Is the writer's controlling question clear? What suggestions for improvement can you offer?

2. *Thesis Statement:* Does the thesis statement directly answer the writer's controlling question? Are the main idea and approach of the essay conveyed by the thesis? What suggestions for improvement can you offer?

3. *Subpoints:* Is each subpoint clear? Are any subpoints too narrow or too broad? Is each subpoint distinct from the others or is there some overlapping of subpoints? Are the subpoints emphatically ordered, with the most important one appearing last? What suggestions for improvement can you offer?

STUDENT SAMPLE A

Controlling Question
What caused the odds to be against me in trying to enter a U.S. college as a newly arrived foreigner?

Opening Paragraph and Thesis
When I first came to the United States, I had to overcome the odds that were against my entering college as a foreigner who had been in the United States for only two years. My experiences in overcoming the odds for entrance to college were that I had a short time to complete all the college preparation requirements compared to other students and the school did not let me take honors or advanced placement classes because of my weak skills in English.

STUDENT SAMPLE B

Controlling Question
What was it about me as a person that allowed me to overcome the odds in order to achieve my goal of becoming one of the top ten students in my high school?

Thesis
Fortunately, two things helped me attain my goal of becoming one of the top ten students in my high school: the motivation to please my

family back in Vietnam and the precious character trait of persever-ance.

STUDENT SAMPLE C

Controlling Question
What steps did I take to overcome the odds in trying to become fluent in English?

Thesis
When I first arrived in the United States, I took two steps to overcome the barrier of my weak English skills.

Plan
1. I obtained after-school tutoring.

2. I practiced speaking English with different people.

❏ *ACTIVITY 9.2:* **PEER RESPONSE**

Now share your work with your writing group. Use the following pro-cedure:

1. One group member should begin by reading aloud his or her work (controlling question, thesis, and plan). The group should then discuss the writer's work in terms of the questions listed on the Peer Response Sheet for Activity 9.2 on page 354. Another group member should record the group's comments on the sheet.

2. After you are finished filling out the sheet, give it to the writer, so that he or she can use it when revising.

3. Repeat the procedure for each group member.

4. Then revise your work as necessary, keeping in mind the suggestions of your writing group.

Drafting the Opening and First Body Paragraphs

Before you begin drafting your essay, check to see if you need to revise your plan, depending on the suggestions of your writing group. If neces-sary, revise your plan or rewrite it.

Next, draft your opening and first body paragraphs. If you need to re-view the techniques for opening paragraphs, look back at Chapter 8. (You will draft the remainder of your essay later, after you work through the peer response procedure for the opening and first body paragraphs.)

Revising the Opening and First Body Paragraphs

Before sharing your draft opening and first body paragraphs with your writing group, practice evaluating the sample paragraphs in Activity 9.3, if time permits.

❏ *ACTIVITY 9.3:* **EVALUATING STUDENTS' OPENING AND FIRST BODY PARAGRAPHS**

After reading this opening paragraph, discuss it in terms of the questions that follow.

OPENING PARAGRAPH

When I arrived as a newcomer at Sequoia High School four years ago, I was at first overwhelmed by the new world I had fallen into—hundreds of students rushing through the halls, students kissing in front of their lockers, and students talking out loud in class and interrupting their teachers. With no friends and not enough English to understand much of what the teachers were saying, I was very scared that I would have to give up my dream, which was to graduate as one of the top ten students in my high school class. Yet I was able to overcome the great odds against me in pursuit of this goal largely because of my perseverance and my motivation to please the family I had left behind in Vietnam.

DISCUSSION QUESTIONS

  1. How does the opening paragraph capture the reader's attention?

  2. Does the opening paragraph tell the reader what approach the writer will take in the essay about overcoming the odds?

  3. If included, are the subpoints of the essay made clear in the opening?

  4. What suggestions for improving the opening paragraph can you offer?

The following sample body paragraph, which uses information from an article in *Quest/80*, describes Vilma Martinez, a Chicano lawyer-activist who was president and general counsel of the Mexican-American Legal Defense and Education Fund (MALDEF). The daughter of a Texas carpenter, Martinez rose from the "poverty and sexism of her background" to become one of the nation's outstanding Chicano lawyers.

As you read the following thesis statement and first body paragraph, determine whether the writer focuses the subpoint clearly. Also look to see if the paragraph includes enough specific evidence as well as thorough analysis to develop the subpoint. Then discuss the questions that follow the paragraph.

THESIS STATEMENT

Two people who were instrumental in helping Vilma Martinez overcome the odds against her in attaining an education were her grandmother and a professor at Columbia University Law School.

FIRST BODY PARAGRAPH

One person who was a key figure in enabling Vilma Martinez to overcome the odds against her was her grandmother. When Martinez speaks of growing up in the barrio of San Antonio, she credits her determination to her grandmother. "She was forthright, she was a coper and a woman of action," recalls Vilma, the eldest of five children. Her grandmother encouraged her, even when her teachers failed to show interest. Vilma got high grades in school, yet her counselors tried to direct her to a nonacademic high school, she says, "because to become a secretary was the highest thing a girl like me could aspire to." With her grandmother's guidance, Martinez became more and more forceful as she grew up. She gained entry into an academic high school and later turned down her father's offer to pay her way to a local Catholic college and instead marched off to the University of Texas, eighty miles from her home. There she lived in a housing cooperative and washed glassware in a biochemistry lab to earn extra money. Because of the determination instilled in her by her grandmother, she was able to achieve her goal of becoming a lawyer and helping Chicano people in a concrete way. She graduated from Columbia Law School, which eleven years later awarded her the university's Medal of Excellence in recognition of her emergence as "a major figure in American civil rights."

DISCUSSION QUESTIONS

1. Is the subpoint of the body paragraph clearly focused? In one sentence, describe the gist or essential message of the paragraph:

_____

_____

2. Does the paragraph include enough specific evidence to develop the subpoint of the paragraph?

3. Does the paragraph include enough analysis? Does it explain how Martinez's grandmother instilled determination in her and how this helped Martinez overcome the odds against her?

❏ *ACTIVITY 9.4:* **MORE PEER RESPONSE**

Now share your opening and first body paragraphs with your writing group. Following the peer response procedure outlined in Activity 9.2, discuss each writer's work in terms of the questions listed on the Peer Response Sheet for Activity 9.4 on page 356. Then revise your opening and first body paragraphs, keeping in mind the suggestions of your writing group.

Drafting the Other Body Paragraphs and Conclusion

You are now ready to draft the remaining body paragraphs, as well as the conclusion for your essay. The following guidelines on the concluding paragraph will help you draft an effective conclusion.

THE CONCLUSION

An effective *conclusion* brings an essay to a satisfying close. Any of the following techniques can be used to make a conclusion effective:

1. Reemphasize the essay's main idea.
2. Broaden the subject by discussing its implications.
3. Close with something specific.
4. Refer back to the opening paragraph.

Reemphasize the Essay's Main Idea

The conclusion may begin by reemphasizing or reaffirming the main idea of the essay. The purpose here is not to review the subpoints covered in the essay, but to leave the reader with a strong sense of the essay's main idea. The reemphasis of the essay's main idea may be a restatement of the thesis but in different words.

In the following example, the student restates the main idea of the thesis (excluding the subpoints) at the beginning of the concluding paragraph:

THESIS STATEMENT

When I first arrived in the United States, I took two important steps to overcome the barrier of my weak English skills.

FIRST SENTENCE OF CONCLUSION

Ultimately, because of the steps I took, I was successful in significantly improving my English skills. . . .

Broaden the Subject by Discussing Its Implications

After restating the main idea, the conclusion can broaden the essay's focus by discussing the implications of the main idea. In discussing implications you answer questions like "What does this all mean?" and "Why is this important?" Discussing the implications of your thesis helps the reader see the importance or meaning of your topic.

Note how the following student broadens the subject by discussing its implications in the conclusion:

DRAFT CONCLUSION

Ultimately, because of the steps I took, I was successful in significantly improving my English skills. I was then able to communicate better with my new friends, and I no longer thought of my schoolwork as impossible. Other newcomers can learn an important lesson from my story: Never give up, no matter how hard English may seem.

Close with Something Specific

Another technique used to make the conclusion effective is closing with something specific, such as an example, a prediction, a call for action, a quotation, or a question.

Use a Specific Example. Note here how the student writer added a small specific example to the concluding paragraph to bring it to a close.

REVISED CONCLUSION

Ultimately, because of the steps I took, I was successful in significantly improving my English skills. I was then able to communicate better with my new friends, and I no longer thought of my schoolwork as impossible. Other newcomers can learn an important lesson from my story: Never give up, no matter how hard English may seem. When newcomers first go through the cafeteria line at their new school and hear only a garble of sounds, they should remember that by taking a few simple steps to improve their English, they will soon hear clear, sparkling words in the cafeteria. Instead of a jumble of sounds, they will hear, "Would you like tuna on whole wheat or pastrami on rye?"

Make a Prediction. A conclusion that makes a prediction turns the reader's thoughts to the future. If the reader accepts your thesis, what will happen in the future? What will be the benefits? What will happen if readers do not accept your thesis? Locate the prediction in the following draft conclusion:

DRAFT CONCLUSION

Thus my perseverance, as well as my desire to please my family in Vietnam, helped me immensely in reaching my goal of graduating as one of the top ten students in my high school class. Because of this success, I know now that I am capable of overcoming great odds, and I believe that this same motivation and perseverance will play important roles in helping me reach my next goal, which is to be accepted to medical school.

Call for Action. An effective conclusion might also speak directly to readers by calling for some direct action on their part. Locate the call for action in the following conclusion:

CONCLUSION

Thus I had to overcome several barriers that were in my way as I tried to enter a U.S. college as a recent foreign arrival. Yet, as you can see, I was able to overcome these almost insurmountable barriers. From my story, you can see that no barriers are truly "insurmountable"; you too can gather courage and leap over even those that seem above your head.

Introduce a Quotation. A relevant quotation—from an expert on your subject, a proverb, or even your grandmother—can help to bring an essay to a satisfying close. For example:

END OF CONCLUSION

. . . As my grandmother always tells me, "Keep your eyes ahead on your dreams and only give a glance to the rocks and boulders in your path."

Ask a Question. Concluding with a question directed at your readers keeps them thinking about your subject after they are finished reading the essay. The question might focus on the essay's main idea or it might be a call for action. For instance:

CONCLUSION

Thus, when I arrived in the United States, the odds were against my being able to go to college because of my weak skills in English and my family's financial problems. Nevertheless, I was able to find the strength to overcome these odds. Now I believe that all of us can be successful in pursuing our goals at least 80 percent of the time, no matter how great the odds are against us. Do you think this can be true in your life, too?

Refer Back to the Opening Paragraph

An effective conclusion might also refer back to some interesting or attention-getting part of the opening. This technique rounds off the essay, giving it a sense of closure.

In the following example, the student writer mentions several concrete details in the opening paragraph, which you saw earlier, and then refers to those details in the conclusion:

OPENING PARAGRAPH

When I arrived as a newcomer at Sequoia High School four years ago, I was at first overwhelmed by the new world I had fallen into—hundreds of students rushing through the halls, students kissing in front of their lockers, and students talking out loud in class and interrupting their teachers. With no friends and not enough English to even understand much of what the teachers were saying, I was very scared that I would have to give up my dream, which was to graduate as one of the top ten students in my high school class. Yet I was able to overcome the great odds against me in pursuit of this goal largely because of my perseverance and my motivation to please the family I had left behind in Vietnam.

CONCLUDING PARAGRAPH

Thus my perseverance, as well as my desire to please my family in Vietnam, helped me immensely in reaching my goal of graduating as one of the top ten students in my high school class. Because of this success, I know now that I am capable of overcoming great odds, and I believe that this same motivation and perseverance will play important roles in helping me reach my next goal, which is to be accepted to medical school. I know that when I have to take admission tests for medical school and go to interviews, I will be just as scared as I was when I first had to face the new world of Sequoia High School. Yet now I know that I have the personal qualities within me to help me reach my next goal.

Now draft the remaining body paragraphs. Then, keeping in mind the suggestions you have just read about conclusions, draft your conclusion paragraph.

Revising the Other Body Paragraphs and Conclusion

If time permits, practice evaluating the student body paragraph and conclusion in Activity 9.5 before sharing your draft essay with your writing group.

❏ *ACTIVITY 9.5:*   **EVALUATING A STUDENT'S BODY PARAGRAPH AND CONCLUDING PARAGRAPH**

After reading the body paragraph and conclusion that follow, discuss the questions with your classmates.

BODY PARAGRAPH

One way I was able to overcome my difficulty in understanding English was by forcing myself to read more. Reading more English books, magazines, and newspapers is good practice for understanding English. Indeed, when I came to the United States, I didn't like reading because whenever I read an article in a newspaper, I only understood half of the writer's ideas. The vocabulary in the articles caused me to misunderstand what was written. One day, my younger cousin, who was an elementary school student, asked me to help her read a story-book. Since I didn't understand the vocabulary, I was confused about the story, and I was unable to help my cousin. She laughed at me and left. I felt ashamed about it so I forced myself to read as many story-books and newspapers as I could. Although I didn't understand some of the vocabulary, I looked up the definitions in the dictionary and mem-orized all of them. As time passed, I built up basic reading comprehen-sion skills. In addition, I recognized that it would take a long time to understand the English language. Therefore, I forced myself to read more in order to improve my ability to understand English.

DISCUSSION QUESTIONS

1. *Topic Sentence:* Does the topic sentence make the subpoint of the para-graph clear?

2. *Evidence:* Is there enough specific evidence to develop the subpoint of the paragraph?

3. *Analysis:* Does the writer analyze the evidence thoroughly in terms of the subpoint being made?

CONCLUSION

Forcing myself to speak more and to read more were the impor-tant solutions to overcoming my difficulties with English. Even though I still lack the ability to speak formal English, I feel comfort-able using everyday English in my life.

DISCUSSION QUESTIONS

1. How does the conclusion reemphasize the main idea of the essay?

2. What techniques should the writer use to improve the conclusion?

❏   *ACTIVITY 9.6:*   **MORE PEER RESPONSE**

Now share your entire essay, including your new body paragraphs and conclusion, with your writing group. Following the peer response procedure outlined in Activity 9.2, discuss each writer's work in terms of the questions listed on the Peer Response Sheet for Activity 9.6 on page 358. Then revise your essay, taking into consideration the suggestions of your writing group.

Editing: More on Logical Connectors

In this editing section, you will learn more about using *logical connectors*—coordinate conjunctions (*and, or, but, for*), transitions (*however, consequently, nevertheless*), and subordinate conjunctions (*although, because, while*).

In earlier chapters, you learned that logical connectors are surface signals that help to bridge the gap between two clauses, two sentences, or two groups of sentences.

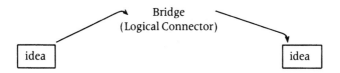

Like other surface signals, logical connectors tell the reader in a direct way (a surface way) the logical relationship between one idea and the next idea.*

> Buchi Emecheta became a successful writer; *in fact,* she has written sixteen books.

Logical connectors help strengthen the coherence of writing. Of course, the most important factor in building coherence is continuity in the developing train of ideas (when one idea emerges from the previous idea and leads smoothly to the next idea). However, sometimes you need to bridge the gap between ideas with a logical connector or another surface signal

---

*Information in the example sentences and exercises in this grammar section is taken from C. Gerald Fraser, "A Writer Who Seeks to Reconcile 2 Worlds," *New York Times* (June 2, 1990).

(such as repetition and synonyms, demonstrative pronouns and adjectives, or pronouns) to help readers see the connections between your ideas.

As you take on the more challenging tasks of academic reading and writing, you will need good control of logical connectors. You will need a good understanding of the meanings of the various logical connectors; in addition, you want to be able to call upon a wide range of logical connectors as you write.

Developing good control of logical connectors will also give you a wide range of possible sentence structures to call upon when you write and thus improve sentence variety in your writing. Rather than being limited to only simple sentences or compound sentences with coordinate conjunctions, you will be able to use various sentence structures, such as compound sentences joined with transitions and adverbial clauses. With the addition of adjective clauses (covered in Chapter 8) and noun clauses (covered in Chapter 10), you will then have a good repertoire or collection of sentence structures to work with as you write and edit.

In this chapter, you will work with a variety of logical connectors—coordinate conjunctions, transitions, and subordinate conjunctions. In the accompanying chart and in the activities that follow, you will see these various types of logical connectors grouped according to the logical relationships that each group signals (addition, contrast, exemplification, and so forth). As you work through these activities, you will build your repertoire of logical connectors, which will in turn help you improve coherence in your writing. In addition, you will become skilled at using different types of logical connectors to vary sentence structure.

Logical Connectors

Logical Relationship	Coordinate Conjunction	Transition	Subordinate Conjunction
Addition	and	moreover furthermore in addition besides	
Reinforcement or Emphasis		indeed in fact	
Choice	or nor		

Logical Relationship	Coordinate Conjunction	Transition	Subordinate Conjunction
Exemplification		for example for instance in particular	
Similarity		likewise similarly	
Contrast	but yet	conversely however in contrast nevertheless nonetheless on the contrary on the other hand otherwise	although though even though while whereas
Cause	for		because since as
Result or Effect	so	consequently thus therefore accordingly hence as a result	
Time		meanwhile subsequently thereafter	when whenever since while before after until as as soon as as long as once
Place			where wherever
Manner			as

STRUCTURING AND PUNCTUATING SENTENCES
WITH LOGICAL CONNECTORS

Before you begin to practice using various logical connectors, you will find it helpful to review the sentence structure and punctuation that each calls for.

Coordinate Conjunctions

Coordinate conjunctions join two independent clauses in order to form a compound sentence:

| Independent Clause | , Coordinate Conjunction | Independent Clause |

Example: Buchi Emecheta was a female raised in a Third World country, *but* she managed to become a successful writer and publisher.

Transitions

Transitions can also join two independent clauses in order to form a compound sentence. Note the difference in punctuation from the preceding compound sentence.

| Independent Clause | ; Transition, | Independent Clause |

Example: Buchi Emecheta was a female raised in a Third World country; *nevertheless,* she managed to become a successful writer and publisher.

Subordinate Conjunctions

Subordinate conjunctions can be used at the beginning of a dependent clause to form a complex sentence. Note the difference in punctuation, depending on whether the dependent clause comes before or after the independent clause:

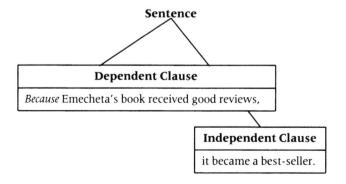

Sentence

Dependent Clause
Because Emecheta's book received good reviews,

Independent Clause
it became a best-seller.

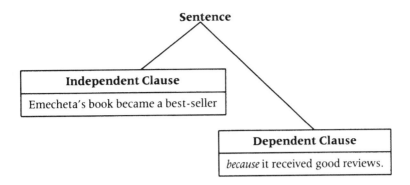

Logical Connectors of Addition

Logical Relationship	Coordinate Conjunction	Transition	Subordinate Conjunction
Addition	and	moreover furthermore in addition besides	

The logical connectors in this diagram signal *addition*. That is, they convey to the reader that to the idea in the first clause, an additional idea is added (in the second clause).

❑ *ACTIVITY 9.7:* **WORKING WITH LOGICAL CONNECTORS OF ADDITION**

First, complete the following sentence by adding a clause that logically fits the first clause, as well as the logical connector:

1. Buchi Emecheta became a successful author, *and* _____

_____.

Next, using the sentence you just created, substitute an appropriate transition of addition for the coordinate conjunction *and*. Be sure to punctuate the new sentence correctly.

2. Buchi Emecheta became a successful author _____

_____.

Logical Connectors of Reinforcement or Emphasis

Logical Relationship	Coordinate Conjunction	Transition	Subordinate Conjunction
Reinforcement or Emphasis		indeed in fact	

The logical connectors in this diagram signal *emphasis* or *reinforcement*. That is, the second idea adds emphasis or reinforcement to the first idea.

❏ *ACTIVITY 9.8:* **WORKING WITH LOGICAL CONNECTORS OF REINFORCEMENT OR EMPHASIS**

Complete the following sentences with a clause that adds reinforcement or emphasizes the first clause.

1. Emecheta's husband objected to her writing; *in fact,* _____.

2. Emecheta's publisher and agent made changes in her manuscript; *indeed,*

_____.

Logical Connectors of Choice

Logical Relationship	Coordinate Conjunction	Transition	Subordinate Conjunction
Choice	or nor		

The logical connectors in the preceding box signal *choice*. *Or* signals a choice between two possibilities—between the idea in the first clause and the idea in the second clause. *Nor* signals that between two things, neither is a possibility. (Remember that *nor* calls for question word order. See Chapter 2 for guidelines on word order with *nor*.)

❏ *ACTIVITY 9.9:* **WORKING WITH LOGICAL CONNECTORS OF CHOICE**

Combine each sentence pair by using the coordinate conjunction *or* or *nor*. You may have to change the word order to complete a sentence.

1. Instead of pursuing her dream, Emecheta could have stayed in Nigeria. She could have stopped writing.

_____

_____.

2. Emecheta did not stay in Nigeria. She did not stop writing.

_____

_____.

Logical Connectors of Exemplification

Logical Relationship	Coordinate Conjunction	Transition	Subordinate Conjunction
Exemplification		for example for instance in particular	

The logical connectors in the preceding box signal *exemplification.* That is, the first clause is a general statement. Then, in the second clause, the logical connector introduces a specific example of the general statement in the first clause.

❏ *ACTIVITY 9.10:* **WORKING WITH LOGICAL CONNECTORS OF EXEMPLIFICATION**

Find the gap between ideas in the following short passage. Then rewrite the passage, using a transition of exemplification to bridge the gap:

When Emecheta came to Britain, she had little money. She had to work hard to support herself and her children. She took a job scrubbing floors.

_____

_____

_____

Logical Connectors of Similarity

Logical Relationship	Coordinate Conjunction	Transition	Subordinate Conjunction
Similarity		likewise similarly	

The logical connectors in the preceding box signal *similarity.* That is, the idea in the second clause is similar to the idea in the first clause.

❑ *ACTIVITY 9.11:* **WORKING WITH LOGICAL CONNECTORS OF SIMILARITY**

In the following passage, find the two sentences that can be joined with a logical connector of similarity. Join the sentences to form a compound sentence. Be careful of how you punctuate the new sentence.

As she pursued her dream of becoming a writer, Emecheta had to take many low-level jobs. In order to support herself and her children, she scrubbed floors. She took a job cleaning at Sandhurst, the Royal Military Academy, in order to do research for a book.

_____

_____

_____

_____

_____

Logical Connectors of Contrast

Logical Relationship	Coordinate Conjunction	Transition	Subordinate Conjunction
Contrast	but yet	conversely however in contrast nevertheless nonetheless on the contrary on the other hand otherwise	although though even though while whereas

The logical connectors in the preceding box signal *contrast*—the idea in the second clause is in contrast to the idea in the first clause.

❑ *ACTIVITY 9.12:* **WORKING WITH LOGICAL CONNECTORS OF CONTRAST**

In each of the following sentences, substitute an appropriate transition of contrast for the coordinate conjunction. Remember to punctuate the new sentences correctly. (To review the different meanings of the transitions of contrast, see Chapter 7.)

1. Emecheta had planned to stay in Britain only two years, *but* she decided to stay permanently.

_____

_____

2. Upon arrival in Britain, Emecheta spoke five languages, *yet* she didn't
speak English.

_____

_____

Now combine each of the following sentence pairs first with a transition of contrast and then with a subordinate conjunction of contrast. Remember to punctuate the new sentences correctly.

1. In Nigeria, Emecheta had received weak educational preparation.
She enrolled in the University of London and earned a degree in sociology
with honors.

_____

_____

_____

_____

2. Many of Emecheta's books describe the struggles of immigrant
women. Others concentrate solely on political conditions in Nigeria.

_____

_____

_____

3. Emecheta's publisher claimed that a chapter of *Destination Biafra* had
been lost. Emecheta knew that her publisher and agent had deleted the
chapter intentionally.

_____

_____

_____

Logical Connectors of Cause

Logical Relationship	Coordinate Conjunction	Transition	Subordinate Conjunction
Cause	for		because since as

The logical connectors in the preceding box signal *cause*. They tell the reader that the logical connector introduces a clause that is a *cause*, while the other clause in the sentence is the *result*.

❏ *ACTIVITY 9.13:* **WORKING WITH LOGICAL CONNECTORS OF CAUSE**

Combine the pair of sentences first with a coordinate conjunction of cause and then with a subordinate conjunction of cause. Punctuate the new sentences correctly.

Emecheta set up her own publishing company.

She wanted to have control over the way her books were published.

1. _____

_____

_____

2. _____

_____

_____

Logical Connectors of Result or Effect

Logical Relationship	Coordinate Conjunction	Transition	Subordinate Conjunction
Result or Effect	so	consequently thus therefore accordingly hence as a result	

The logical connectors in the preceding box signal *result.* They tell the reader that the first clause gives the cause and the second clause (introduced by the logical connector) gives the result.

❏ *ACTIVITY 9.14:* **WORKING WITH LOGICAL CONNECTORS OF RESULT OR EFFECT**

Combine the pair of sentences first with a coordinate conjunction of result and then with a transition of result. Remember to punctuate the new sentences correctly.

Emecheta and her children had no experience in book publishing.

Starting a publishing company meant having on-the-job training.

1. _____

_____

_____

2. _____

_____

_____

Logical Connectors of Time

Logical Relationship	Coordinate Conjunction	Transition	Subordinate Conjunction
Time		meanwhile subsequently thereafter	when whenever since while before after until as as soon as as long as once

The logical connectors in the preceding box signal *time.* Some mean *time before* (before, until), some mean *same time* (meanwhile, when, while, once, as soon as, as long as), some mean *time after* (subsequently, thereafter, since, after), and some mean *anytime* (whenever).

❑ *ACTIVITY 9.15:* **WORKING WITH LOGICAL CONNECTORS OF TIME**

Combine each sentence pair first with a transition of time and then with a subordinate conjunction of time. Remember to punctuate the new sentences correctly.

1. Some of Emecheta's children worked at printing and assembling the books. Others went out to stores as sales representatives.

_____

_____

_____

2. For the *New Yorker,* John Updike wrote a favorable review of Emecheta's book *Double Yoke.* The book became a best-seller.

_____

_____

_____

Logical Connectors of Place

Logical Relationship	Coordinate Conjunction	Transition	Subordinate Conjunction
Place			where wherever

The logical connectors in the preceding box signal *place. Where* refers to a definite place, and *wherever* refers more generally to any place.

❑ *ACTIVITY 9.16:* **WORKING WITH LOGICAL CONNECTORS OF PLACE**

Combine each sentence pair with a subordinate conjunction of place. You may need to delete some words.

1. Emecheta's books have been published in many places. They have been praised in all these places.

_____

_____

_____

2. Emecheta came from a place. At that place, women were not encouraged to become writers.

_____

_____

_____

Logical Connectors of Manner

Logical Relationship	Coordinate Conjunction	Transition	Subordinate Conjunction
Manner			as

The logical connector in the preceding box signals *manner*—in the manner or way that.

❏ *ACTIVITY 9.17:* **WORKING WITH LOGICAL CONNECTORS OF MANNER**

Combine the following sentences with a subordinate conjunction of manner. You may need to delete some words.

Emecheta never gave up her dream of becoming a writer.
Her husband had urged that.

_____

_____

✓ *EDITING CHECKLIST* _____

After revising your essay for content, you are ready to edit it. Check for the following:

    ☐ Check for *coherence problems*. Ask a classmate or friend to read your essay aloud to you. Listen for breaks in coherence, where one sentence does not smoothly follow another. If you find breaks in coherence, ask yourself the following questions:

    • Can I use the principle of "something old/something new"—picking up "something old" from a previous sentence and adding to it "something new"?

    • Can I use a surface signal to link one sentence to the next—repetition and a synonym, a demonstrative pronoun or adjective, a pronoun, or a logical connector (coordinate conjunction, subordinate conjunction, or transition)?

☐ Check for *sentence variety*. Mark each sentence in your essay as simple, compound, or complex. Then ask these questions:

• Does each paragraph have good sentence variety—a good mixture of simple, compound, and complex sentences?

• Do I have too many simple or compound sentences?

• Can I combine some logically related simple sentences with adjective or adverbial clauses?

If time permits, also check your draft for the following:

☐ Check for *correct verb tense.*

☐ Check for *sentence structure problems:* fragments, run-on sentences, and comma splices.

CHAPTER 10

Writing about the Way Males and Females Are Raised

In this chapter, you will write a compare/constrast essay about the ways male and females are raised in your culture, drawing upon your own experience, as well as ideas you get from the readings. Researchers in the academic world call this topic (the ways males and females are raised) "gender roles" or "sex roles." Researchers in this area examine, for example, the roles males and females are expected to assume as adults.

Before beginning work on your essay, you will read several selections about the way males and females are raised in two very different societies—Japan and Saudi Arabia. A number of selections are included here to give you several viewpoints on this very complex topic. If time permits, you can read all the selections, or you can choose just a few for your study. Reading these selections will give you ideas for your own essay comparing the way males and females are raised in your culture.

You will first read three selections about how males and females are raised in Japan and how this upbringing affects the roles they are expected to assume in adulthood. As you read these selections and the following two on Saudi Arabia, you may want to begin thinking about the readings as "sources." In this text, you are reading selections and using these sources as "springboards" for your own writing. That is, you will read each selection, think about the ideas of the author, and use these ideas as jumping-off points for your own ideas on the subject. As you write, you will draw upon your personal experience as a source of evidence for your essay. Later, as you make the transition into academic writing, you will work more closely with the sources themselves, using ideas and evidence from sources in your essays and research papers. You may, for example, respond directly to a reading, agreeing or disagreeing with the author's ideas, or you may gather ideas and evidence from a number of sources in order to write a research paper on a topic. Later, you may write up the results of your original

231

experiments or research, drawing upon outside sources to support your conclusions. In each of these cases, you will need to evaluate the sources you are using, determining which are the most authoritative and reliable sources of evidence for your writing. Now, you can practice evaluating sources by looking closely at the readings in this chapter and the next. In evaluating a source, you will want to think about the author, purpose, and audience: Is the author objective? Does the author present the evidence logically, rather than emotionally? Is the author an expert in the field? How has the author gathered evidence? Is the evidence presented accurate? factual? If the evidence is from personal experience, is that experience representative? Is the author writing to inform or persuade readers? Is the reading published in the popular press (magazines and newspapers) or in a prestigious scholarly publication (in a research journal or by a press devoted to publishing academic research)?

You will notice that the first and third readings that follow were written by journalists, who gathered their evidence by interviewing people and by reading about and observing people in the culture. The second reading, however, is by an academic researcher who has gathered her evidence from her own scientific surveys and observations, as well as from other scholarly articles and books. You will want to discuss with your classmates how your knowledge of these readings as sources would affect how you would use them, if, for example, you were using them as sources for a research paper.

In the first reading about Japan (from *National Geographic*, April 1990), American journalist Deborah Fallows describes the way females are raised in Japan and the roles adult males and females assume in Japanese society today.

Readings about Japan

▶ *BEFORE YOU READ*

1. Where is Japan? Can you locate it on the map that appears in the front of this book?

2. How traditional do you think Japanese culture is today? Do you think males and females in Japan are raised in the same way?

3. What roles do you think males and females are expected to assume as adults?

from *JAPANESE WOMEN*

DEBORAH FALLOWS

Customs play a fundamental role in binding Japanese women to their **traditional** role as mother-housekeeper-wife. Training for that **complex** and demanding role begins early.

My best Japanese friend, Keiko Wada, and I took our 12-year-olds, Sachiko and Tommy, shopping for gym clothes at the start of the school year. Tommy went into the changing room, leaving his shoes outside the curtain. When he stepped out and walked over to me to show off his selection, Keiko whispered into Sachiko's ear. Sachiko **discreetly retrieved** Tommy's shoes and **knelt** to place them beside him. What was **embarrassing** for Tommy and surprising to me was perfectly natural for Japanese friends—Sachiko was a well-brought-up Japanese girl doing the expected thing.

Some Japanese women still help dress their husbands in the morning and routinely serve them the choicest morsels from the family rice pot. And once, on a crowded **bullet train** out of Yokohama, I watched a **harried** woman in her 50s rush onto the train weighted down with suitcases, shopping bags, and various parcels. She **scrambled** to claim the last free seat. A moment later her husband **strolled** onto the train, cool and collected, and slipped into the seat his wife had saved for him. While he read the newspaper, she stood in the aisle, bags and purse still **dangling,** all the way to Kyoto, a two-and-a-half-hour trip. . . .

Times are changing for women in Japan, but change is slow. Most Japanese women I know say that they are raising their daughters and sons by the same rules and standards, yet I never saw a Japanese boy do for anyone what Sachiko did for Tommy in that clothing store. . . .

Spinsterhood remains a **dreaded** fate. (An only slightly outdated **slang** term for an unmarried woman over twenty-five is "Christmas cake," because the **latter** drops sharply in value after December 25.) For wedding halls and hotels the Japanese wedding spells big business, as I saw when I visited the Tokyo Hilton's spring wedding show one Sunday afternoon. **Engaged** couples and their eager mothers turned out by the hundreds in their best clothes, **sampling** food trays and studying pricey menus. **Bedazzled** brides-to-be tried on the different **costumes** that every Japanese bride rents or buys for the greatest occasion of her life. . . .

Women have always worked in Japan, many of them at hard **manual labor**—in rice fields, farms, and fisheries—and others in the same few **occupations,** on factory lines or as nurses or teachers. Now some women are **venturing out** in new directions: Housewives are taking part-time jobs; university graduates are breaking into **fast-track lanes. Individualists,** always rare in Japan regardless of **gender,** are becoming "firsts"—first woman **skipper,** soldier, bank manager. . . .

Women in managerial positions still number only 160,000, about one percent of all working women. Those few women who have "made it" tend to be **feminine**—that is, **humble**—about their success. They **resist** calling themselves **role models** and offer little encouragement to young women starting out. Patience is still the key word.

The second reading about Japan is from *The Japanese Woman* (Free Press, 1993) by Sumiko Iwao, an academic researcher. Notice how this more scholarly source differs from the first reading, which is from a popular magazine (*National Geographic*). As you'll see below, the fact that Iwao's book has footnotes tells you that this is a scholarly source.

In the selection below, Iwao tells of the different ways in which one Japanese mother, Akiko Noda, raises her son and daughter. According to Iwao, Akiko's parenting practices are typical of modern Japanese parents.

from *THE JAPANESE WOMAN*

Sumiko Iwao

Today Akiko's children are 16 and 14. When they were small, their father was among the **middle-echelon** managers of his company and was often absent on business trips abroad. At one point, when his son was three and his daughter an **infant,** he spent 18 months in the United States. Today we might call their marriage at that stage a "**commuting** marriage." . . . It was a rule of Kazuo's company that if an employee was stationed overseas for a year or less, he did not take his family along. Kazuo's original assignment had been for a year, but it had been **extended;** during the 18 months he had been able to come home only once for two weeks.

As a mother, Akiko's life was not much different whether Kazuo was abroad or in Japan. She trained and **lavished** affection on her children according to her own childrearing policy, with little **participation** or **intervention** from her husband. Her son and daughter **doted** on her and **rebelled** against her **authority** in the same way that children do in any other country. When they were small, she **indulged** the majority of their **whims** while firmly guiding them in the direction of expected **norms.**

The older they grew, the more strictly the children had to **toe the line,** as society expected of them. Akiko's daughter became helpful around the house at an early stage, quickly **absorbing** the model of caretaking behaviors **exhibited** by her mother and other females surrounding her. Mother and daughter have a close **rapport, appreciating** the same pleasures and enjoying each other. Akiko's daughter is **instinctively** neat and aware of her surroundings. Her son was never expected to perform any **chores voluntarily,** but beginning when he was 10, Akiko made a deal with him to clean and fill the bathtub every day and put out the trash in the morning in exchange for his weekly allowance. Akiko lavished physical affection on her son in his preschool years, but by age 7 or 8 he had become more distant and there were frequent battles of wills. Akiko had difficulty in understanding his needs and in getting him to **cooperate** with family activities or to attend to personal **hygiene,** like brushing his teeth and taking a bath. They often **clash** over routine matters, like unfinished homework, a messy desk, and the way he treats his sister. By the time he entered junior high school, he had become somewhat more responsible about his own activities, but Akiko is worried that she has not made her son help more with household chores and that he depends on her too much for his daily needs. She knows that males of his **generation** are growing up with females who expect men to be more involved in **domestic** matters and feels that he ought to learn to cook and take care of his own personal needs. Kazuo has very little involvement with the daily lives of his children, although he helps Akiko make important decisions involving their schooling. When the children were small, he was a very indulgent and doting father, often behaving more like a big brother or playmate with them than a father. The older they grew, the more **stern** he tended to become. Now he is concerned mainly with whether they are studying properly and in good health. . . .

As in many societies, disciplining (punishment) of the children in the Japanese family was traditionally more the role of the father than the mother, but this is no longer the role among **contemporary** Japanese, largely because of the absence of the father from the home. Surveys show that in 49 percent of cases studied, the mother plays a greater role in disciplining the children than the father, while another 43 percent think it is a role played by both parents equally. Only 4 percent think discipline is to be left to fathers.* In short, all **facets** of childrearing become part of the mother's role.

Unlike their mothers, who had a very clear set of guidelines, aptly expressed in an array of old **proverbs** designed to prevent **disgrace** of the family name and dishonor to the ancestors,** Japanese mothers

*Prime Minister's Office Survey, 1986.

**For example: *"Baka na ko o motaba, kaji jori tsurai* [A stupid child is a worse catastrophe than a fire]" and *"Haji wa ie no jamai* [Shame is the ruin of the family]."

today have less to guide them and a **tendency** to be very **permissive.** Without the support or cooperation of the fathers, the mothers' tendency to spoil their children becomes all the stronger; mothers often do little to control their children, giving them much freedom to do as they like (sons always have the greater freedom).

Mothers have **infinite** love for their sons, especially when they are small. No matter what a young son does, his mother quickly forgives him. A common sight is that of a **toddler** traveling with his mother on the train; bored and restless, perhaps also hungry and tired, he begins to hit his mother hard with his tiny fists. His mother does not try to stop him, merely **enduring** his blows. Rather than **scolding** him, she gently asks him to be patient. She appears to think that this is part of her role as mother, and she tends to be even more **lenient** and indulgent because he is a boy.

The popular comic strip artist Saimon Fumi describes this common pattern in an essay that describes how a mother will give her seven-year-old daughter a bitter scolding, resulting in a quarrel between them, but is immediately forgiving no matter what her three-year-old son does.*** Occasionally, the mother in this essay realizes that she should try harder to keep her son in line, but her **severity** is transparent and the little boy knows it; as she **glowers** at him, he runs circles around her, grinning. The mother tries to be stern, but the insincerity of her scolding delights the boy, and the testing and tension between them provide a certain kind of closeness. Such situations, the essay **concludes,** may provide "moments of perfect happiness." As Saimon's title for this essay ("Now I Know How the Woman Feels Who Will Lend Her Life's Savings to a Hopelessly Untrustworthy Man") illustrates, Japanese women's willingness to accept any misbehavior on the part of their small sons extends to older males as well. No matter how **bungling, miscreant,** or foolish he is, if the man in question is one a woman loves, she is willing to forgive **virtually** anything. The **obverse** of the mother-son relationship can be observed in father-daughter relations, although the latter tend to be much weaker when the father is away from home a great deal.

In the third reading about Japan, "Many Japanese Women Are Resisting Servility" (*The New York Times*, July 9, 1995), Sheryl WuDunn describes contemporary views toward male and female roles in that country, including the problems these views and expectations have caused in recent times.

***Fumi, Saimon, Ren'ai ron [On infatuation and love] (Tokyo: PHP Institute, 1990), 62.

from *MANY JAPANESE WOMEN ARE RESISTING SERVILITY*

Sheryl WuDunn

Tokyo, July 8—For centuries, Japanese women have **trailed** behind their husbands, **scrubbing** away their muddy footprints, preparing and draining their baths and, once upon a time, paying for **infidelity** with their delicate heads.

They bore their **femininity** proudly, even blackening their teeth in the 17th century in a bow to fashion. The servitude was so extreme that a Spanish trader in the 16th century described the women as "**pious**" and "excellent," and the Japanese men as "cruel."

No longer, however, are these women so silently **resigned.** These days, in their homes, over tea with their friends and at luncheons for women only, many could scarcely be more **scathing** about what they see as the unfair sex.

"My father almost never steps inside the kitchen," said Chie Suzuki, a 23-year-old systems engineer. "If Mom is around, he wouldn't even serve tea—he'd just yell, 'Tea!' But of course if my mother isn't around, he has to do it by himself. Would I marry someone like my dad? No way!"

Japan has much less of a **feminist** movement than the United States, but still women of all ages are quietly **rebelling,** calling newly stablished [*sic*] **hot lines,** organizing pressure groups and nationwide **rallies** and even filing **discrimination** suits. Japanese women are also putting more **emphasis** on careers, with the result that they are marrying later and having fewer children, much to the **alarm** of the (male) authorities.

Kayo Enomoto, a 23-year-old travel agency worker who spent a year in America, wonders how she will find an acceptable husband in Japan.

"I think Japanese men are dreaming," said Miss Enomoto, an independent-minded woman who lives alone. "They have this ideal figure of a woman that's very different from reality. Men like women who will make them three square meals a day and who will wait patiently for their return home."

To explore her doubts about Japanese men, Miss Enomoto **conducted** an experiment. One evening at a drinking party with more than a dozen men and women, she decided to play the role of the **docile** woman.

She sweetly poured beer for the men. She **dashed** to their sides after they drained their cups. She wiped the tables with her handkerchief when they **spilled** their beer.

"At the end of the party, I was the most popular girl," she said, angrily. "Half of the guys wanted my phone number. I was so disappointed. I wondered how stupid the guys could be. It was **obvious** that they like obedient girls."

Miss Enomoto says the Japanese male's **conservatism** shocks her. When she tells them she likes to cook—and adds that she is good at it—they **respond** with a smile that she would make a good wife and mother.

"I am **stunned,**" she said. "They think that just because I can cook, I can make a very good wife or a very good mother. But a mother is someone who raises children, not a cook. A wife is a partner, not a cook." . . .

"Men are raised to be spoiled," said Yumiko Hamada, a writer who lived with her husband and two children in the United States for eight years. She successfully **remolded** her husband's behavior, but as in many households all over Japan, the problem was her in-laws.

When her husband went back to his mother's house one time and began helping with the dishes as he does at home, his parents were **horrified.** That is women's work, they said.

"Now when we go over there, it's constant work for me," she said. "I don't let him do anything; otherwise, his family will hate me."

Readings about Saudi Arabia

In the following section, you will read two selections about Saudi Arabia.

In thinking about how males and females are raised in your culture, one of the important areas you might consider is education: Do males and females have the same educational opportunities? Are academic expectations the same for males and females? In the first selection from *Nine Parts of Desire: The Hidden World of Islamic Women* (Anchor Books, 1995), author Geraldine Brooks describes the difference between education for males and females in Saudi Arabia, both historically and at present. In the reading, Brooks refers to the "driving demonstration" of November 1990, when 47 Saudi women (mostly professionals) protested Saudi Arabia's ban on women driving by driving a few blocks.

▶ *BEFORE YOU READ*

1. Where is Saudi Arabia? Can you locate it on the map that appears in the front of this book?

2. What do you know about the differences in the ways males and females are raised in traditional countries such as Saudi Arabia? Share your knowledge with your classmates.

3. What roles would you imagine that adult males and females in Saudi Arabia are expected to assume?

from *NINE PARTS OF DESIRE: THE HIDDEN WORLD
OF ISLAMIC WOMEN*

GERALDINE BROOKS

Today in Saudi Arabia, fathers like Mohamed al-Ghazi can still make . . . a choice for their daughters. Schooling for girls, although now **widespread,** has never been **compulsory** if their fathers disapprove. Many men believe in the saying that educating women is like allowing the nose of the camel into the tent: eventually the beast will edge in and take up all the room inside.

Saudi Arabia didn't get its first girls' schools until 1956. Its opening was **contrived** by Iffat, the wife of King Faisal, and the only Saudi ruler's wife ever **referred** to as queen. Iffat, who had been raised in Turkey, wanted to broaden education to include more science and more Western subjects, but she had to **proceed cautiously** even in opening such a school for her own sons. The girls' school was an **infinitely** more delicate matter. When Dar al Hanan, the House of Affection, opened in Jeddah in 1956, it did so in the **guise** of an **orphanage.** Since the Koran repeatedly orders Muslims to care for orphan girls, such an **institution** was beyond **reproach.** It had been running a year before Iffat felt able to risk explaining the institution's real intention.

In an article in a local paper titled "The Mother Can Be a School in Herself If You Prepare Her Well," the **objectives** of Dar al Hanan were described as producing better mothers and homemakers through Islamically guided instruction.

Iffat, through Faisal, based her case for women's education on a famous set of verses in the Koran that have become known as Umm Salamah's verses. . . .

What the verses made clear was that the **obligations** of the faith fell without **differentiation** on men and women. To carry out those obligations, Iffat argued, women had to be educated and informed. By 1960 the **ulema** had been brought to **grudging** acceptance of this principle, and cautiously agreed to the spread of girls' schools throughout the country. The **provisos** were that the schools would remain under the control of the ulema and that no father who objected would be **obliged** to send his daughters to them.

But for some Saudis that wasn't enough. In the town of Burayda, not far from Insaf, men **rioted** in **protest** at the opening of the first girls' school in 1963. At around the same time as the United States was calling out its National Guard to **enforce** racial **desegregation** of schools in the American South, King Faisal had to call out the National Guard to keep the Burayda school open by force. For a year, the only pupil in the school was the **headmistress's** daughter.

Many fathers continued to exercise their **option** of keeping daughters **ignorant.** By 1980, only 55% of Saudi girls were attending primary school, and only 23% were enrolled in secondary education. Only 38% of women were **literate,** compared with 62% of men.

Still, some girls managed to get the best education that money could buy. At Dar al Fikr, a private school for girls in Jeddah, the German-built campus is about as **magnificent** a school building as it's possible to imagine. Inside the privacy of a towering white wall, glass doors swish open into a crisply air-conditioned foyer of polished stone. The **layout** is star-shaped, with classrooms **radiating** from large indoor recreation areas. High ceilings and huge panes of glass give an open, airy feeling to art studies, a gymnasium, science labs and a computer center **humming** with Commodore and Macintosh desktops.

No class has more than twenty pupils. There is a day-care center, being used when I visited by the teachers' infants, but **available** to the students in a country where early marriage and pregnancy are accepted and encouraged. In addition to an academic **curriculum** that stressed languages, girls could choose courses in cookery or dressmaking, **karate** or ballet, **desktop publishing** or motor mechanics. The motor mechanics course puzzled me, since Saudi women weren't allowed to drive. "If her driver says there's something the matter with the car, I want her to know if he's telling the truth," explained the headmistress, Basilah al-Homoud.

The pupils had the **well-tended** look of the very rich. They were tall, with **lustrous** hair swept back in thick braids. The headmistress, a **svelte,** silk-clad thirty-eight-year-old, had the unlined skin of a teenager and **taut** body of an **aerobics addict.** "The gym is the most important room in my house," she said. Twenty years earlier, her older sister had wanted to study dentistry, impossible then for women in Saudi Arabia. Basilah's father had moved the whole family to Syria so her sister could study at Damascus University. She came home as the first Saudi dentist and opened a clinic to treat both men and women. But she soon found that some Saudi men used to **strict** segregation couldn't **cope** with having a strange woman touch them, even with a dentist's drill. Tired of **propositions** and misunderstandings, she separated her clinic into men's and women's sections and hired male dentists to treat the men.

Basilah, too, **preferred** professional segregation. Dar al Fikr had a neighboring school for boys and a male board of directors. When Basilah had to have a meeting with the board, or with her boys' school **counterpart,** she used closed-circuit TV. "I might need a **colleague's** support, but I don't need to be sitting in a room with him," she said. "If the men could come in here and only be with us, they would end up **dominating** and telling us how to run things. I prefer to run my own show."

Basilah also used closed-circuit TV at the university, where she was studying for her MBA. Women were first admitted to university in Saudi Arabia in 1962, and all women's colleges remain strictly seg-regated. Lecture rooms come **equipped** with closed-circuit TVs and telephones, so women students can listen to a male professor and question him by phone, without having to **contaminate** themselves by being seen by him. When the first dozen women graduated from university in 1973, they were **devastated** to find that their names hadn't been printed on the **commencement** program. The old tradi-tion, that it dishonors women to mention them, was **depriving** them of recognition they believed they'd earned. The women and their families protested, so a separate program was printed and a segregated graduation ceremony was held for the students' female relatives. Two thousand women attended. Their celebratory **ululations** raised the roof.

But while the opening of women's universities widened **access** to higher learning for women, it also made the educational experience much **shallower.** Before 1962, many **progressive** Saudi families had sent their daughters abroad for education. They returned to the king-dom not only with a degree but with experience of the outside world, whether in the West or in more progressive Arab countries such as Egypt, Lebanon or Syria, where they'd breathed the air of desegrega-tion and even caught a breath of **secular** culture. Now a whole gener-ation of Saudi women have completed their education entirely within the country. While thousands of Saudi men benefit from higher edu-cation abroad at government expense, women haven't been **granted** such scholarships since 1980. The government's position is that women's educational needs, as set out in a Ministry of Higher Educa-tion **policy** paper, are "to bring her up in a sound Islamic way so that she can fulfill her role in life as a successful housewife, ideal wife and good mother, and to prepare her for other activities that suit her na-ture such as teaching, nursing and medicine."

The result is a **cadre** of older Saudi women professors who are **vastly** more **liberal** than the younger women students they now are teaching. When some of these women professors took part in the driving **demonstration,** it was their women students who turned on them first. One student **barged** into one professor's office and started pulling at the professor's hair and **abusing** her for demonstrating. Young women objecting to the drivers led an angry protest from the campus **mosque.** Among the calls of the **zealots** following the demonstration was for the women's university to be **permanently** closed.

Lack of opportunity for education abroad means that Saudi women are trapped in the **confines** of an education system that still **lags** men's. Subjects such as geology and petroleum engineering—tickets to **influential** jobs in Saudi Arabia's oil economy—remain closed to women. Three of Saudi Arabia's seven universities—Iman

Mohamed bin Saud Islamic University in Riyadh, the University of Petroleum and Minerals and the Islamic University in Medina—don't accept women. Few women's colleges have their own libraries, and libraries shared with men's schools are either entirely **off limits** to women or open to them only one day per week. Most of the time women can't **browse** for books but have to **specify** the titles they want and have them brought out to them.

But women and men sit the same degree examinations. Professors quietly **acknowledge** the women's scores routinely **outstrip** the men's. "It's no surprise," said one woman professor. "Look at their lives. The boys have their cars, they can spend the evenings **cruising** the streets with their friends, sitting in cafes, buying **black-market** alcohol and drinking all night. What do the girls have? Four walls and their books. For them, education is everything."

In the second reading about Saudi Arabia, "Saudi Women Try New Ways to Overcome Bars to Advancement," from *The Washington Post* (August 31, 1994), journalist Nora Boustany discusses the roles women now play in Saudi Arabia and the limitations they face.

from *SAUDI WOMEN TRY NEW WAYS TO OVERCOME BARS TO ADVANCEMENT*

Nora Boustany

RIYADH, Saudi Arabia—Three years after the Persian Gulf War **prompted** the first **stirrings** of a movement by Saudi women for greater freedoms, the public **campaign** has long since been **suffocated** by the new official **restrictions,** and a **lower-profile** struggle has **ensued** for advancement in the business and professional world.

The brief **spark** from a drive-in protest by 47 women in downtown Riyadh on Nov. 6, 1990, has been **extinguished.** Saudi women are forbidden from driving, and many of those involved in the protest lost their jobs temporarily and were **reprimanded** for causing **embarrassment** to the kingdom at a time of more pressing national issues. In addition, the **setback** has left even the most **outspoken** of women fearful of voicing their **frustrations** or views.

As Saudi women **groom** themselves for careers in business and the professions—outnumbering men in some of the sciences and medical fields and mastering the use of computers—they are still **excluded** from public debate.

Women run **investment** firms, manage shops and work in hospitals. Except for the hospitals, however, all work **sites** in Saudi Arabia are **segregated.** The secret hope many **harbor** is that changing needs will reshape the role and **participation** of women. "But whatever we do, we are in a **pioneering** role," said Shuaa Rashed, a radio broadcaster.

One **prominent** businesswoman running her father's investment firm said she **ignores** the rules. "I deal with men. Am I legal? No, but I do it. Everybody knows and nobody is stopping me," she said with a **shrug** as she served Thai carry-out food in her kitchen while **fielding** calls from male employees **seeking** instructions. "The worst thing you can do in the Arab world is ask for permission. It will always be no," she said.

"There are all these fields for men. Somehow, we are struggling and getting through the holes, pushing forward," said Leila Thulaima, the head of a Studies Committee on Preventive Medicine.

Abdullah Dabbagh, secretary general of the Saudi Chamber of Commerce and Industry, said that in his **extended family,** "I have six male doctors and 10 female doctors, which gives you an **indication** that women are out there getting ready."

Women who want to **survive** work within a system of social segregation to **maintain** an **aura** of respect and untouchability. At the Institute of Public Administration, where hundreds of young women train for management jobs, accounting, publishing and computer work, the only link to the male world is by telephone or **fax.** When **terminals** break down, male technicians come at night.

"This is a Third World country; men and women have problems. But if I am strongly rooted in my **heritage** and religion, I can **adapt** and drill a path ahead of me," Thulaima said forcefully.

"Before, we had to beg girls to get trained. We had five or six women in each course. Now we have a waiting list of 600 to 700 for each of the 160 programs," Ilham Dakheel, a **consultant** in workforce and resource development, said of the all-female institute. "There is a difference between **veiling** and **seclusion**—they are not **synonymous.**"

It is custom here for women, in the presence of men other than their father, **spouse** or brother, to wear the ankle-length *abaya,* cover their heads and pull a black veil over their faces. But the way they dress in public is the least of their worries. "Before driving and taking off the abaya, we need more important things—you need your **identity** as a woman. Here we are still part of the men," commented a Saudi **psychologist.**

The bravado of the **high-profile** driving protest by 47 middle-aged professional women shook a kingdom where everything is solved quietly and behind the scenes, but the issue remains **unresolved.** When **confronted** with an emergency and a relative has to be driven to hospital, what should a woman do?

"These are extremely limited incidents. She will not drive, because she won't know how and she does not have a license," Prince

Nayef, the interior minister, answered **matter-of-factly.** "A woman is **compelled** to seek the assistance of a man."

"Before the establishment of the kingdom, women were considered as cattle. Ask women in their seventies and eighties what it was like when they were 5 or 6 years old," noted one prominent prince, adding that what has been **accomplished** so far should not be overlooked.

May Rimajy, an obstetrician, said the first generation of female doctors in Saudi Arabia had to go into research. Now more patients are asking to be treated by female physicians.

But in the hearts of those who are **trailblazing** on the narrow path allowed them in Saudi Arabia, there is a strong desire for recognition.

A married Saudi woman who moved from being director of a women's bank to successfully running an **antique** dealership, a beauty salon and other stores **confessed** that "if I see a [male] customer making the wrong choice on an antique table I **interfere** though I am not supposed to."

"We are doing everything, but there is one thing missing," she said. "I want to be **legitimate.** I should feel proud of what I am accomplishing. I feel bad that people abroad think of us Saudi women as **passive.**"

"We want to be part of decision-making. We are not dreaming of the impossible. We would like to have committees at the Shura Council who are in touch with women's issues," said Johara Angari, a **columnist** and writer, **referring** to a **consultative** body appointed by the king.

"If that writer wants to start that process by writing a **petition** to the **authorities,** she should do it," a senior security official suggested, adding that the wives of members of the Shura Council could **initiate** it by telling their husbands.

In a country where the **motto** seems to be "**progress** without change," female artists are **cautiously** addressing the issue of the role of women. Princess Fahda, daughter of the late King Saud, still keeps three of her favorite watercolors. One shows a woman from the back, in a **fading** black robe, walking barefoot in the sand toward a range of mountains. "She is walking away from her destiny. Mountains represent power and strength," Fahda explained.

Women's faces painted by Shadia Alem show angled lines of **anxiety** that disappear behind veils. Her subjects are in **contortions,** wrapped around themselves. Long, delicate hands and feet **accent repressed** sensuality—an artist's **rendering** of undeclared dreams.

"Art is a window to our soul," **confided** another young princess over dinner after she had **exhausted** the limits of **benign** chatter about children, dieting and **macrobiotic** food. . . .

"I feel women, wherever they are, seem always sad," said Princess Fahda. "It is their **karma** from the day they are born till the day they die."

Women of Saudi Arabia (Jodi Cobb, © National Geographic Society)

▶ *AFTER YOU READ*

1. In the first reading, Fallows says that "most Japanese women [she knows] say that they are raising their daughters and sons by the same rules and standards." After reading the selections on Japan, would you say that males and females are raised similarly or differently in Japan? Why?

2. What would you say are the roles that Japanese males and females are expected to assume as adults? Are these roles similar or different? How do you think Japanese males and females feel about the roles they are expected to assume?

3. In what ways, do you think, are males and females raised similarly or differently in Saudi Arabia? If differently, do you think this is true of all parents?

4. What would you say are the roles that adult males and females are expected to play in Saudi Arabia? What do you think are their feelings about these roles?

5. In your culture, are males and females raised similarly or differently?

6. Do you think it is beneficial to raise males and females differently? Why or why not?

✏️ **WRITING ASSIGNMENT:** *Writing about the Way Males and Females Are Raised*

In this chapter, you will first learn about writing compare/contrast essays and then work through the stages of the writing process to develop your own essay. Before you begin work on the essay, discuss the following

---

Supplemental Reading List—Chapter 10

If you would like to learn more about gender roles, read the annual "Women in Science" section in *Science* magazine. (You will most likely find *Science* magazine in your library or on the newsstand.)

For example, in its "Women in Science '93" issue (April 16, 1993), the magazine includes articles on such topics as the alleged "female style" in science, the place of women in science education, and women entrepreneurs in industry. One particularly interesting article tells the story of three women anthropologists who not only suc-ceeded in their fields but also have had enormous impact on the methods and the knowledge in primatology (the study of primates). Similar articles may be found in *Science* magazine, March 4, 1993, and March 11, 1993.

---

question with your classmates. Your answer to this question will become the focus of your compare/contrast essay.

Question: In what ways are males and females raised differently or simi-larly in your culture?

In many cultures around the world, males and females are raised dif-ferently by their parents. For example, parents in some cultures raise males and females differently in terms of education, household responsibilities, and even the expectations they have for their children. Yet parents in the same culture might also raise males and females similarly in terms of teach-ing them respect for their elders.

Write an essay in which you compare and/or contrast the ways in which males and females are raised in your culture. Remember to include in the essay specific, concrete evidence for each subpoint as well as thorough analysis.

Guidelines on Writing Your Compare/Contrast Essay

In this chapter, you will write a compare/contrast essay, which may be a very challenging task. At first, it may seem confusing to be writing about two subjects and to be comparing and/or contrasting them in several ways. Also, designing an organizational structure for your compare/contrast essay may at first seem difficult. Yet keep in mind that you will not have to learn everything about compare/contrast writing at once; instead, you will work on the challenging tasks of compare/contrast writing in a step-by-step manner, confronting each challenge as it arises naturally in the writing process. After writing this essay, you will feel much more confident about comparing and contrasting, something which you will be asked to do often in your college writing assignments.

Prewriting: Generating, Focusing, Ordering, and Planning

CONTROLLING QUESTION

Think about the controlling question for your compare/contrast essay. If necessary, reread the writing assignment. Then write down the one-sentence question you will answer in the essay.

Controlling Question:

_____

_____

GENERATING IDEAS: BRAINSTORMING WITH A T-SQUARE

After writing your controlling question, you are now ready to generate some ideas about your topic. Use one of the prewriting techniques you learned in earlier chapters or try brainstorming with a "T-square." As shown in the example on page 248, you draw a large "T" and write the names of the two subjects being compared or contrasted (in this case, males and females in your culture) at the top of the two columns. Then you brainstorm as many ideas as you can think of about the way males and females are raised in your culture.

FOCUSING YOUR TERMS OF COMPARISON

After you have generated as many ideas as possible about your two subjects, you are ready to focus the subpoints of your essay. In the case of a compare/contrast essay, your subpoints are your terms of comparison.

Controlling Question:
    In what ways are males and females raised similarly or differently in Laotian culture?

Males	Females

An Example T-Square

What are *terms of comparison*? In compare/contrast analysis, you analyze two related subjects in a way that reveals how those subjects are similar or different. You compare and/or contrast these subjects by using the same terms of comparison for both. For example, in comparing two brands of chocolate ice cream, you might compare them in terms of taste, texture, and cost (see the diagram on page 249). In comparing two apartments you are thinking of renting, you might, for instance, compare them in terms of size, location, and monthly cost.

Look back at the ideas you have brainstormed on your T-square and think of ways you might gather these ideas into several groups or terms of comparison. In the example on page 250, the student grouped the brainstormed ideas into five terms of comparison. Then the student chose three terms of comparison to write about (marking them with an asterisk) and eliminated the other two—support and household duties.

ORDERING AND PLANNING

Thesis

After focusing your terms of comparison, write a rough thesis statement. Remember that the thesis statement should directly answer your controlling question, as well as convey the essay's main idea to the reader.

SUBJECT A   SUBJECT B

Terms of Comparison

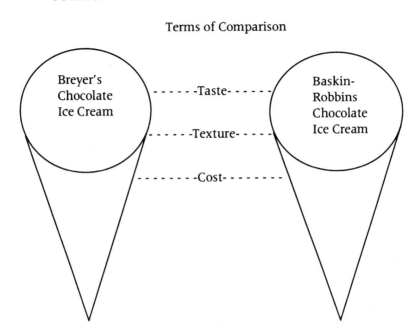

Thus, your thesis should tell the reader what you are comparing or contrasting—that is, the way males and females are raised in your culture. In addition, if you wish, you may announce the subpoints of your essay—your terms of comparison—in your thesis.

For example:

Controlling Question:

In what ways are males and females raised similarly or differently in Chinese culture?

Thesis without Subpoints:

Although girls and boys in Chinese culture are raised somewhat similarly, in most ways, they are brought up differently.

Thesis with Subpoints or Terms of Comparison:

Although males and females are both raised to give respect to elders in Chinese culture, they are raised quite differently in terms of education and freedom in their social lives.

Preliminary Plan

Now draw up a preliminary plan for your essay. This might, for instance, be an outline or a tree diagram. In drawing up your plan, you might choose

Controlling Question:
    In what ways are males and
females raised similarly or
differently in Laotian culture?

Males	Females
Can go out late at night	*Freedom
Can't have girlfriend while in school	Stay home with parents
	Can't stay out late
	Can't have boyfriend while in school
Taught respect for boss, teacher, parents, relatives	→ Same
No bad language	
*Respect for Elders	
	Household Duties
Sit around and watch T.V.	Girls wash dishes — work, do laundry plus clean house
Boys get the favor and support plus high expectations	Seem to be on their own
More attention	Not as much support as boys
*support	
More education College → M.D., Ph.D.	*Education Not as much education (high school)

Example T-Square with Five Terms of Comparison

to use one of two very common compare/contrast organizational structures: (1) the point-by-point method or (2) the block-by-block approach.

Point-by-Point Organization. In this essay, you will have two subjects (males and females) and two or more terms of comparison. Using point-by-point organizational structure, you organize each body paragraph (or group of body paragraphs) around one term of comparison (one subpoint). Within each subpoint, you then present evidence for each of the two subjects (males and females). The sample outline on page 251 shows how a point-by-point essay could be organized.

Block-by-Block Organization. Using block-by-block organizational structure, you focus each group of body paragraphs around one of your

Point-by-Point Outline

Opening Paragraph

Thesis: Although both males and females are raised to give respect to elders in Chinese culture, they are raised quite differently in terms of education and freedom in their social lives.

Term of Comparison 1:
  both males and females taught to respect elders
    Evidence—males taught to respect elders
    Evidence—females taught to respect elders

Term of Comparison 2:
  males and females educated differently
    Evidence—males' education
    Evidence—females' education

Term of Comparison 3:
  males and females raised differently in terms of freedom in their social lives
    Evidence—males' social freedom
    Evidence—females' social freedom

Restatement of Thesis

Conclusion

---

two subjects (males or females). Under each subject, you present evidence for each of the terms of comparison. Thus you present all your evidence for one subject (males) in the first block of paragraphs and then all your evidence for the other subject (females) in the second block of paragraphs. The sample outline on page 252 shows how an essay using the block-by-block approach can be organized.

Analysis. As you see from the preceding outlines, you need specific evidence for each term of comparison. Now you will want to think about where and how you will analyze this evidence.

In point-by-point organization, the analysis immediately follows the evidence presented for each subject, as shown in the sample outline on page 253.

In block-by-block organization, you will probably find it easiest to analyze the similarities or differences immediately after presenting the evidence in the *second* block. In the case of the block-by-block outline on page 252, the student plans to analyze the similarities or differences between male

Block-by-Block Outline

Opening Paragraph

Thesis: Although both males and females are raised to give respect to elders in Chinese culture, they are raised quite differently in terms of education and freedom in their social lives.

Subject A: Males
    Term of Comparison 1—taught respect for elders
        Evidence—males
    Term of Comparison 2—education
        Evidence—males
    Term of Comparison 3—social freedom
        Evidence—males

Subject B: Females
    Term of Comparison 1—taught respect for elders
        Evidence—females
    Term of Comparison 2—education
        Evidence—females
    Term of Comparison 3—social freedom
        Evidence—females

Restatement of Thesis

Conclusion

---

and female upbringing immediately after presenting evidence for the second subject—the females.

In analyzing the similarities or differences between males and females for each term of comparison, you might consider answering one or more of the following questions:

Why are males and females different/similar for this term of comparison?

How are males and females different/similar for this term of comparison?

What are the effects of this difference/similarity?

Who has the "best of the situation" for this term of comparison—males or females?

When to Use Block-by-Block or Point-by-Point. If you have three or more terms of comparison, point-by-point structure is probably easier for

Point-by-Point Outline with Analysis

Opening Paragraph

Thesis: Although both males and females are raised to give respect to elders in Chinese culture, they are raised quite differently in terms of education and freedom in their social lives.

Term of Comparison 1:

both males and females taught to respect elders

Evidence—males taught to respect elders

Evidence—females taught to respect elders

Analysis of similarity

Term of Comparison 2:

males and females educated differently

Evidence—males' education

Evidence—females' education

Analysis of difference

Term of Comparison 3:

males and females raised differently in terms of freedom in their social lives

Evidence—males' social freedom

Evidence—females' social freedom

Analysis of difference

Restatement of Thesis

Conclusion

readers because evidence and analysis for each subpoint (each term of comparison) is kept together in the essay.

The block-by-block method is easier for readers when you have only two terms of comparison or fewer. If you have three or more terms of comparison, then readers have to hold in their minds all the evidence you presented for Subject A (all three terms of comparison) until they reach the presentation of evidence for Subject B.

As you draw up your preliminary plan and begin thinking about how you will organize evidence and analysis, you will find it helpful to see a sample of a student body paragraph. In the activity following, you will see how the student who created the point-by-point outline with analysis above wrote a body paragraph for the third term of comparison—social freedom.

Block-by-Block Outline with Analysis

Opening Paragraph

Thesis: Although both males and females are raised to give respect to elders in Chinese culture, they are raised quite differently in terms of education and freedom in their social lives.

Subject A: Males
    Term of Comparison 1—taught respect for elders
        Evidence—males
    Term of Comparison 2—education
        Evidence—males
    Term of Comparison 3—social freedom
        Evidence—males

Subject B: Females
    Term of Comparison 1—taught respect for elders
        Evidence—females
        Analysis of similarity to males
    Term of Comparison 2—education
        Evidence—females
        Analysis of difference from males
    Term of Comparison 3—social freedom
        Evidence—females
        Analysis of difference from males

Restatement of Thesis

Conclusion

❏ *ACTIVITY 10.1:* **EVALUATING EVIDENCE AND ANALYSIS IN A COMPARE/CONTRAST BODY PARAGRAPH**

Practice evaluating evidence and analysis in the paragraph below. After one student has read aloud the following student body paragraph, discuss the paragraph according to the questions that follow.

In Colombian culture, young males and females are given different limitations on their social lives. Males always have more freedom than females, and females always have more restrictions than males. For example, Araceli is a friend of mine from my high school in Colombia, and she has one older brother. Although Araceli is only two years younger than her brother, they have lived under different standards. Araceli told me that she could not go out at night even if her girlfriends came along with her, and her parents did not let her talk on the phone with boys. Once when her parents found out that she got a letter from a boy, they punished her by making her kneel down and then they burned that letter. Her brother, however, was much more fortunate than she. He could stay out late, and his parents allowed him to have girlfriends when he was only twelve. In contrast, Araceli has a very confined social life because she is very protected by her parents. In old Colombian society, a well-educated female was not allowed to step out the door of the house until she got married, but males could go out to work, make friends, and have their own social lives. Most Colombian parents set a lot of limitations for their daughters because they want to keep them safe from the temptations of sex; the purity of virginity is the most important thing that an unmarried female has to be aware of. In addition, most Colombians think that females are weaker than males physically; therefore, males are thought to be strong enough to protect themselves when they leave home. As a result, males seem to have the privileges to do what they want, but females have to live under the shadow of many limitations. Araceli's parents, like most Colombian parents, raise their children with different standards for males and females, and the traditional thought about males and females having different limitations on their social lives still applies today.

DISCUSSION QUESTIONS

1. Does the paragraph have enough specific evidence to prove the subpoint—that males and females have different limitations on their social lives?

2. In the analysis, which of the following analytical questions is the writer answering?

Why are males and females different or similar for this term of comparison?

How are males and females different or similar for this term of comparison?

What are the effects of this difference or similarity?

Who has the "best of the situation" for this term of comparison—males or females?

3. Does the writer provide enough analysis? What suggestions for improvement can you offer?

An Alternative Outline: A Tree Diagram. Instead of a traditional outline, you might try using a tree diagram to visualize your preliminary plan. The following example shows how one student used a tree diagram to create a plan.

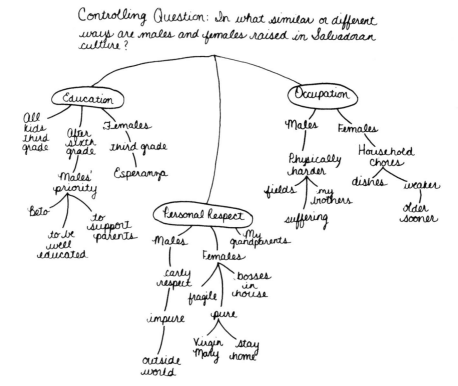

An Example Tree Diagram

Revising the Thesis and Plan

Before sharing your thesis and plan with your writing group, practice evaluating the thesis statements in Activity 10.2, if time permits.

❑   *ACTIVITY 10.2:*   **EVALUATING THESIS STATEMENTS**

After reading the two following thesis statements, discuss each one in terms of the questions that follow.

Thesis Statement A:

In Chinese culture, parents raise their male and female children differently in terms of education, rules and regulations, and marriage.

Thesis Statement B:

Cambodian parents raise boys and girls differently in terms of housework, education, and relationships.

DISCUSSION QUESTIONS

1. Does the thesis make clear what two subjects are being compared?

2. Does the thesis convey the main idea of the essay—that the two subjects are similar or different?

3. Are the terms of comparison made clear in the thesis?

4. Are any terms of comparison too broad or too narrow? Why or why not?

5. Are the terms of comparison distinct or do some overlap with one another in terms of focus? Explain.

❑   *ACTIVITY 10.3:*   **PEER RESPONSE**

Now share your thesis and plan with your writing group. Use the following procedure:

1. One group member should begin by reading aloud his or her work (thesis and plan). The group should then discuss the writer's work in terms of the questions listed on the Peer Response Sheet for Activity 10.3 on page 360. Another group member should record the group's comments on the sheet.

2. After you are finished filling out the sheet, give it to the writer so that he or she can refer to it when revising.

3. Repeat the procedure for each group member.

4. Then revise your thesis and plan, keeping in mind the suggestions of your writing group.

Drafting and Revising the First Body Paragraph

After revising your thesis and plan, you are ready to begin drafting your essay. Remember, though, that as you draft and then revise the essay, you are free to change your original plan as new ideas come to mind.

If you wish, you may write your opening paragraph first, or wait until later to complete it. At this point, though, complete at least your first body paragraph.

Revising the First Body Paragraph

Before meeting with your writing group, practice evaluating the body paragraphs in Activity 10.4, if time permits.

Note: The activities that follow as well as the Peer Response Sheets that go with this chapter are all based on the point-by-point organizational format. When evaluating a paragraph or essay that uses the block-by-block method, you need to remember that the analysis will come later in the essay, within the blocks covering the second subject.

❑ *ACTIVITY 10.4:* **EVALUATING TWO STUDENTS'**
   BODY PARAGRAPHS

After reading the two body paragraphs that follow, discuss each one in terms of these questions:

DISCUSSION QUESTIONS

1. Is the subpoint or term of comparison clearly stated in a topic sentence near the beginning of the paragraph?

2. Does the paragraph contain enough specific, concrete evidence for both males and females?

3. Which of the analysis questions listed on page 255 is the writer answering? Does the writer provide sufficient analysis? What suggestions for improving the analysis can you offer?

4. Did you find any problems in coherence in the paragraph? How might the writer solve the problem?

BODY PARAGRAPH A

One of the differences in terms of how females and males are raised in traditional Hispanic culture is the standard of sexual behavior. The female is expected to be pure and clean of "sin." She must stay home and cannot go out unless a family member comes along. In order to go to a dance, her parents must be invited so that the whole family can go. Above all, a girl must never lose her virginity, unless she has found the right man and gets married. Males, however, are taught to be "macho." Although men want to marry a woman who is a virgin, they are expected to go out to the world and lose their virginity as soon as they can. Males are given the permission to go out on their own. Also, males are given the authority to scold females whenever they consider the females are misbehaving. Thus, males and females are raised differently in traditional Hispanic society in terms of sexual behavior.

BODY PARAGRAPH B

One of the most important differences in the way males and females are raised in Salvadoran culture is in terms of education. The government requires children to finish at least the sixth grade; then it is up to the parents to decide if their children will continue in school. In poor families, parents do their best to send their sons to school because males are expected to support the parents when they get old. For example, my cousin Beto is in college not only because he has the intelligence to be there but also because he will one day need to support his parents. In contrast, the females are very lucky if they get past the sixth grade. My next-door neighbor, Esperanza, knows that she is smarter than her brothers, but she cannot go to school because her parents cannot afford to send her, just her brothers. Esperanza is always sad because she has to stay at home and take care of her little brothers and is expected to get married; she wants a better future for herself than she can get by marrying. I feel inspired to study hard because I have an opportunity to attend a university in the United States, an opportunity I would not have if I lived in El Salvador. Generally, Salvadoran men receive a better education than women because they are expected to support their families and aging parents. Male sons are also considered more intelligent because they hold all the responsible positions within the society. However, women do not receive as good an education as men because they are considered to be less smart than men. In addition, Salvadorans believe women do not need much education to maintain households, raise children, or serve their "superior" husbands.

❏ *ACTIVITY 10.5:* **MORE PEER RESPONSE**

Now share your first body paragraph with your writing group. Following the peer response procedure outlined in Activity 10.3, discuss each writer's first body paragraph in terms of the questions listed on the Peer Response Sheet for Activity 10.5 on page 361. Then revise your first body paragraph, keeping in mind the suggestions of your writing group.

Drafting and Revising the Rest of the Essay

As you draft the remaining body paragraphs, refer to your writing group's comments about your first body paragraph. Now draft the other body paragraphs, the opening (if not done earlier), and the conclusion for your essay.

If necessary, refer to Chapter 8 for ideas about writing an opening paragraph and Chapter 9 for ideas about writing a conclusion for your essay. As you draft, refer to the plan you have created for this essay, although you will want to keep in mind that you may need to revise your plan as you draft or after you draft.

If time permits, before sharing your completed essay with your writing group, practice evaluating the student body paragraph in Activity 10.6.

❑ *ACTIVITY 10.6:* **EVALUATING A STUDENT'S BODY PARAGRAPH**

After reading this body paragraph, discuss it in terms of the questions that follow.

BODY PARAGRAPH

In addition to the differences in social freedom, males and females in Vietnamese culture are raised differently in that males are valued more highly than females. Traditional Vietnamese parents say that they love their children equally, but deep inside their hearts they favor males over females. This is because males carry on the family name, follow in their dad's footsteps to success, and live with their parents after they are married in order to take over the family financially. Thus, parents feel more secure when a son is born. For example, my parents, who have three girls and three boys, have always told us that they love us equally. However, as a child, that was not what I saw in the ways they treated my brothers. They gave my brothers more of an allowance than they gave my sisters and me. We, along with my parents, had to wait to start dinner when the boys were late. Yet when my sisters and I were late for dinner, my parents and brothers started dinner without us. Furthermore, one time my parents asked us how we wanted to spend some extra money the family had. My sisters and I wanted to replace our old television with a new one, but my brothers wanted a video game system. My parents said the video game system was the better choice because the boys could experiment with new ideas on it. All in all, Vietnamese parents give males whatever they ask for and expect males to care for them in old age. In contrast, parents treat females as if they are less important to the family. Females are treated like strangers in the family, as things not worth spending extra money on.

DISCUSSION QUESTIONS

1. Where is the paragraph's topic sentence? Does it announce the sub-point or term of comparison of the paragraph?

2. Does the writer present enough specific, concrete evidence to develop the term of comparison? What suggestions for improvement can you offer?

3. Does the writer sufficiently analyze the differences in how males and females are raised? Which analysis question (see page 255) is the writer answering?

❏ *ACTIVITY 10.7:* **MORE PEER RESPONSE**

Now share your entire draft essay, including your new body paragraphs, opening, and conclusion, with your writing group. Following the peer response procedure outlined in Activity 10.3, discuss each writer's essay in terms of the questions listed on the Peer Response Sheet for Activity 10.7 on page 363. Then revise your essay until you are satisfied with its organizational structure (as revealed in the thesis and topic sentences) and development (of the body paragraphs, introduction, and conclusion). As you revise, remember to consider the suggestions of your writing group.

Editing: Noun Clauses

After you are satisfied with your revised essay in terms of its organization and development, you are ready to edit it. During the editing stage, you need to check the essay for sentence variety, as you have done in previous chapters.

In this section, you will learn about *noun clauses,* which are dependent clauses that function like nouns in a sentence. Once you have practiced using noun clauses, you can add them to the storehouse or collection of sentence structures you have built up in past chapters. As you create sentences and as you edit for sentence variety, you will then be able to call upon a wide range of structures—simple and compound sentences, as well as complex sentences using adverbial, adjective, and noun clauses.*

*The information in the example sentences and exercises in this grammar section is taken from Deborah Fallows, "Japanese Women," *National Geographic* (April 1990).

WHAT IS A NOUN CLAUSE?

A noun clause performs the same job that a noun does in a sentence. It can serve as subject, object, or complement. In the following example, the noun clause serves as an object in the sentence:

SUBJECT	VERB	OBJECT
I	like	*Japan.*

SUBJECT	VERB	NOUN CLAUSE AS OBJECT
I	know	*that Japan has a very traditional culture.*

THE FORM AND USE OF NOUN CLAUSES

Some of the words used to introduce a noun clause include the following:

who/whom/whose	when	why
what	which	where
why	that	how

Noun clauses are most commonly used as the following:

- subjects
- objects
- subject complements
- objects of a preposition
- adjective complements
- noun complements

The study of noun clauses that follows is divided according to the grammatical functions of the noun clause in a sentence—whether it functions as a subject, object, complement, or object of a preposition.

Noun Clause as Subject (*That, Whether, WH-Words*)

That Noun Clause *as Subject.* A *that noun clause* may serve as the *subject* of a sentence:

SUBJECT
That Japanese women are raised differently is not surprising.

Whether Noun Clause *as Subject.* A *whether noun clause* may also serve as the subject of a sentence. These clauses come from Yes/No questions.

Example Yes/No Question:

Do Japanese women want to be equal to men?

SUBJECT

| *Whether Japanese women want to be equal to men* | is an important question.

WH-Word Noun Clause *as Subject*. *WH-word noun clauses* may also function as the subject of a sentence. *WH-word* clauses come from *WH-word* questions and thus can begin with any one of the following *WH-words:*

who   whom   whose   what   which   when   why   how

Example WH-Word Question:

What does the modern Japanese woman want?

SUBJECT

| *What the modern Japanese woman wants* | is still unknown.

Word Order. Note that both *whether* and *WH-word* noun clauses do not use question word order (in which the auxiliary verb comes before the subject), even though they come from question form. Rather, these two noun clauses use the normal word order of English, where the subject comes before the verb.

Question Word Order:

AUXILIARY VERB   SUBJECT   VERB

Do   Japanese women want to be equal to men?

Noun Clause Word Order:

SUBJECT   VERB

Whether Japanese women want to be equal to men is an important question.

Question Word Order:

AUXILIARY VERB   SUBJECT   VERB

What does the modern Japanese woman want?

Noun Clause Word Order:

SUBJECT   VERB

What the modern Japanese woman wants is still unknown.

Using it *as Subject*. To make a sentence with a noun clause less formal, you can place *it* in the subject position and move the noun clause to the end of the sentence:

That Japanese women are raised differently is not surprising.

It is not surprising *that Japanese women are raised differently.*

However, *it* can replace an *if* or *whether* or *WH-word* noun clause only when you add the following type of phrase to the beginning of the sentence:

SUBJECT   VERB   ADJECTIVE
It   +   be   +   evident, obvious, clear

WH-Word Noun Clause:

What the modern Japanese woman wants is still unknown.

It Phrase:

It isn't clear what the modern Japanese woman wants.

❏   *ACTIVITY 10.8:*   **WORKING WITH NOUN CLAUSES**
      AS SUBJECTS

Step 1: Using ideas from the first sentence, fill in the blanks in the second sentence with a noun clause that functions as a subject. Remember to check word order.

1. Chang missed the deadline for the spring essay contest.
That _____ made him angry.

2. Could Chang have won the essay contest?
Whether _____ is worth knowing.

3. How would Chang have spent the prize money?
How _____ is a mystery.

4. After Chang's sister won the contest, she gave the prize money to her school.
What _____ is very surprising.

Step 2: Now try revising the sentences with noun clauses to begin with *it*. Which sentence or sentences can be changed to begin with *it*? Which cannot be changed to begin with *it*?

Noun Clause as Object (*That, If, Whether, WH-Words*)
      That Clause *as Object*. A *that clause* may also serve as the *object* in a sentence:

OBJECT

Deborah Fallows thinks │*that times are changing for Japanese women.*│

***Omitting* That.** Often you can omit *that* before a noun clause:

Deborah Fallows thinks t~~h~~at times are changing for Japanese women.

However, you cannot omit *that* when it follows certain verbs, such as *answer* or *imply:*

Incorrect:

Fallows *implies that* this change is coming slowly.

If, Whether, *and* WH-Word Noun Clauses *as Objects.* *Whether* and *WH-word noun clauses* can also function as the object in a sentence:

OBJECT

She doesn't know | *whether women will ever become equals of men in Japan.*

OBJECT

She wonders | *if Japanese women will assume leadership positions.*

Word Order. Like noun clauses in the subject position, *if, whether,* and *WH-word noun clauses* that serve as objects do not take question word order (in which the auxiliary verb comes before the subject). Even though such clauses come from questions, they take the usual subject-verb word order. Here are some examples:

Question Word Order:

AUXILIARY VERB   SUBJECT   VERB

Why are unmarried Japanese women over age twenty-five called "Christmas cake"?

Noun Clause Word Order:

SUBJECT   AUXILIARY VERB   VERB

Why Japanese women over age twenty-five are called "Christmas cake" is obvious. Christmas cake drops sharply in value after December 25th.

Sequence of Tense. To determine the correct sequence of tense for a noun clause used as an object, you need to look at the tense of the main verb in the independent clause. That verb's tense determines the tense of the verb in the noun clause.

1. *Main Verb in the Present Tense:* When the main verb in the independent clause is in the present tense, the verb in the noun clause may be in one of the following tenses, depending on whether its action takes place before, at the same time as, or after the time of the verb in the independent clause.

Main Verb in Independent Clause	**Tense of Verb in Noun Clause**		
	Time Before	*Same Time*	*Time After*
Present	Past	Present	Future (*will* + base)
	Present perfect		

Examples:

Deborah Fallows *says* that many Japanese women today *work* outside the home.

She *says* that Japanese women *have* always *worked*, normally in manual labor.

She *believes* that young Japanese women *will need* to be patient in order to succeed in the professional world.

2. *Main Verb in the Past Tense:* When the main verb in the independent clause is in the past tense, the verb in the noun clause may only be in the past tense, the past perfect tense, or the past form of the modal (*would, could, should*) plus the base verb form. This depends on whether the action of the verb in the noun clause takes place in time before, at the same time as, or after the time of the verb in the independent clause.

Main Verb in Independent Clause	**Tense of Verb in Noun Clause**		
	Time Before	*Same Time*	*Time After*
Past	Past perfect	Past	Past form of modal + base verb form

Examples:

Long ago, the Japanese *expected* that women *would* only *work* in the rice fields and fisheries.

They *knew* that women *had worked* on farms for centuries.

3. *Base Form of the Verb in a Noun Clause:* When certain verbs are followed by a noun clause that functions as an object, the verb in the noun clause must be in its base form (the infinitive without the *to* or the dictionary entry form of the verb):

advise	insist	recommend
command	order	request
demand	prefer	require
desire	propose	suggest

Examples:

Many Japanese men *prefer* that a woman *remain* feminine.

They *prefer* that women *focus* their attention on their children.

❏ *ACTIVITY 10.9:* **WORKING WITH NOUN CLAUSES AS OBJECTS**

After you have read the first sentence, complete the second sentence with a noun clause that functions as an object. Be careful of verb tense, verb form, and word order.

1. Kuljinder's parents want her to become a nurse.

In fact, Kuljinder's parents insist that she _____

_____.

2. Kuljinder wants to study physics and become an astronaut, but she is concerned about going against her parents' wishes.

Kuljinder doesn't know whether _____

_____.

3. When Kuljinder was young, her parents gave her a doll and dollhouse. Yet Kuljinder was unhappy about having to stay inside to play with her dollhouse.

Kuljinder didn't understand why _____

_____.

4. Kuljinder's favorite activity was shooting off rockets in the street with her brothers.

Kuljinder already knew what _____

_____.

❏ *ACTIVITY 10.10:* **WORKING WITH VERB TENSES IN NOUN CLAUSES**

For each of the following sentences, circle the correct tense in the noun clause.

1. While living in Japan, Deborah Fallows learned that Japanese women (*had worked, have worked*) for centuries.

2. Before interviewing Japanese women, Fallows decided what questions she (*would, will*) ask them.

3. In her article, Fallows says that the number of women executives in Japan (*doubled, has doubled*) over the past decades.

Noun Clause as Subject Complement (*That, If, Whether, WH-Words*)

That, if, whether, and *WH-word noun clauses* can all serve as complements of the subject of a sentence. A *subject complement* is a noun, adjective, or pronoun that follows a linking verb such as *be, seem,* or *appear*. The subject complement completes (or "complements") the meaning of the subject by telling us something about the subject. For example:

SUBJECT   SUBJECT COMPLEMENT

Saudi Arabia is *a country in the Middle East.*

SUBJECT   VERB   SUBJECT COMPLEMENT

The question is *whether women are raised differently from men.*

SUBJECT   VERB   SUBJECT COMPLEMENT

The truth   is *that women are raised differently from men.*

❏ *ACTIVITY 10.11:* **WORKING WITH NOUN CLAUSES AS SUBJECT COMPLEMENTS**

Match each phrase on the left with an appropriate clause on the right to form a complete sentence.

1. The truth is   **a.** how educators can compare male and female education.

2. The question is   **b.** that many Saudi Arabian women receive an education.

3. The problem is   **c.** whether females are given the same education that males receive.

Noun Clause as Adjective Complement (*That*)

A *that* clause can serve as an *adjective complement* in a sentence. As an adjective complement, the noun clause complements or completes the meaning of the adjective. For example:

ADJECTIVE   ADJECTIVE COMPLEMENT

People are surprised *that males and females are still raised differently.*

ADJECTIVE   ADJECTIVE COMPLEMENT

People are aware *that boys and girls play with different toys.*

Noun Clause as Noun Complement (*the Fact That* and *the Idea That*)

A noun clause can also serve as a *noun complement* in a sentence, particularly with expressions like *the fact that* and *the idea that*. In this case, the noun clause complements or completes the meaning of a noun in the sentence. For example:

NOUN NOUN COMPLEMENT

The idea that boys are better at math is untrue.

NOUN NOUN COMPLEMENT

The fact that girls are taught to use more polite language should not be surprising.

Here the noun clause *that girls are taught to use more polite language* complements or completes the meaning of the noun *The fact*.

❏ *ACTIVITY 10.12:* **WORKING WITH NOUN CLAUSES AS ADJECTIVE AND NOUN COMPLEMENTS**

Combine each of the following sentence pairs so that the new sentence has a noun clause that functions as an adjective complement or as a noun complement.

1. Michelle always uses a polite question when she wants something. That is a fact.

_____

_____

_____

2. Her brother Dan always uses a command when he wants something. That makes Michelle uncomfortable.

_____

_____

_____

3. Other people will do what Dan wants. He feels confident of this.

_____

_____

_____

4. Dan does not need to be polite. This is his idea.

_____

_____

_____

Noun Clause as Object of a Preposition (*WH-Words*)

A noun clause that functions as the object of a preposition can begin with any of the following *WH-words:*

who   whom   whose   what   which   where   when   why   how

Here are some examples of how such noun clauses are used as the object of a preposition in a sentence:

OBJECT OF PREPOSITION

Mercia didn't tell him about │ *why she wants to go to the race-car driving school.* │

OBJECT OF PREPOSITION

Her father asked her about │ *how she would pay for her lessons.* │

❑   *ACTIVITY 10.13:*   **WORKING WITH NOUN CLAUSES AS OBJECTS OF PREPOSITIONS**

Complete each of the following sentences by adding a noun clause that functions as the object of a preposition. Make certain that the noun clause begins with a *WH-word.*

1. Everyone on the race track was looking at _____

_____.

2. Mercia's mother was worried about _____

_____.

3. Mercia, however, was only interested in _____

_____.

4. She didn't want to think about _____

_____.

❑   *ACTIVITY 10.14:*   **WORKING WITH NOUN CLAUSES**

In each of the following blanks, add a noun clause that functions as the subject of the sentence. The noun clause should answer the question indicated. Remember to check for correct word order in the new sentences.

1. *Did you play with dolls when you were young?*

_____ is a secret.

2. *How did you feel about playing with toy guns when you were young?*

_____ is (or is not) surprising.

3. *When do you think boys and girls will be treated equally?*

_____ is a puzzling question.

4. *What role do you think women would like to play in your culture?*

_____ is an interesting question.

✓ EDITING CHECKLIST

After revising your essay for content, you are ready to edit it. Check for the following:

☐ Check for *sentence variety.* Mark each sentence in your essay as simple, compound, or complex. Then ask these questions:

- Does each paragraph have good sentence variety—a good mixture of simple, compound, and complex sentences?
- Do I have too many simple or compound sentences?
- Can I combine some logically related simple sentences with adjective, adverbial, or noun clauses?

☐ Check for *coherence problems.* Ask a classmate or friend to read your essay aloud to you. Listen for breaks in coherence where one sentence does not smoothly follow another. If you find breaks in coherence, ask yourself the following questions:

- Can I use the principle of "something old/something new"—picking up "something old" from a previous sentence and adding to it "something new"?
- Can I use a surface signal to link one sentence to the next—repetition and a synonym, a demonstrative pronoun or adjective, a pronoun, or a logical connector (coordinate conjunction, subordinate conjunction, or transition)?

If time permits, also check your draft for the following:

☐ Check for *correct verb tense.*

☐ Check for *sentence structure problems:* fragments, run-on sentences, and comma splices.

✓

CHAPTER 11

Writing about Arranged Marriages

In this chapter, you will write an argumentative essay about arranged marriages. In the traditional arranged marriage, parents and elders choose a person they believe is the most suitable marriage partner for their son or daughter. The arranged couple then usually meets briefly, if at all, before the actual marriage. After marriage, the husband and wife learn to know and, hopefully, love one another.

Before beginning work on your essay, you will read a selection about an arranged marriage from Ved Mehta's autobiography, *The Ledge between the Streams* (1984). Reading this selection will make you more aware of the benefits and drawbacks of arranged marriages and give you ideas for your essay.

In Chapter 2, you learned that writer Ved Mehta, who had been blind since the age of four, left his native India in 1949 to attend the Arkansas School for the Blind. Later, after studying at Pomona College, Oxford University, and Harvard University, Mehta went on to become a successful author as well as a staff writer for the *New Yorker*.

In the reading, Mehta tells of a time when his sister, Pom, became engaged to marry Kakaji, a young Indian dentist—a marriage arranged by both their families. As you read, note that Mehta refers to his father as Daddyji and to his mother as Mamaji. In addition, Umi, Usha, and Nimi are Mehta's other sisters, and Gian Chand is his family's household servant.

Before reading, you need to know something about the Indian caste system. In this system, individuals in Indian society are assigned at birth to one of four castes or to the group of outcasts. From the highest to the lowest in terms of status, these castes are the Brahmin (priests and teachers), the Kshatriya (rulers and warriors), the Vaishyas (merchants and landowners), and the Shudras (servants and workers). The fifth category consists of Harijans, who have long been considered outcasts in India and called the

272

"Untouchables." People in a particular caste traditionally marry among themselves and avoid contact with those in other castes.

The Mehta family lives in Lahore, a city in the Punjab province of India, whereas Kakaji, the bridegroom, resides five hundred miles away in the Punjab city of Dehra Dun, India. At the beginning of the story, Daddyji has just returned from the mountain resort of Mussoorie.

▶ *BEFORE YOU READ*

1. Where is India? Locate it on the map that appears in the front of this book.

2. Are you familiar with the tradition of arranged marriage? Share your knowledge with your classmates.

3. In the United States today, most young people marry for romantic love. How do you think an arranged marriage differs from one based on romantic love?

4. In your culture, are most marriages arranged or do young people usually marry for romantic love?

5. How would you feel if your parents announced that you or your sibling would soon be married to someone they chose?

from *THE LEDGE BETWEEN THE STREAMS*

VED MEHTA

Before we moved to Lahore, Daddyji had gone to Mussoorie, a hill station in the United Provinces, without telling us why he was going out of the Punjab. Now, several months after he made that trip, he gathered us around him in the drawing room at 11 Temple Road while Mamaji mysteriously hurried Sister Pom upstairs. He started talking as if we were small and he were **conducting** one of our "dinner-table-school" discussions. He said that by right and tradition the oldest daughter had to be given in marriage first, and that the ripe age for marriage was nineteen. He said that when a girl **approached** that age her parents, who had to take the **initiative,** made many inquiries and followed many leads. They **investigated** each young man and his family background, his relatives, his friends, his classmates, because it was important to know what kind of family the girl would be marrying into, what kind of company she would be expected to keep. If the girl's parents decided that a particular young man was suitable, then his people also had to make their investigations, but, however favorable their findings, their decision was **unpredictable,** because good, well-settled boys were in great demand and could afford to be choosy. All this took a lot of time. "That's why I said noth-

ing to you children about why I went to Mussoorie," he concluded. "I
went to see a young man for Pom. She's already nineteen."

We were **stunned.** We have never really faced the idea that Sister Pom might get married and suddenly leave, I thought.

"We won't lose Pom, we'll get a new family member," Daddyji
said, as if reading my thoughts.

Then all of us started talking at once. We wanted to know if Sister
Pom had been told; if she'd agreed; whom she'd be marrying.

"Your mother has just taken Pom up to tell her," Daddyji said.
"But she's a good girl. She will agree." He added, "The young man
in question is twenty-eight years old. He's a dentist, and so has a profession."

"Did you get a dentist because Sister Pom has bad teeth?" Usha
asked. Sister Pom had always been held up to us as an example of
someone who, as a child, had **spurned** greens and had therefore
grown up with a mouthful of poor teeth.

Daddyji laughed. "I **confess** I didn't think of anyone's teeth when
I chose the young man in question."

"What is he like?" I asked. "What are we to call him?"

"He's a little bit on the short side, but he has a happy-go-lucky
nature, like Nimi's. He doesn't drink, but, unfortunately, he does
smoke. His father died at an early age of a heart attack, but he has a
nice mother, who will not give Pom any trouble. It seems that everyone calls him Kakaji."

We all laughed. Kakaji, or "youngster," was what very small boys
were called.

"That's what he must have been called when he was small, and
the name stuck," Daddyji said.

In spite of myself, I pictured a boy smaller than I was and imagined him taking Sister Pom away, and then I imagined her having to
keep his pocket money, to arrange his clothes in the **cupboards,** to
comb his hair. My mouth felt dry.

"What will Kakaji call Sister Pom?" I asked.

"Pom, silly—what else?" Sister Umi said.

Mamaji and Sister Pom walked into the room. Daddyji made a
place for Sister Pom next to him and said, "Now, now, now, no reason
to cry. Is it to be yes?"

"Whatever you say," Sister Pom said in a small voice, between
sobs.

"Pom, how can you say that? You've never seen him," Sister Umi
said.

"Kakaji's uncle, Dr. Prakash Mehrotra, himself a dentist, has
known our family from his student days in Lahore," Daddyji said. "As
a student dentist, he used to be welcomed in Babuji's Shahalmi Gate
house. He would come and go as he pleased. He has known for a long

time what kind of people we are. He remembered seeing you, Pom, when we went to Mussoorie on holiday. He said yes immediately, and his approval seemed to be enough for Kakaji."

"You promised me you wouldn't cry again," Mamaji said to Sister Pom, patting her on the back, and then, to Daddyji, "She's agreed."

Daddyji said much else, sometimes talking just for the sake of talking, sometimes laughing at us because we were **sniffing,** and all the time trying to make us believe that this was a happy occasion. First, Sister Umi took issue with him: parents had no business arranging marriages; if she were Pom she would run away. Then Sister Nimi: all her life she had heard him say to us children, "Think for yourself— be **independent,**" and here he was not allowing Pom to think for herself. Brother Om took Daddyji's part: girls who didn't get married became a burden on their parents, and Daddyji had four daughters to marry off, and would be **retiring** in a few years. Sisters Nimi and Umi **retorted:** they hadn't gone to college to get married off, to have some young man following them around like a leech. Daddyji just laughed. I thought he was so wise, and right.

"Go and bless your big sister," Mamaji said, pushing me in the direction of Sister Pom.

"I don't want to," I said. "I don't know him."

"What'll happen to Sister Pom's room?" Usha asked. She and Ashok didn't have rooms of their own. They slept in Mamaji's room.

"Pom's room will remain empty, so that any time she likes she can come and stay in her room with Kakaji," Daddyji said.

The thought that a man I never met would sleep in Pom's room with Sister Pom there made my heart race. A sob shook me. I ran outside.

The whole house seemed to be in an uproar. Mamaji was shouting at Gian Chand, Gian Chand was shouting at the bearer, the bearer was shouting at the sweeper. There were the sounds of the kitchen fire being **stoked,** of the drain being washed out, of water running in bathrooms. From behind whichever door I passed came the rustle of *saris, salwars,* and *kemises.* The house smelled of fresh flowers, but it had a **ghostly** chill. I would climb to the landing of Sister Pom's room and **thump** down the stairs two at a time. Brother Om would shout up at me, "Stop it!" Sister Umi would shout down at me, "Don't you have anything better to do?" Sister Nimi would call to me from somewhere, "You're giving Pom a headache." I wouldn't **heed** any of them. As soon as I had thumped down, I would **clatter** to the top and thump my way down again.

Daddyji went past on the back **veranda.** "Who's coming with Kakaji?" I asked. Kakaji was in Lahore to buy some dental equipment, and in a few minutes he was expected for tea, to meet Sister Pom and the family.

"He's coming alone," Daddyji said, over his shoulder. "He's come from very far away." I had somehow imagined that Kakaji would come with at least as many people as we had in our family, because I had started thinking of the tea as a kind of **cricket match**—the **elevens facing off.**

I followed Daddyji into the **drawing room.** "Will he come alone for his wedding, too?"

"No. Then he'll come with the bridegroom's party."

We were joined by everyone except Mamaji and Sister Pom, who from the moment we got the news of Sister Pom's marriage had become inseparable.

Gian Chand came in, the tea things rattling on his tray.

Later, I couldn't remember exactly how Kakaji had arrived, but I remember noticing that his footfall was heavy, that his greeting was **affectionate,** and that his voice seemed to float up with laughter. I don't know what I'd expected, but I imagined that if I had been in his place I would have **skulked** in the **gulli,** and perhaps changed my mind and not entered at all.

"Better to have **ventured** and lost than never to have ventured at all," Daddyji was saying to Kakaji about life's battles.

"Yes, Daddyji, just so," he said, with a little laugh. I had never heard anybody outside our family call my father Daddyji. It sounded odd.

Sister Pom was sent for, and she came in with Mamaji. Her footsteps were shy, and the **rustle** of her sari around her feet was slow, as if she felt too **conscious** of the noise she was making just in walking. Daddyji made some **complimentary** remark about the silver border on her sari, and told her to sit next to Kakaji. Kakaji and Sister Pom exchanged a few words about a family group photograph on the **mantelpiece,** and about her studies. There was the **chink** of china as Sister Pom served Kakaji tea.

"Won't you have some tea yourself?" Kakaji asked Sister Pom.

"Kakaji, none of my children have ever tasted tea or coffee," Daddyji said. "We consider both to be bad habits. My children have been brought up on hot milk, and lately Pom has been taking a little **ghi** in her milk at bedtime, for health reasons."

We all protested at Daddyji's broadcasting family matters.

Kakaji **tactfully** turned the conversation to a visit to Mussoorie that our family was planning.

Mamaji offered him onion, potato, and cauliflower **pakoras.** He accepted, remarking how hot and crisp they were.

"Where will Sister Pom live?" Usha asked.

"In the summer, my practice is in Mussoorie," Kakaji said, "but in the winter it's in Dehra Dun."

It struck me for the first time that after Sister Pom got married people we didn't know, people she didn't know, would become more important to her than we were.

Kakaji had left without formally **committing** himself. Then, four days later, when we were all sitting in the drawing room, a servant brought a letter to Mamaji. She told us that it was from Kakaji's mother, and that it asked if Sister Pom might be **engaged** to Kakaji. "She even wants to know if Pom can be married in April or May," Mamaji said excitedly. "How **propitious!** That'll be the fifth wedding in the family in those two months." Cousins Prakash and Dev, Cousin Pushpa (Bhaji Ganga Ram's adopted daughter), and Auntie Vimla were all due to be married in Lahore then.

"You still have time to change your mind," Daddyji said to Sister Pom. "What do you really think of him?"

Sister Pom wouldn't say anything.

"How do you expect her to know what her mind is when all that the two talked about was a picture and her **bachelor's exam** in May?" Sister Umi demanded. "Could she have fallen in love already?"

"Love, Umi, means something very different from 'falling in love,'" Daddyji said. "It's not an act but a lifelong process. The best we can do as Pom's parents is to give her love every **opportunity** to grow."

"But doesn't your 'every opportunity' include knowing the person better than over a cup of tea, or whatever?" Sister Umi persisted.

"Yes, of course it does. But what we are discussing here is a simple matter of choice—not love," Daddyji said. "To know a person, to love a person, takes years of living together."

"Do you mean, then, that knowing a person and loving a person are the same thing?" Sister Umi asked.

"Not quite, but understanding and respect are **essential** to love, and that cannot come from talking together, even over a period of days or months. That can come only in good time, through years of experience. It is only when Pom and Kakaji learn to consider each other's problems as one and the same that they will find love."

"But, Daddyji, look at the risk you're taking, the risk you're making Pom take," Sister Nimi said.

"We are trying to **minimize** the risk as much as we can by finding Pom a family that is like ours," Daddyji said. "Kakaji is a dentist, I am a doctor. His life and way of thinking will be similar to mine. We are from the same **caste,** and Kakaji's family originally came from the Punjab. They eat meat and eggs, and they **take** religion **in their stride,** and don't pray every day and go to temples, like Brahmans. Kakaji knows how I walk into a club and how I am greeted there. The atmosphere in Pom's new home will be very much the same as the atmosphere here. Now, if I were to give Pom in marriage to a Brahman he'd expect Pom to live as he did. That would really be **gambling.**"

"Then what you're doing is **perpetuating** the caste system," Sister Nimi said. She was the **pivotal rebel** in the family. "You seem to **presuppose** that a Kshatriya should marry only a Kshatriya, that a Brahman should marry only a Brahman. I would just as soon marry a shopkeeper from the Bania [Vaishya] caste or an Untouchable, and help to break down the caste barriers."

"That day might come," Daddyji said. "But you will admit, Nimi, that by doing that you'd be increasing the odds [of your being unhappily married]."

"But for a cause I believe in," Sister Nimi said.

"Yes, but that's a whole other issue," Daddyji said.

"Daddyji, you say that understanding and respect are necessary for love," Sister Umi said. "I don't see why you would respect a person more because you lived with him and shared his problems."

"In our society, we think of understanding and respect as coming only through **sacrifice,**" Daddyji said.

"Then you're **advocating** the **subservience** of women," Sister Nimi said, "because it's not Kakaji who will be expected to sacrifice—it's Pom. That's not fair."

"And why do you think that Pom will learn to respect Kakaji because she sacrifices for him?" Sister Umi said, pressing her point.

"No, Umi, it is the other way around," Daddyji said. "It is Kakaji who will respect Pom because she sacrifices for him."

"But that doesn't mean that Pom will respect Kakaji," Sister Umi **persisted.**

"But if Kakaji is moved by Pom's sacrifice he will show more consideration for her. He will grow to love her. I know in my own case I was moved to the depths to see Shanti suffer so because she was so ill-prepared to be my wife. It took me long enough—too long, I believe—to reach that understanding, perhaps because I had broken away from the old traditions and had given in to Western influences."

"So you admit that Pom will have to suffer for years," Sister Umi said.

"Perhaps," Daddyji said. "But all that time she will be **striving** for **ultimate** happiness and love. Those are precious gifts that can only be cultivated in time."

"You haven't told us what this ultimate happiness is," Sister Umi said. "I don't really understand it."

"It is a **uniting** of ideals and purposes, and a **merging** of them. This is the tradition of our society, and it is the means we have adopted to make our marriages successful and beautiful. It works because we believe in the goodness of the individuals going into the marriage and **rely on** the strength of the **sacred** bond."

"But my ideal is to be independent," Sister Nimi said. "As you say, 'Think for yourself.'"

"But often you have to choose among ideals," Daddyji said. "You may have to choose between being independent and being married."

"But aren't you struck by the fact that all the suffering is going to be on Pom's part? Shouldn't Kakaji be required to sacrifice for their happiness, too?" Sister Nimi said, **reverting** to the old theme.

"There has to be a start," Daddyji said. "Remember, in our tradition it's her life that is joined with his; it is she who will **forsake** her past to build a new future with him. If both Pom and Kakaji were to be **obstinate,** were to compete with each other about who would sacrifice first, who would sacrifice more, what hope would there be of their ever getting on together, of their ever finding love?"

"Daddyji, you're evading the issue," Sister Nimi said. "Why shouldn't he take the initiative in this business of sacrifice?"

"He would perhaps be expected to if Pom were working, too, as in the West, and, though married, leading a whole different life from his. I suppose more than this I really can't say, and there may be some injustice in our system, at that. In the West, they go in for romantic love, which is unknown among us. I'm not sure that method works any better than our method does."

Then Daddyji said to Sister Pom, "I have done my best. Even after you marry Kakaji, my responsibility for you will not be over. I will always be there in the background if you should need me."

"I respect your judgment, Daddyji," Sister Pom said obediently. "I'll do what you say."

Mamaji **consulted** Shambu Pandit. He compared the **horoscopes** of Sister Pom and Kakaji and set the date of the marriage for the eleventh of May—the year was 1946—between the wedding of Cousin Pushpa and the wedding of Auntie Vimla. "That's just three days after she finishes her B.A. finals!" we cried. "When will she study? You are sacrificing her education to some silly **superstition.**"

But Shambu Pandit would not be **budged** from the date. "I am only going by the horoscopes of the couple," he said. "You might as well protest to the stars."

We **appealed** to Daddyji, but he said that he didn't want to **interfere,** because such matters were up to Mamaji. That was as much as to say that Shambu Pandit's date was a settled thing.

I recall that at about that time there was an engagement ceremony. We all—Daddyji, Mamaji, Sister Pom, many of our Mehta and Mehra relatives—sat cross-legged on the floor of the front veranda around Shambu Pandit. He recited the Gayatri Mantra, the simple prayer he used to tell us to say before we went to sleep, and made a thank offering of incense and ghi to a fire in a **brazier,** much as Mamaji did—behind Daddyji's back—when one of us was going on a trip or had recovered from a **bout** of illness. Servants passed around a platter **heaped** up with crumbly sweet balls. I heard Kakaji's sister, Billo, saying something to sister Pom; she had just come from Dehra Dun bearing a sari, a veil, and the engagement ring for Sister Pom, after Romesh Chachaji, one of Daddyji's brothers, had gone to Dehra Dun bearing some money, a silver platter and silver bowls, and sweetmeats for Kakaji. It was the first time that I was able to think of Kakaji both as a **remote** and frightening dentist who was going to take Sister Pom away and as someone ordinary like us, who had his own family. At some point, Mamaji **prodded** me, and I **scooted** forward, **crab fashion,** to **embrace** Sister Pom. I felt her hand on my neck. It had something cold and metallic on it, which sent a **shiver** through me. I realized that she was wearing her engagement ring, and that until then Mamaji was the only one in our family who had worn a ring.

In the evening, the women relatives **closeted** themselves in the drawing room with Sister Pom for the engagement singsong. I **crouched** outside with my ear to the door. The door **pulsated** with the beat of a barrel drum. The pulse in my forehead throbbed in sympathy with the beat as I caught snatches of songs about bedsheets and **henna,** along with explosions of laughter, the songs themselves rising and falling like the **cooing** of the doves that nested under the **eaves** of the veranda. I thought that a couple of years earlier I would have been playing somewhere outside on such an occasion, without knowing what I was missing, or been in the drawing room **clapping** and singing, but now I was crouching by the door like a thief, and was feeling ashamed even as I was **captivated.**

▶ *AFTER YOU READ*

1. Most young people in the United States choose a marriage partner on the basis of romantic love. What problems can result from a marriage based on romantic love?

2. In the reading, Daddyji describes the kind of love he believes can grow in an arranged marriage. In your view, how does the love that grows in an arranged marriage differ from the love in a marriage based on romantic love?

3. Draw a T-square like the one that follows on the board. Then brainstorm with your classmates all the reasons you can think of "for" and "against" Pom's arranged marriage. You might include the arguments presented by her father and sisters as well as your own ideas about the benefits and drawbacks of Pom's arranged marriage.

Question: Should Pom agree to the arranged marriage?

For	Against

4. In your opinion, should young people today return to the tradition of arranged marriage? Why or why not?

Supplemental Reading List—Chapter 11

Divakaruni, Chitra Banerjee. *Arranged Marriage.* New York: Anchor Books, 1995.

    In this collection of stories, author Divakaruni tells the tales of a number of Indian women who entered into arranged marriages either in India or as immigrants in the United States.

📝 **WRITING ASSIGNMENT:** *Writing about Arranged Marriages*

In this chapter, you will first learn about writing argument essays and then work through the stages of the writing process to develop your own essay. Before you begin work on your essay, discuss the following question with your classmates. Your answer to this question will become the focus of your argumentative essay.

Question: Should young people in the United States today consider arranged marriage instead of marriage based on romantic love? Why or why not?

Although most young people marry on the basis of romantic love, over half of the marriages in the United States end in divorce. Some experts suggest arranged marriage as an alternative, arguing that these marriages are more enduring than marriages based on romantic love.

    Write an essay in which you argue for or against the proposal that young people should adopt the tradition of arranged marriage. For each point in your argument, include specific, concrete evidence and thorough analysis.

Guidelines on Argumentative Writing

WHAT IS ARGUMENTATION?

Argumentation is a common form of writing. You will see arguments in the "Letters to the Editor" column of local and city newspapers, and you will write argumentative essays in many of your academic classes, such as history, political science, and English. In addition, argumentation will play a role in many of your scientific papers.

In writing an argumentative essay, you try to convince readers to accept your point of view—the stand you take on a debatable or two-sided issue. The issue must be one about which you can take a stand—for or against. For example, the proposal to serve some vegetarian meals in your school cafeteria is an issue that is debatable. The issue has two sides—one side arguing for the proposal because the meals would be healthier for students, and the other side arguing against the proposal because only a few students would want the meals.

STATING THE PROPOSITION

At the heart of every argument is a **proposition,** which is the writer's "for" or "against" stand on the issue. The proposition answers the controlling question of the argument and can usually be written as a one-sentence statement containing the words *should* or *should not:*

Controlling Question:

Should Lahey College Food Services offer a small selection of vegetarian meals for students who do not eat meat?

One Possible Proposition:

Lahey College should offer a small selection of vegetarian meals for students who do not eat meat.

As you can see, the proposition is the writer's stand on the issue of vegetarian meals. In a published argument, the writer's proposition might be implied or suggested instead of directly stated, as it would most often be in the thesis of an academic essay.

In addition to a proposition, an argument also consists of *reasons for or against the proposition.* These reasons form the subpoints of the argument.

❏ *ACTIVITY 11.1:* **IDENTIFYING THE WRITER'S PROPOSITION**

After reading the following letter to the editor from *The New York Times* (June 24, 1995), discuss the questions that follow with your classmates. In the letter, the author addresses the question of whether motorcyclists should be required to wear helmets.

To the Editor:

Re "The Case for No Helmets" (Op-Ed, June 17): While Dick Teresi and other motorcycle enthusiasts delight in feeling "the wind in their hair," the rest of us are feeling their hands in our pockets. Bikers without helmets cost the rest of us big money.

Mr. Teresi's "facts" don't add up. He makes statistically invalid comparisons between states and ignores the fact that every state that enacts a universal helmet law experiences fatality reductions and every state that has repealed a helmet law has seen motorcycle deaths go up.

He also rejects conclusions reached by the nation's premier public health institution, the Centers for Disease Control and Prevention, because it doesn't support his position, but he accepts a study by an obscure college economics professor who does.

The facts are simple:

• Helmets work. According to the United States Department of Transportation, helmets reduce the risk of fatal injury by nearly 30 percent and are highly effective in preventing head injuries, the leading cause of motorcyclist deaths.

• Helmet laws work. Between 1976 and 1980, helmet laws were weakened or repealed in 28 states. Motorcycle fatalities increased 60 percent (registration went up only 15 percent). The 25 states currently with all-rider helmet laws have use rates near 100 percent, compared with 36 percent in states without.

• The rest of us pay. Taxpayers assume the majority of the cost for the care of injured motorcyclists—up to 80 percent of the acute and long-term costs. Between 1984 and 1993, if motorcycle helmet use had been 100 percent, we could have saved an additional 4,100 lives, prevented more than 2,500 injuries and saved approximately $4 billion.

• The public supports these laws. A recent public opinion poll found that 79 percent of Americans oppose weakening or repealing motorcycle helmet laws and 63 percent believe doing so will place a greater burden on taxpayers.

Judith Lee Stone
President, Advocates for Highway and Auto Safety
Washington, June 19, 1995

DISCUSSION QUESTIONS

1. What is the writer's proposition? In one sentence, write the proposition here:

_____

_____

2. What are some of the reasons the writer gives for this proposition? Write them here:

_____

_____

_____

_____

Prewriting: Generating Ideas

Before you begin drafting your essay about arranged marriages, take some time to generate ideas about the topic. Use one of the prewriting techniques you learned in earlier chapters—clustering (pages 10–11), freewriting (pages 31–32), tree diagraming (page 54), or brainstorming (pages 101–102)—or try the "T-square" technique described here.

BRAINSTORMING WITH A T-SQUARE

First, write your controlling question—the one-sentence question you will answer in the essay—at the top of a blank piece of paper. If necessary, reread the writing assignment on page 281. Then draw a T-square like the one shown on page 281. Next, spend about ten or fifteen minutes brainstorming all the reasons you can think of both for and against the proposition.

FOCUSING AND PLANNING

After generating ideas about your topic, group the related ideas of the *for* and *against* columns. Then select what you believe are the most important reasons for *both* sides of the issue and list those reasons on another T-square like the one that follows.

Reasons *for* Arranged Marriage	Reasons *against* Arranged Marriage
Reason 1: _____	Reason 1: _____
Reason 2: _____	Reason 2: _____
Reason 3: _____	Reason 3: _____

Now you need to decide which side of the issue you feel most strongly about; this will form the main part of your proposition. Write your proposition—a one-sentence *should* or *should not* statement. List below the proposition at least two reasons you will use to support it in the essay. For example, if you feel that young people *should not* return to the tradition of arranged marriage, then your main proposition should be supported by reasons *against* arranged marriage.

Main Proposition:

Young people *should not* return to the tradition of arranged marriage because

Reason 1 (against): _____

Reason 2 (against): _____

However, if you feel that young people today *should* adopt the tradition of arranged marriage, then your main proposition should be supported by reasons *for* arranged marriage.

Main Proposition:

Young people *should* return to the tradition of arranged marriage because

Reason 1 (for): _____

Reason 2 (for): _____

Adding a Concession

Now that you have your main proposition and reasons to support it, you are ready to strengthen your argument by acknowledging the opposing viewpoint in a *concession*. For example if, in your main proposition, you argue *for* a return to arranged marriage, you may want to first bring in one or more reasons *against* this proposition. In the concession section of your argument, you "concede" to one or more points of the opposition. That is, you present the opposing point or points and then show why they are not significantly damaging to your main proposition. Building a concession into your argument or "conceding" one or more points to the opposition also shows that you are being fair, which, in turn, strengthens your argument.

Look at the T-square you have already created and select one or more opposing points that you believe need to be discussed. Then write the concession point(s) at the beginning of your plan, before the main proposition.

Concession:

Reason A (for): _____

Young people *should not* return to the tradition of arranged marriage because

    Reason 1 (against): _____

    Reason 2 (against): _____

Concession:

Reason A (against): _____

Young people *should* return to the tradition of arranged marriage because

    Reason 1 (for): _____

    Reason 2 (for): _____

Developing the Thesis and Preliminary Plan

You can now use what you have written to create your thesis and preliminary plan. If you choose to include a concession in the thesis, you can use one of the following logical connectors: *even though, although, while,* or *however.* If you choose to include your reasons for or against the main proposition in your thesis, you can use one of the following cause-and-effect logical connectors: *because* or *since.*

A thesis statement that includes the subpoints of the argument (that is, the reasons for and against) might be set up in one of the following ways:

Sample Thesis 1:

Even though **(reason for)** _____ ,
young people today *should not* return to the tradition of arranged marriage since

    (reason against) _____ and

    (reason against) _____.

Sample Thesis 2:

Although **(reason against)** _____ ,
young people today *should* return to the tradition of arranged marriage since

    (reason for) _____ and

    (reason for) _____.

Your preliminary plan should then set up the subpoints of the essay (that is, your reasons for or against arranged marriage) in the order they are presented in the thesis:

Sample Thesis and Plan 1

Thesis:

Even though **(reason for)** _____ ,
young people today *should not* return to the tradition of arranged marriage since

     (reason against) _____ and

     (reason against) _____ .

Plan:

First subpoint (reason for): _____

Second subpoint (reason against): _____

Third subpoint (reason against): _____

Sample Thesis and Plan 2

Thesis:

Although **(reason against)** _____ ,
young people today *should* return to the tradition of arranged marriage since

     (reason for) _____ and

     (reason for) _____ .

Plan:

First subpoint (reason against): _____

Second subpoint (reason for): _____

Third subpoint (reason for): _____

Planning Support for Subpoints

As you draw up your preliminary plan, think about how you want to develop each body paragraph in the essay. You can do so in the following two ways:

1. Developing the reasons that support the main proposition with evidence and analysis.

2. Developing the reasons that oppose the main proposition (the concession) with evidence and analysis.

1. In order to *develop a subpoint that supports your main proposition,* you need to provide specific, concrete evidence for that point. The evidence might include specific facts or examples from your own experience and observations. Then you need to analyze the evidence by explaining to the reader how it supports your main proposition.

2. In order to *develop a concession point* (a subpoint that opposes your main proposition), you need to provide specific, concrete evidence for the point, such as facts or examples.

In analyzing concession evidence, though, you may choose one of two common argumentative techniques: a) *conceding to* the point of the opposition or b) *refuting* it. If you concede to a point from the opposing side, you first admit that this concession point is true or valid (that is, you explain why the evidence presented proves the point). You go on to explain why admitting to the truth or validity of this one concession point does not significantly weaken the main proposition of your argument. You might, for example, give reasons why this is not an important point in the overall argument. If you choose to refute a point from the opposing side, you explain why this concession point is actually untrue or not valid. You might, for instance, point to weaknesses in the evidence. Or, you might explain why the evidence presented does not actually prove the point to be true. Whether you concede to or refute an opposition point, you show your own fairness and thus strengthen your argument by bringing in a point from the opposing side, rather than ignoring the opposing side.

At this point, then, work on your preliminary plan by jotting down a few rough ideas about the evidence and analysis you will use in each body paragraph. Also decide on how you plan to support your subpoints.

Drafting the Thesis and Body Paragraphs

Before meeting with your writing group, you will draft the thesis and body paragraphs of your essay. (Later you will draft your opening and conclusion paragraphs.) Referring to the thesis and preliminary plan you have just created, revise your thesis (if necessary) and draft the body paragraphs. When drafting your body paragraphs, refer to the "Planning Support for Subpoints" section in this chapter (page 287).

Revising the Thesis and Body Paragraphs

If time permits, before sharing your draft with your writing group, practice evaluating the student samples in Activity 11.2.

❑ *ACTIVITY 11.2:* **EVALUATING STUDENTS' THESES AND BODY PARAGRAPHS**

Read these three sample paragraphs and discuss the questions that follow each one. Note that sample A is a body paragraph that supports the writer's main proposition; samples B and C are concession paragraphs.

STUDENT SAMPLE A

Thesis
Marriage based on romantic love is better for today's young couples because romantic memories will later help them get through hard times, because young people today are too independent to let parents choose their marriage partners, and because arranged marriages will not solve the divorce problem in the United States.

Body Paragraph of Support
One reason young couples today should not return to the tradition of arranged marriage is because the memories they share of their dating experience are important after marriage to maintain that feeling of falling in love. For example, my parents always try to tell me about their romantic memories when they are feeling stressed or when they are tired after work. Often, they tell me how they fell in love and how they got married. While they are talking about their experiences of falling in love and dating, they wear a smile on their faces, and they look at each other in a special way. Every time I see their actions, I understand how they came to love each other so much. Moreover, I can see that they are relaxing and falling in love again. I really like to hear about their memories because I like to see my parents' happy faces. I realize that their romantic memories are important in order to keep their love for each other alive. Thus, I believe that a marriage based on romantic love, because of its beautiful memories of falling in love and dating, is better than an arranged marriage that has no such memories.

DISCUSSION QUESTIONS

1. Is the point of the paragraph clearly focused in a topic sentence?

2. Does the writer present enough specific, concrete evidence to make the point convincing?

3. Does the writer analyze the evidence, explaining why it proves the reason stated in the topic sentence?

4. What suggestions for improvement can you offer?

STUDENT SAMPLE B

Thesis

Even though arranged marriage does not allow partners to get to know each other before they marry, young people today should adopt the tradition of arranged marriage because in it couples can learn to have a deeper love for each other than romantic love allows. In addition, the arranged couple can build a permanent, stable family life for their children.

Body Paragraph of Concession

Granted, arranged marriage does not give partners a chance to know each other well before marriage. For example, in Japan, arranged marriage is very common, and many arranged couples go through a similar process before they marry. In a fancy restaurant, someone introduces them. If they like each other, then they date several times; however, such a date is a formal date. They wear good clothes and go to dinner in fancy restaurants. Also, they talk about their hobbies, favorite books, and favorite music; thus, their conversation is limited. As a result, they see only the good side of their partner. After several dates, they may decide to get married. Yet, after marriage, they may find out another side of the partner and be surprised. Thus one of the drawbacks of an arranged marriage is that partners do not have a chance to know each other before marrying; nevertheless, most young couples discover after the marriage that their parents used good judgment in choosing a partner for them—one who is a good person and who shares the same values and many of the same dreams for the future of their new family.

DISCUSSION QUESTIONS

1. In this paragraph, the writer is conceding to one point of the opposition. Is the concession point clearly focused in a topic sentence?

2. Does the writer present enough specific, concrete evidence to make the point convincing—that partners in an arranged marriage do not get to know each other well before marriage?

3. In analyzing the evidence presented, does the writer concede to or refute the point? That is, does the writer admit that this point is true and then explain why this concession point does not significantly damage the main proposition of the argument? Or, does the writer refute the point, explaining why this concession point is actually not true?

4. What suggestions for improvement can you offer?

STUDENT SAMPLE C

Thesis

Although arranged marriages would likely result in lower divorce rates, in the United States we should not return to this tradition because the partners in arranged marriages tend not to understand each other well and this might result in less happiness in married life.

Body Paragraph of Concession

On the one hand, arranged marriages would most likely result in fewer divorces. During the "old days," it was considered wrong to divorce. Hence, returning to the tradition of arranged marriage would reinforce that old custom. Moreover, couples in arranged marriages do not divorce as often as those in marriages based on romantic love. However, things have changed much. Today, many young people marry for love, not because their parents want them to marry a particular person. Thus, divorce rates have increased tragically because couples have no obligation to their parents. Couples divorce if the marriage does not work out. Therefore, some people believe that we should return to the tradition of arranged marriage. They think arranged marriages will result in fewer divorces because the partners have an obligation to their parents to stay together. My aunt and uncle, for example, were married as a result of an arranged marriage. He was an alcoholic. Every time he got drunk, he became very violent and aggressive. Although my aunt wanted to divorce him, she could not because divorce is not acceptable in the old Chinese tradition. In addition, my aunt did not want to disappoint her parents by divorcing. As a result, she had to live with a husband whom she did not love. Hence, arranged marriages would result in fewer divorces. Sometimes, they lead to a tragic ending.

DISCUSSION QUESTIONS

1. Is the point of the paragraph clear? Why or why not?

2. Has the writer chosen evidence that is appropriate for developing the point of the paragraph? Explain.

3. Is it clear whether the writer is conceding to or refuting the point? Why or why not?

4. What suggestions for improvement can you offer?

❏ *ACTIVITY 11.3:* **PEER RESPONSE**

Now share your draft thesis and body paragraphs with your writing group. Use the following procedure:

1. One group member should begin by reading aloud his or her thesis and body paragraphs. The group should then discuss the draft in terms of the questions listed on the Peer Response Sheet for Activity 11.3 on page 367. Another group member should record the group's suggestions on the sheet.

2. After you are finished filling out the sheet, give it to the writer so that he or she can refer to it when revising.

3. Repeat the procedure for each group member.

4. Then revise your thesis and body paragraphs, keeping in mind the suggestions of your writing group.

DRAFTING AND REVISING YOUR OPENING AND CONCLUSION PARAGRAPHS

After you have revised your thesis and body paragraphs, you are now ready to draft your opening and conclusion paragraphs. If necessary, refer to Chapter 8 for ideas about developing your opening paragraph. Refer to Chapter 9 for ideas about writing your conclusion paragraph.

❏ *ACTIVITY 11.4:* **MORE PEER RESPONSE**

You are now ready to share your opening and conclusion paragraph with your writing group. Use the group procedure outlined in Activity 11.3, but use the Peer Response Sheet for Activity 11.4 on page 370 for discussion and for recording the group's suggestions about the opening and conclusion paragraphs.

After meeting with your group, revise your draft once again. Once you are satisfied with its content, you are ready to edit it.

Editing: Using Multiple Verb Tense Centering Points in a Paragraph

In earlier chapters, you learned about centering a paragraph in the "world of the present" or in the "world of the past." In this editing section, you will learn how to use multiple centering points within one paragraph. Your ability to use multiple centering points will not only help you revise your essay on arranged marriage; it will also be essential to the academic writing you will do throughout college.

CENTERING A PARAGRAPH AROUND ONE CENTERING POINT

Think about what you learned from earlier chapters about centering a paragraph in the "world of the present" or the "world of the past." As you read the review that follows, make certain you have a good sense of how to choose verb tenses within these two "worlds" of time.

Centering in the "World of the Present"

In Chapter 4, you learned how to center a group of sentences or a paragraph in the "world of the present" to describe a world of people and events that is still happening now. Events in this "world" revolve around a centering point in present time. Once you choose to center a group of sentences in the "world of the present," you need to keep this centering point uppermost in your mind in order to choose verb tenses in relation to it. As you see from the diagram below, you use certain verbs to refer to events that occur at the "same time" as the present centering point, at "time before" the present centering point, or at "time after" the present centering point.

Centering in the "World of the Past"

In Chapters 1 and 5, you learned how to center a group of sentences or a paragraph in the "world of the past" to describe events that took place entirely in the past—events that are no longer happening now. Within the "world of the past," events revolve around a centering point in past time. As you write, you keep this centering point uppermost in your mind and choose verb tenses in relation to it. As you see from the diagram on page 294, you use certain verbs to show that events occurred "time before" the past centering point, "same time" as the past centering point, or "time after" the past centering point.

"World of the Present"

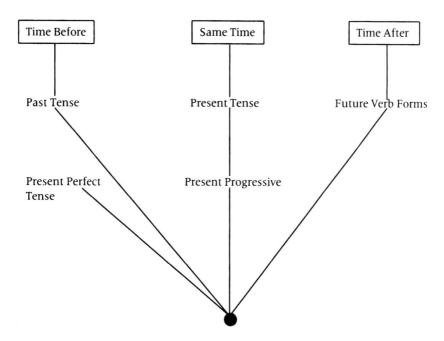

| Time Before | Same Time | Time After |

Past Tense   Present Tense   Future Verb Forms

Present Perfect   Present Progressive
Tense

"World of the Past"

| Time Before | Same Time | Time After |

Past Perfect Tense   Past Tense   Past Tense

Past Progressive

In addition, you learned in Chapter 1 that the present tense is rarely used within the "world of the past." It is used in this way only for the following purposes:

- To convey a present perspective on past events:

    I *remember* living in China when I was a child.

- To describe a "timeless truth" that would sound awkward or misleading if phrased in past tense:

    I learned in my anthropology class that different cultures around the world *have* different marriage customs.

USING MULTIPLE CENTERING POINTS IN A PARAGRAPH

One of the most difficult tasks in writing, especially for the non-native speaker, is using multiple centering points in a paragraph. Whether you are writing a lab report, a history paper, or an English essay, it probably contains paragraphs that should use multiple centering points. For example, a paragraph might begin with a group of sentences centered in the "world of the present," follow with an example centered in the "world of the past," and conclude with a group of analysis sentences centered in the "world of the present."

Therefore, in addition to being able to choose the correct verb tenses for the "world" of the past or present, you also need to be able to use multiple centering points within a paragraph.

❏ *ACTIVITY 11.5:* **IDENTIFYING MULTIPLE CENTERING POINTS IN A PARAGRAPH**

As you read the following passage about arranged marriage from Elisabeth Bumiller's *May You Be the Mother of a Hundred Sons: A Journey among the Women of India* (1990), note how the paragraphs contain multiple centering points, both in the "world of the present" and in the "world of the past."

In India, an estimated 95 percent of marriages are still arranged, including the majority of those among the educated middle class. As with so many other statistics in India, no one is certain of the accuracy of this estimate, and in fact many sociologists and much of the general public believe the percentage of arranged marriages to be even higher. When I first came to India, this astonished me. I knew arranged marriage was standard among villagers and the rural poor—in other words, most of the country—but I did not expect that an Indian man who had lived in the United States would come home after years of dating American women to marry someone he had met only three times. I did not expect college women in the big cities to gladly give their parents the task of finding them good husbands. I was more amazed when some would say yes to a prospective groom after a half-hour meeting. "I could decide maybe in a day," a twenty-year-old New Delhi commercial-arts student told me. Then she thought a minute. "Well, maybe that's a bit rushed. Maybe in a week."

Arranged marriage survives among the Indian middle class partly because a new kind of system has emerged. (The term *middle class,* as it is used in India, refers not to those in the middle economic group but to the people in the top 10 percent, who can afford to buy consumer products and live what the West would consider a semblance of a middle-class life.) A generation ago, a bride and groom rarely spoke to each other before the wedding. In many cases they had never even laid eyes on each other. They had no veto power over their parents' choice, and if the marriage was miserable, so be it. Even now, for the majority of Indians, marriage still works this way.

But these days middle-class couples are allowed to meet several times before making a decision, and a few can go out once or twice alone. Although most marriages are still arranged among members of the same caste, engagements may last six months and more, and women may reject the choice of their parents. . . .

When you are composing a paragraph that contains two or more centering points, keep the following guidelines in mind.

Guidelines for Using Multiple Centering Points in a Paragraph:

1. *When you are composing a group of sentences, be aware of your centering point in time.* Ask yourself whether you are centering in the "world of the present" or the "world of the past." Then choose the appropriate verb tenses to refer to "time before," "same time," or "time after" the centering point of that "world."

2. *When shifting from one "world" to another, clearly announce this shift to the reader* with one of the following:

• A transitional word or phrase (such as *for example, on the other hand,* or *in conclusion*).

• A time signal (such as *yesterday, today, now,* or *at that time*).

• A phrase or sentence that bridges the gap from one group of sentences to the next (*As this example shows, . . .*). (See Chapter 6 for a review of the principle of "something old/something new.")

❏ *ACTIVITY 11.6:* **MARKING MULTIPLE CENTERING POINTS IN A PARAGRAPH**

As you read the sample student paragraph that follows, note where the writer shifts from one centering point to another. In the right-hand margin, draw brackets to mark each group of sentences that is centered around one centering point and label it "Present World" or "Past World." Also, underline the transitions, time signals, and bridging phrases that the writer uses to signal a shift from one "world" to another. The following example (from the Bumiller passage you read in Activity 11.5) shows how the paragraph should be marked.

Example:

Arranged marriage survives among the Indian middle class partly because a new kind of system has emerged. (The term *middle class,* as it is used in India, refers not to those in the middle economic group but to the people in the top 10 percent, who can afford to buy consumer products and live what the West would consider a semblance of a middle-class life.) A generation ago, a bride and groom rarely spoke to each other before the wedding. In many cases they had never even laid eyes on each other. They had no veto power over their parents' choice, and if the marriage was miserable, so be it. Even now, for the majority of Indians, marriage still works this way.

[right margin annotations:] Present World · Past World · Present World

SAMPLE STUDENT PARAGRAPH

A form of arranged marriage would be good for today's young people because in an arranged marriage, the mate is selected on the basis of wisdom, not passion. Few young people today use wisdom when selecting a marriage partner. Instead, they rely on "chemistry"; they choose the person they find most attractive. My sister, for example, fell in love with a handsome young man with black hair and big brown eyes. She called him her "movie star." She loved to ride around town with him in his convertible and be seen by her friends. Then she ran away from home and married him. A month after the marriage, my sister discovered that her new husband supported himself by stealing cars. Young people today should think about the example of my sister. Instead of selecting a mate based on passion, as my sister did, young people should lean on the wisdom of their parents and other elders, who can select for them a partner with strong character traits and a good economic future. Since parents' eyes are not clouded by romantic love, they are able to select the best mate for their son or daughter.

As you can see in this paragraph, the use of multiple tenses is not confusing because, within the past and present "worlds," the writer carefully limits the verb tenses to those appropriate to each "world." In addition, the writer uses clear signals when shifting from one centering point to another.

PROBLEMS WITH USING MULTIPLE CENTERING POINTS IN A PARAGRAPH

There are three common problems that writers have in paragraphs with multiple centering points:

1. Choosing inappropriate verb tenses within one "world."
2. Failing to stay within one "world."
3. Failing to signal a shift from one "world" to another.

The following discussion shows you how to avoid these problems when composing paragraphs with multiple centering points.

Choosing Inappropriate Verb Tenses within One "World"

A common tense problem occurs when a writer composing a group of sentences centered around one centering point (either in the "world of the present" or the "world of the past") chooses inappropriate verb tenses within that particular "world."

To solve this problem, think about which "world" you are centering your group of sentences in (the "world of the present" or the "world of the past"). Then refer to the tense chart for that "world" (see page 293 or page 294) and select the appropriate tenses to refer to events that took place at "time before," "same time," or "time after" the centering point of that "world."

❏ *ACTIVITY 11.7:* **CORRECTING VERB TENSE ERRORS IN EACH "WORLD"**

The following student paragraph contains several centering points (or "worlds"), as well as a number of errors in verb tense usage within these "worlds." As you read the paragraph, draw brackets to mark each group of sentences that is centered in the past or present "world" and label it "Present World" or "Past World." Then underline the transitions, time signals, and bridging phrases that the writer uses to signal shifts from one "world" to another. Finally, circle and correct any errors you find in the writer's use of verb tenses within each "world" of time.

I believe love, romance, and passion are essential for two lovers to be happy. When a couple marries without love, as often happens in an arranged marriage, it is very difficult for them to be happy together. My grandparents, for instance, have been married for forty-five years, and they still have love and passion for each other. They did not marry because of some arrangement made by their parents; rather, they married because they loved each other. During all of their years together, there have been many arguments and conflicts, but they have stayed together because they love each other so much, and I believe they will continue to stay together until one of them dies. One time, five years ago, my grandfather has a situation of financial disaster. Because of this financial situation, he has to ask my grandmother to sell all of her jewelry. In fact, my grandmother did not complain about selling all her jewelry because she loves and cares for her husband very much. When couples marry for love, as my grandparents did, they are better able to survive the hard times in their marriage, and they will be happy. A couple without love is not likely to survive life's hardships as well.

Failing to Stay within One "World"

Another common tense problem occurs when a writer has not made a definite decision about whether to center a group of sentences in the "world of the past" or the "world of the present." Instead of choosing one world, the writer uses tenses from both worlds. As a result, the reader becomes confused by the "drifting" tenses and cannot determine whether the events described occurred in the "world of the past" or the "world of the present."

To solve this problem, you need to decide—before you compose the group of sentences—whether you want to center it in the present or past "world." Then you can use the appropriate verb tenses within that "world."

❏ *ACTIVITY 11.8:* **CORRECTING VERB TENSES THAT "DRIFT"**

As you read the following student paragraph, note where the verb tenses "drift" between the present and past "worlds." Draw brackets in the right-hand margin to mark where you think groups of sentences should be centered around one centering point (one "world") and identify each as "Present World" or "Past World." Then circle incorrect verb tenses within each world and make the necessary corrections.

> Young couples in the Western world should not adopt the tradition of arranged marriage because a bad arranged marriage can turn into a death trap. Because there is a low percentage of divorces in arranged marriages, they show up well on surveys. However, because the tradition often does not allow arranged couples to divorce, unhappy couples are forced to stay together and live through the suffering and hatred between them. For example, when I was in Vietnam, I have a friend whose aunt's marriage is arranged. His aunt was arranged to marry a middle-class man who had a good job, but whom she did not love. After they got married, she tries to love him, but she cannot because he is always drunk coming home from work, and he yelled at her and sometimes beat her. She is very depressed. She wish she can get a divorce, but the elders who arranged her marriage will not permit it, and divorce would give her parents a bad reputation. As this woman's example shows, an arranged marriage can lead to a great deal of suffering and even physical violence if the partner does not turn out to be a good person and if divorce is not permitted.

Failing to Signal a Shift from One "World" to Another

In a paragraph with multiple centering points, a writer sometimes fails to signal to the reader when shifting from one "world" to another (such as from the "world of the present" to the "world of the past"). To solve this problem in your writing, you first want to become aware of when you are shifting from one centering point, or "world," to another. Then you need to signal this shift clearly to the reader with a transition, a time signal, or a bridging phrase.

❏   *ACTIVITY 11.9:*   **SIGNALING SHIFTS**
     FROM ONE "WORLD" TO ANOTHER

As you read the following paragraph, note where the writer fails to signal shifts between the past and present "worlds." Draw brackets to mark where groups of sentences are centered around one centering point (one "world") and label each as the "Present World" or "Past World." Then, mark an "*X*" where a signal is needed to announce a shift from one "world" to another. Finally, provide those signals—transitions, time signals, or bridging phrases.

Arranged marriage is better than marriage for romantic love because in an arranged marriage, the partners learn a love that is deeper than romantic love. My parents' marriage was arranged. Over the years, they learned to care for and cherish each other, but not in a romantic way. While my father was still alive, he helped my mother with the house cleaning on the weekends. When she was sick, he would cook meals for the family. My mother turned her full attention to my father each night when he came home from his ten-hour shift at the garment factory. She listened to how he felt and let him know that she cared how his day had gone. Love in an arranged marriage is not based simply on physical attraction; instead, it is based on a deep sense of respect and genuine caring for the other person.

 EDITING CHECKLIST ———————————————————

After revising your essay for content, you are ready to edit it. Check for the following:

☐ Check for *correct verb tenses* by using the following procedure:

1. For each paragraph, identify each group of sentences that should be centered in either the "world of the present" or the "world of the past."

2. For each group of sentences in the past or present "world," check that you have used the appropriate verb tenses to refer to events that took place "time before," "same time," or "time after" the centering point of that "world."

3. Look for the areas where you shift from one "world" to another (such as from the present to the past "world") and check to see that you have signaled those shifts with a transition (such as *for example, on the other hand,* or *in conclusion*), a time signal (*yesterday, today, now, at that time*), or a bridging phrase or sentence (*As this example shows, . . .*). (For more on how to use the principle of "something old/something new," see Chapter 6.)

□ Check for *coherence problems.* Ask a classmate or friend to read your essay aloud to you. Listen for breaks in coherence where one sentence does not smoothly follow another. If you find breaks in coherence, ask yourself the following questions:

- Can I use the principle of "something old/something new"—picking up "something old" from a previous sentence and adding to it "something new"?

- Can I use a surface signal to link one sentence to the next—repetition and a synonym, a demonstrative pronoun or adjective, a pronoun, or a transition?

If time permits, also check your draft for the following:

□ Check for *sentence variety.*

□ Check for *sentence structure problems:* fragments, run-on sentences, and comma splices.

APPENDIX A

Logical Connectors

Logical Relationship	Coordinate Conjunction	Transition	Subordinate Conjunction
Addition	and	moreover furthermore in addition besides	
Reinforcement or Emphasis		indeed in fact	
Choice	or nor		
Exemplification		for example for instance in particular	
Similarity		likewise similarly	
Contrast	but yet	conversely however in contrast nevertheless nonetheless on the contrary on the other hand otherwise	although though even though while whereas
Cause	for		because since as

Logical Relationship	Coordinate Conjunction	Transition	Subordinate Conjunction
Result or Effect	so	consequently thus therefore accordingly hence as a result	
Time		meanwhile subsequently thereafter	when whenever since while before after until as as soon as as long as once
Place			where wherever
Manner			as

APPENDIX B

Principal Parts of Irregular Verbs

Base Form	Past Form	Past Participle
be	was/were	been
beat	beat	beaten
become	became	become
begin	began	begun
bend	bent	bent
bet	bet	bet
bite	bit	bitten
bleed	bled	bled
blow	blew	blown
break	broke	broken
bring	brought	brought
build	built	built
buy	bought	bought
catch	caught	caught
choose	chose	chosen
come	came	come
cost	cost	cost
cut	cut	cut
deal	dealt	dealt
dig	dug	dug
do	did	done
draw	drew	drawn
drink	drank	drunk
drive	drove	driven
eat	ate	eaten
fall	fell	fallen
feed	fed	fed
feel	felt	felt

Base Form	*Past Form*	*Past Participle*
fight	fought	fought
find	found	found
flee	fled	fled
fly	flew	flown
forget	forgot	forgotten
forgive	forgave	forgiven
freeze	froze	frozen
get	got	gotten
give	gave	given
go	went	gone
grow	grew	grown
hang	hung	hung
have	had	had
hear	heard	heard
hide	hid	hidden
hit	hit	hit
hold	held	held
hurt	hurt	hurt
keep	kept	kept
know	knew	known
lay	laid	laid
lead	led	led
leave	left	left
lend	lent	lent
let	let	let
lie	lay	lain
light	lit, lighted	lit, lighted
lose	lost	lost
make	made	made
meet	met	met
pay	paid	paid
put	put	put
quit	quit	quit
read	read	read
ride	rode	ridden
ring	rang	rung
rise	rose	risen
run	ran	run
say	said	said
see	saw	seen
seek	sought	sought
sell	sold	sold
send	sent	sent
set	set	set

Base Form	Past Form	Past Participle
shake	shook	shaken
shine	shone, shined	shone, shined
shoot	shot	shot
shut	shut	shut
sing	sang	sung
sit	sat	sat
sleep	slept	slept
slide	slid	slid
speak	spoke	spoken
spend	spent	spent
spin	spun	spun
split	split	split
spread	spread	spread
stand	stood	stood
steal	stole	stolen
stick	stuck	stuck
strike	struck	struck
swear	swore	sworn
swim	swam	swum
swing	swung	swung
take	took	taken
teach	taught	taught
tear	tore	torn
tell	told	told
think	thought	thought
understand	understood	understood
wake	woke, waked	woken, waked
wear	wore	worn
weave	wove	woven
weep	wept	wept
win	won	won
wring	wrung	wrung
write	wrote	written

APPENDIX C

Present and Past Progressive Tenses

THE PRESENT PROGRESSIVE

Form the *present progressive tense* with the present tense of *be* plus the *-ing* verb form:

Vladimir *is studying*.

The present progressive tense conveys to the reader the idea of *an action in progress right now* (an action that is not yet ended). The action usually has some duration; that is, it is continuing over a period of time.

It *is raining* outside.

The children *are playing* games in the den.

In addition, the present progressive tense can signal that an action is happening right now *in a repeated manner:*

Someone *is knocking* at the door.

The present progressive tense can also convey the idea that the action is only a *temporary state of affairs*. In the following sentences, note the difference in meaning between the present tense for a habitual action and the present progressive for a temporary state of affairs:

Present:

Mother usually *cooks* dinner for the family.

Present Progressive:

Father *is cooking* dinner tonight.

STATIVE VERBS

Stative verbs, which describe a state of being, not a dynamic or active situation, usually do not occur in the progressive tense. Stative verbs fall into the groups shown in the accompanying table.

Stative Verbs

States of Being	be
States of Knowing (through the Mind)	believe imagine know realize suppose think understand wonder
States of Emotion	disagree dislike intend like pity want wish hate
States of Knowing (through the Senses)	feel hear see smell taste
States of Measurement	cost equal measure weigh
States of Relationship	belong (to) contain have own

Occasionally, some stative verbs can be used in the progressive. When used in this way, they signal the *active meaning* of the verb, not the stative or state of being.

Present Tense for a State of Being:

I *think* calculus is difficult.

Progressive Tense for an Active Mental Process:

I *am thinking* about this calculus problem.

THE VERBS *LIVE, STAND, SIT, LIE*

One group of verbs in English—*live, stand, sit,* and *lie*—can be used in either the progressive or nonprogressive tense. In the progressive tense, these verbs show that the state is temporary; in the nonprogressive, they show that the state is more permanent or habitual.

Permanent:

My parents *live* in San Francisco.

Temporary:

I *am living* in the dormitory at San Juan College.

Permanent:

The mosque *stands* in the center of the city.

Temporary:

Marta *is standing* behind the door.

The present progressive can also be used to signal the future:

Sinja and Payim *are coming* to see us on Friday.

THE PAST PROGRESSIVE

Form the *past progressive tense* with the past tense of *be* plus the *-ing* verb form:

Vladimir *was studying* last night.

Deladier *was talking* on the phone.

The past progressive conveys the idea of *an action in progress in the past.* Past progressive actions had some *duration*—they continued for a period of time in the past.

Yesterday Sabrina *was cleaning* the house from noon until 3 P.M.

The past progressive tense is also used to show the *relationship between two events in past time.* As the following examples show, the past progressive may be used to show that an action was in progress at a particular time in the past:

Particular Time in the Past	Event in Progress in the Past
When the doorbell rang,	Sabrina was cleaning the oven.
At 6 A.M.,	Sabrina was sweeping the walk.
The phone rang	while Joo was washing windows.

Notice that *when* is often used to signal a particular time in the past (with the past tense), and *while* is used to signal an ongoing event in progress in the past (with the past progressive).

APPENDIX D

Overview of Verb Tenses

The accompanying table gives examples for the twelve tenses in English. Note that the future perfect and future perfect progressive tenses are used less often than the other verb tenses.

Verb Tenses	
Present Tense Manuel's parents *live* in Argentina.	**Present Progressive** Manuel *is living* in the dorm at his college.
Past Tense Manuel *came* to the United States last summer.	**Past Progressive** Manuel *was flying* over the equator on July 4, 1996.
Future Tense Manuel *will visit* his family in Argentina next summer.	**Future Progressive** Manuel *will be visiting* his sister on his twenty-first birthday.
Present Perfect Tense Manuel *has been* in the United States for six months.	**Present Perfect Progressive** Manuel *has been trying* to call his friend Eduardo for two days.
Past Perfect Tense At the time he boarded the plane for the United States, Manuel *had* never *flown* before.	**Past Perfect Progressive** When Manuel's plane landed in Miami last summer, he *had been flying* for ten hours.
Future Perfect Tense By next May, Manuel *will have lived* in the United States for nine months.	**Future Perfect Progressive** By the time he arrives home, Manuel *will have been sitting* in an airplane seat for twelve hours.

In addition to being able to select the appropriate verb tense for a sentence, you need to be able to center a group of sentences in the "world of

312

the present" or the "world of the past." Moreover, within each of these "worlds," you need to select the appropriate verb tenses to signal an event or fact that took place at "time before," "same time," or "time after" the centering point of that world. For more information, see Chapter 4 for the "world of the present," and see Chapters 1, 4, and 5 for the "world of the past." For a discussion of how to use more than one centering point or one "world," see Chapter 11.

In addition to the "worlds" of the present and past, there are two others: the "world of the future" and the "world of the conditional."

The "world of the future," which is very rarely used in English, describes events that will take place around a centering point in future time:

> By next May, Manuel *will have lived* in the United States for nine months.

> Manuel *will visit* his home in Argentina next summer.

> When Manuel travels to Argentina next summer, he *will be flying* for the second time in his life.

The "world of the conditional" is used to discuss events or facts that are either hypothetical (unreal) or untrue:

> If Manuel *were* a millionaire, he *would buy* his own plane to fly to Argentina.

> If Manuel *were* a woman, he *would have* fewer opportunities to work as an engineer in Argentina.

APPENDIX E

Avoiding Comma Splices and Run-On Sentences

Comma splices and run-on sentences—two common sentence errors—result from the improper joining of two independent clauses in a compound sentence.

COMMA SPLICE

A *comma splice* occurs when two independent clauses are incorrectly joined only by a comma:

Comma Splice:

Neshat likes to vacation in the mountains, her sister prefers the beach.

Correct:

Neshat likes to vacation in the mountains, *but* her sister prefers the beach.

RUN-ON SENTENCE

A *run-on sentence* occurs when two independent clauses are joined, or "run together," without the necessary punctuation or logical connector:

Run-On:

Nicolai could clean his apartment this weekend he could visit his favorite art museum.

Correct:

Nicolai could clean his apartment this weekend, *or* he could visit his favorite art museum.

EDITING STRATEGIES FOR CORRECTING COMMA SPLICES AND RUN-ON SENTENCES

To correct a run-on sentence or comma splice, use one of the following strategies:

1. Insert a period between the two independent clauses. (This may, however, give your writing a choppy effect, with too many simple sentences.)

Incorrect:

The water in Hawaii is warm, swimming is a favorite activity of tourists.

Correct:

The water in Hawaii is warm. Swimming is a favorite activity of tourists.

2. Join the two independent clauses with a comma and a coordinate conjunction (see the discussion of coordinate conjunctions as logical connectors in Chapter 2):

Correct:

The water in Hawaii is warm, *and* swimming is a favorite activity of tourists.

3. Join the two independent clauses with a semicolon alone, if this is logical:

Correct:

Hawaii is a wonderful place to visit; some people even call it paradise.

4. Join the two independent clauses with a transition (see the discussion of transitions as logical connectors in Chapter 7):

Correct:

Hawaii is a wonderful place to visit; *indeed,* some people even call it paradise.

5. Make one of the clauses dependent by adding a subordinate conjunction (see the discussion of subordinate conjunctions as logical connectors in Chapter 3):

Correct:

Because Hawaii is such a wonderful place to visit, some people call it paradise.

❏ *ACTIVITY:* **CORRECTING COMMA SPLICES AND RUN-ON SENTENCES**

For each of the following sentences, circle the independent clauses. Then mark the run-on sentences as "RO" and the comma splices as "CS." Finally, using any of the editing strategies described earlier in this appendix, correct the comma splices and run-on sentences.

1. I may go to Singapore for the holidays I may stay in San Francisco.

2. My sister is going to Disneyland for Easter, her best friend will meet her there.

3. They hope to go to the beach one day, however, the weather may not be warm enough.

4. They plan to visit art museums they will spend one day at the Movie Museum at Universal Studios.

Glossary of Vocabulary Words

abandon (*noun*) complete freedom of expression (sometimes uncontrolled)

abandon (*verb*) to leave behind or give up

abaya a long, dark, cloaklike garment entirely covering a woman's head, arms, body, and legs, worn in keeping with the Islamic belief in women's modesty

abrasive causing a surface to wear away

abruptly suddenly, without expectation

absolute state of complete perfection, without doubt

absorb to take in or take great interest in

abundance a great amount of

abuse to hurt or use wrongly

accede to finally agree to a demand

accelerate to speed up or advance

accent (*verb*) to bring attention to

access means of entry or ability to reach

accompany to go along with

accomplish to do something successfully

acknowledge to recognize as true or real

acquire to take on or possess

acquisitive getting ideas or things

acute sharp; not long lasting

adapt to change in order to fit a new situation

adaptive done in order to be suitable for new conditions

addict (*verb*) to attach oneself to habitually

Adirondacks mountains in northern New York State

adjust to make changes to fit a new situation

adolescence youth, from 12 to 18 years of age

advocate (*verb*) to support

aerobics vigorous exercise that makes one breathe hard

affect to cause to change

affectionate showing love and care

aghast suddenly very surprised; shocked

aglow lit up

alarm (*noun*) something that sounds to warn of danger

algae small, one-celled plants that live in water

alien something that is not familiar

Allah God, in the Islamic religion

ally a person providing support

amoeba a tiny, one-celled creature (protozoan)

amplify to increase or make larger

amulet an object thought to protect a person from evil

ancestors family members born in earlier generations

317

ancestral having to do with one's ancestors

anchor a heavy metal or stone piece, attached to a rope and thrown into the water to hold a ship in place

anesthesiologist a doctor who gives drugs to make a patient sleep deeply during surgery

antique something that was made in a much earlier time

anxiety strong uneasiness or worry

aplomb self-confidence

apparent clearly seen

appeal to ask (someone) for help

applaud to show praise by clapping one's hands together

appreciate to be thankful for or grateful to; to understand or enjoy

apprenticeship the period of time when one works for low wages in order to learn a trade or skill

approach to come near in space or time

appropriate suitable or proper

approximate to be nearly the same

arc something shaped like a curve

archaeology the study of things in human history and culture in earlier times

archetype the original type or model for things that came later

array a collection or group

assert to state or put forward forcefully

assure to say something in order to remove doubt

astonishing amazing or very surprising

at her disposal available for her use

atmosphere the surroundings or feelings of a place

auditorium a large room with a stage where people gather for school events, plays, etc.

aura a feeling surrounding a person or place

auspicious promising later success

authority position of power or control; a person with great knowledge on a subject

avail (*noun*) usefulness

available ready to be of use

aversion a great dislike for something

awe a sense of great wonder

bachelor's exam set of final tests one needs to pass to obtain a college/university degree

bait very small fish or worms used on fish hooks to catch larger fish

baling wire very strong wire such as that used to tie up large portions of hay

bamboo a very tall grass with thick, hard stems

banish to send away by order

barge (*verb*) to suddenly rush in, possibly interrupting or intruding

barrier a wall or fence, for example, built to keep persons and things out

bastard of inferior origin

batch a group of things

BBC British Broadcasting Corporation, Great Britain's worldwide television and radio networks

beam (*noun*) a large, square wooden log used as support in a structure

beam (*verb*) smile brightly

bedazzled filled with wonder to the point of confusion

behemoth something extremely large, such as a very large animal

benediction a prayer or blessing

benign something that brings about good, not harmful, consequences

bestow to give

binoculars field glasses with two lenses, used for seeing things at great distances

biotechnology the engineering and biological investigation of relationships between humans and machines

black market a market where goods are sold illegally, despite government restrictions

Blake, William British poet of the early nineteenth-century Romantic movement

blanket a heavy, square cloth (often wool), used for covering

blobby shaped like a blob (a round mass)

blurt to suddenly say something, without thinking

board (*verb*) to provide food and housing for

bookkeeping a system for keeping business accounts

bottlenose porpoises small members of the whale family who have long, thin, pointed noses

bough a main branch

boundary something that indicates the edge or limit of an area, such as land

bout a short time of much activity

bowels (of ship) the lowest, inner parts of a ship

bracing giving one energy and alertness

Braille round printed marks raised on a surface, for example, a page, for reading by blind people

brazier a container where coal is burned

brew (*verb*) to make a drink (such as tea or coffee) with hot water

brief (*verb*) to give important information about something

brook (*verb*) to allow to happen

browse to look at a collection of objects casually

Buddhist having to do with Buddhism, a religion of Asia begun by Gautama Buddha

budding just beginning to bloom or develop

budge to cause to move or change

bulging curving outward

bullet train an extremely fast train (Japan)

bundle objects wrapped together like a package

bungling doing something badly or carelessly

Bunsen burner a small gas burner for laboratory experiments

burden a heavy weight or responsibility

bust a failure

buzzing making a sound like a bee

cadge to get by begging

cadre a group of trained people in the middle of an organization

campaign a plan of action designed to achieve a certain purpose

candidate a person who is seeking to be elected to office; a person wanting to be chosen for a job or position

capability the ability to do something

captivate to attract

captured taken prisoner

cardamom an East Indian spice made from a fruit

carefree having no worries

Casals, Pablo a world-famous musician (played the cello)

cast (*noun*) a mold or model for something

cast (*verb*) throw

caste one of the groups/classes people are divided into (for example, in India)

catalyst a substance that modifies or increases a chemical reaction

cataract cloudiness in the lens of the eye (a medical condition)

caterwauling unpleasant noises, such as the wailing of a cat

cautious very careful

celebrate to rejoice about something, often with ceremony

ceramics research the science of manufacturing ceramics (artificial materials that are not metal or organic), such as heat-resistant materials for space vehicles

challenge something needing one's full energy, thought, and effort

challenging questioning the truth or rightness of

charcoal a black material for fuel, made by distilling wood

chattel movable property

Chesterfield a brand of American cigarettes

chink small sound made by two things hitting together

chore a task performed on a regular basis

Churchill, Winston prime minister of England during World War II

circumstance a condition or fact surrounding a person or event

clap to make a sound by hitting the inside of the hands together

clash (*verb*) to be in opposition to; to conflict with

classify to put items into groups by similarity

clatter loud noise resulting from movement

claustrophobia a fear of being in closed-in spaces

claw (*verb*)   to scratch fiercely with the nails of fingers or toes

claw (*noun*)   a sharp, curved limb

cleat   a piece of wood or metal used as a support

cling   to stick to

cloak   a long coat (without sleeves) that wraps around

closed-circuit television   a television network that is produced for broadcast within a group only, such as within a school or business

closet (*verb*)   to put into a small, closed space

cluster   a group of things gathered closely together

cobweb   a network of threads that spiders make

colleagues   those who work in one's office or work group

colonial   having to do with colonies (countries under the control of distant countries)

colony   a group of plants or animals of the same kind living together

columnist   a writer who writes short pieces, often daily, for a newspaper or magazine

combustion science   the study of the burning of material (such as fuel)

comedy   stories or works that are funny

comely   attractive

commencement   the ceremony where students receive their academic degrees

comment (*verb*)   to express an opinion about

commercial   an advertisement for a product

commit   to promise (oneself) to something

commuting   traveling back and forth (often long distances) between work and home

companion   a person who goes along with another person

compel   to force

compelling (*adjective*)   demanding one's attention

complex   having many parts

complicate   to make more difficult or complex

complimentary   expressing admiration

component   a single part of a system

compose   to be made up of or formed from

compulsive   uncontrollably done, often repeatedly

concentrate   to put all one's thoughts on

concept   a general or abstract idea

concerto   a piece of music for one or more instruments and orchestra

conclude   to end; to believe or decide after considering the facts

conduct (*noun*)   behavior

conduct (*verb*)   to carry out

cone   a geometric shape with a small pointed end and a large circular end

confess   to admit having done wrong

confide   to tell something secret or private

confines   within a border or boundary

conflict (*noun*)   struggle between opposing ideas or desires; disagreement

confront   to face

Confucian   having to do with the ethical system developed by K'ung-Fu-tzu ("Confucius") in China

conscious   aware of

consciousness   the state of thinking; awareness of one's surroundings

conservative   wanting to keep things as they are

conspirator   one who makes secret plans with another

constriction   a tightening or narrowing of

consult   to ask the opinion of

consultant   a person who gives advice

consultation   the act of giving one's opinion or advice on

contamination   loss of purity due to contact with dirt or other matter

contemporary   during the same period of time; modern

context   what comes before or after; the situation

contingency   having to do with a possible future event

contort   to twist

contract   a legal agreement

contradictory   not agreeing

contrive   to plan cleverly

convalescent   getting well from an illness

convention   the practices or matters that are acceptable to the group

coo   to make a low, soft sound

cooperate   to work together

cope   to manage under difficult conditions

core   the central or innermost part of something

cork   a light, springy material made from the bark of the cork tree

correspondence   exchange of letters or papers

cosmopolitan   having people from many parts of the world

costume   clothes for a special occasion

counterpart   a person from a different group who has the same job or purpose

courteous   polite

crab   a sea animal with a wide flat shell and large front claws

crab fashion   to crawl sideways, as crabs do

crawl   to move on one's hands and knees

create   to make (something) exist; to produce

credential   the certificate or paper that shows one has the knowledge and right to do something

crew   people working together on a task, such as those on a ship

cricket   a British game played with balls and bat

critical   judging harshly; a very important time, such as a turning point

crouch   to bring the body close to the ground, with bent knees

cruise   to move about leisurely, usually for pleasure

crystal   a solid, see-through mineral looking like ice

culture   the beliefs, arts, and ways of doing things of a society

culture shock   surprise at how behaviors in one culture differ from those in one's own culture

cupboard   built-in cabinet

curious   wanting to know more about; puzzling or strange

curriculum   the types of studies offered in a school

curse   a saying of words thought to bring evil or harm

daily grind   everyday work, may be long, hard, repeated

dandy (*adjective*)   very good

dangling   hanging loose

daphniae   tiny creatures living in fresh water (crustaceous)

dash   to move very quickly or to do something hastily

data   information, sometimes in numbers

decorum   the display of proper manners

dedicate   to set aside for special use or to fully give oneself

defect   something wrong or imperfect about something

defer   to delay or postpone

defiantly   openly refusing to obey

deformity   of unnatural shape

delete   to remove

deliberately   done on purpose or by plan

demeaning   reducing in status or rank

demonstration   the act of proving or showing; a public expression of protest or support

demonstrative   showing one's feelings outwardly

departure   the act of leaving

deprivation   the state of being prevented from having something

deprive   to take away from

descending   going down

desegregation   the end of racial separation in public places

desktop publishing   using a computer and special software to make a document that is ready to be published

despite   without being prevented by

destined   intended for a certain purpose, perhaps by fate

detect   to discover or find

detective   a policeman or private person who searches for information about crime

devastated defeated or destroyed completely

devoid empty

devoted showing great care or loyalty

dialect a variety of languages specific to a certain region

dictation the act of speaking words to a person or into a tape machine so that they can be written down

differentiation the process of finding differences between

dingy dark and dirty

disappear to go out of sight or vanish

disastrous causing great damage

discard to throw away

discipline training that brings self-control or obedience

discreetly with sensitivity in a socially careful way

discriminate to treat differently, often because of race, ethnicity, or gender

disgraceful bringing shame

disgusting offensive

disinfectant an agent that destroys germs

dismay a feeling of great fear and helplessness

disparagement viewing or speaking of with no respect

display the showing of

dispute an argument

distinguish (*verb*) to see as distinct, different

distract to draw attention away from

disturbing breaking up a calm or settled state

ditto the same as something mentioned above/previously

divorce the legal end of a marriage

dizzying making one feel out of balance/light-headed

DNA the acids that are the building blocks of all living things; they hold the "codes" for how the living things will be structured

docile tame, obedient

domestic having to do with the family or household

dominate to rule over or control

donate to give as a gift, esp. for a useful purpose

dorsal on or near the back

dote on to shower with excessive love and attention

double over to bend over from the middle of the body, from laughter or pain

dowry goods and money a female brings to her marriage

dramatically done in an unusual or forceful way

drawing room a formal room in a house, for receiving guests

dread to fear

dredge to scrape over the bottom of a lake or river

drift (*verb*) to be carried along, often without direction

drift (*noun*) the area at the ocean's edge where material is left by the waves

drip to fall in small drops

duality having two parts

duration the period of time in which something happens or exists

dusk the time of decreasing light, after sunset

dwarfism the medical condition of stunted or arrested growth

dwell to live somewhere

ease to make easier

eaves the edges of a roof that hang beyond the house

echo (*noun*) a reminder of

eelgrass underwater grasslike plants

efficient that which works best and most quickly

eldest the oldest person (esp. in a family)

electronic having to do with machines that use electric current, such as radios, televisions, etc.

electronic listening post a place where one gathers information from radio or shortwave radio broadcasts

electrophoresis gel a jellylike, electrically charged material in which electrophoresis takes place (electrophoresis is the spreading out of the particles within a gel when the particles are electrically charged)

elegant beautiful and graceful

elementary the first five or six grades of school

the elevens facing off the two eleven-member cricket teams as the game begins

elite the most privileged people in a society or group

elopement the act of running away to marry secretly

elude to escape from

embarrassing feeling social discomfort

embody to give bodily form to or to have bodily form

embrace to take in one's arms; to accept

emotion any of the strong human feelings, such as love, hate, sorrow

emotional in the area of feelings

emphasis special importance

enable to make possible; to allow

encampment the place where a group of people has set up tents

enchant to put under a spell or to delight with charm

encounter a meeting

endorsement approval

endure to bear something painful for a long time

enforce to bring about obedience

engaged having promised to marry

enhance to enlarge or increase

ensuing happening afterward

enthusiasm a feeling of great interest

entomologist a scientist who studies insects

environment physical surroundings or conditions

equip to provide with the necessities

era a time period

erode to wear away

essential absolutely necessary

essentially basically; in reality

estimate to loosely calculate cost, quantity, etc.

ether a gas used as an anesthetic to put patients to sleep during surgery

ethnic concerning a certain race, nation, or tribe

etiquette formal rules of behavior or manners

euglena a one-celled freshwater creature with a red eye spot

evaluate to judge the worth or value of

eventually at last

evolve to develop gradually and continuously

exception something existing outside the normal rules

excess more than is reasonable

exclude to keep out

excruciating severely painful

excursion a short trip or outing

execution the act of killing for punishment

exhaust (*verb*) to let out or to use up

exhibit to show or display

expanse a wide area, such as of land, water, or sky

expedition a highly organized trip taken by a group, with a purpose and destination

explore to study or examine

exquisite very beautifully made

extended made longer

extended family a family made up of parents, children, and other relatives, such as grandparents, aunts and uncles, etc.

extension an added-on, longer part

extent the length or amount that something extends

extinguish to put out, such as a fire or light

extract to remove from or pull out of

exuberance unrestrained joy or enthusiasm

fabled made known by oral or written stories

facet a small surface of (gemstone or tooth); an aspect of

fade to slowly lose brightness or volume

famine a period when many people have to go without food

fan (*verb*) to cause currents of air to move over; to stimulate

fanatical having very strong, unreasonable keenness for something

fancy (*adjective*) very decorative

fancy (*verb*) desire

fantasy   something imagined

farewell   the act of saying good-bye

fascination   a great interest

fast-track lane   the most competitive ways of advancing in the business and professional world

fauna   the animals of a region

fax   a printed message sent over telephone lines

FBI   the United States' Federal Bureau of Investigation, an agency for investigating federal crime

feminine   having the characteristics of a female

feminist   a person who believes in equal rights for women

fertile   able to reproduce

fester   to decay or rot

fez   a round, tall hat with a flat top, tassels, and no brim

field (*verb*)   to handle (such as questions) or to catch (such as a ball)

field hockey   a game that eleven players play with sticks and a ball

fin   a winglike part of a water animal, used for moving through the water and for balance

flash bulletin   an important news story announced during a break in regular broadcasts of radio or television

flat   apartment (British)

flats   land having no curves

flotilla   a group of small ships moving together

fluid dynamics   the study of the behavior of fluids at rest and in motion

flutter   to wave quickly (such as curtains)

foreboding   suggesting a feeling of evil/unpleasantness

forefinger   the finger next to the thumb

foresight   the ability to look ahead in order to plan ahead

forge   to form

forsake   to leave or abandon

fortuitous   by chance or accident; not planned

foul play   unfair play or action; crime

frail   weak in body; delicate

frantically   done with great emotion such as fear, worry, or pain

frenzy   a state of being wildly excited or extremely agitated

friable   easily broken into powder

frock   a pretty dress

frustration   the state of being prevented from doing or accomplishing something

fuel   something (wood, gasoline, oil, coal) used to produce energy

Fu Manchu   a Chinese character with a long, drooping mustache

furious   very angry

furiously   wildly

gamble   to risk something with an uncertain result

Ganda   the ethnic group of people who live in the Buganda region of Uganda

Gandhi, Mahatma   national leader in India

gap   an empty space between two objects or things

gauze   a thin, loosely woven fabric often used for bandages

gaze   to look steadily

gender   male or female

generation   a group of people born during the same era

genetics   within biology, the study of heredity, how traits and variations are passed biologically from parents to their children

genius   a person with extremely high intelligence and often creativity

gesture   a movement of a body part, such as a hand or other appendage, to express an idea or to emphasize a spoken message

Ghana   a republic in western Africa

ghetto   an area of a city where people of a similar culture are forced to live, usually because of poverty or discrimination

ghi (ghee)   a semifluid, clarified butter made from buffalo or yak milk

ghostly   resembling or reminding one of a ghost—a dead person's spirit

glide   to move smoothly, as though without effort

glimpse   to look at briefly

glower   to look at with anger or displeasure

gnash   to strike the teeth together or grind them together harshly

gobble up to eat something very rapidly or study with great enthusiasm

godmother a woman who promises to help a child at its first important religious ceremony

grace notes light musical notes added for decoration

graffiti artwork and words painted on public areas (often offensive)

grainy looking like covered with hard, tiny seeds

grant (*verb*) to agree, permit, or give

grasp (*verb*) to hold firmly in the hand, wrapping one's fingers around; understand

gratifying bringing pleasure to; satisfying

grind to crush into pieces or powder

grit courage; tiny pieces of stone or sand

groom (*verb*) to brush and clean (such as an animal) or to train

groundbreaking (*adjective*) new and inventive

growl to make a harsh sound from deep in the throat, showing anger or warning

grudging unwilling to do or to give something

guff meaningless talk

guise a false appearance

gulli (gulley) a channel or ravine worn in the earth by water, may serve as a drain for storm water

halt to stop

handicapped (*adjective*) having a disability of body or mind that results in difficulty or disadvantage

haphazard by chance

harass to annoy repeatedly

harbor (*verb*) to give shelter to

hard knocks difficulties and disappointments from which a person can learn

hardware mechanical electronic or computer parts, as opposed to software

harried worried

headmistress the female principal of a school, usually a boarding school

heap to pile up

heat shield on a space shuttle, the surface parts designed to protect the shuttle from the intense heat upon reentry into the earth's atmosphere

heed to listen to or consider

henna a red-brown dye used for the hair and skin

hereditary that which can biologically be passed down from parents to children

heritage the property one may inherit or those traditions passed down from previous generations

hesitate to hold back from acting or doing something

high profile very well known or widely publicized

Himalayas high mountains in southern Asia, running through Pakistan, India, Tibet, and other countries

Hirohito [Kirohito] emperor of Japan during World War II

Hitler, Adolf Nazi leader of Germany before and during World War II

hoard to save things, often secretly

hold to keep something

honeymoon the trip a young couple takes immediately after their wedding

honor to hold in high respect

hop to move forward in a walking motion, using only one foot

horoscope a description of one's character and future based on the position of the stars

horrify to cause to react with shock

hospitable friendly and welcoming toward visitors

hot line a telephone answering service using experts to answer questions or counsel a distressed person

hum (*verb*) to make a low sound like the "m" sound, with the lips closed; to make a buzzing noise, such as made by an insect or electronic equipment

humble not openly proud; unassuming

hunched over sitting with the shoulders rounded forward

hydra a freshwater creature with a long, round body and a hole surrounded by long, snakelike limbs

hygiene behaviors used to clean the body

hypnotic bringing the mind close to a sleeplike state

hysterical extremely upset; laughing uncontrollably

idealize to think of as perfect

identify (with) to think that one has similar ideas or feelings to another

identity the personal characteristics of an individual

ideology a set of (economic or political) beliefs

idiosyncratic possessing a characteristic peculiar to a certain group or individual

idol an image one worships like a god

ignites becomes set on fire

ignorant lacking knowledge

ignore to not pay attention to

illustrate to provide pictures of a subject

immensity very great size

immobilized made unable to move

impact the influence or effect of

impervious unable to be penetrated

import to bring in from outside (the country)

impress to make a good impression on others

impression an image or feeling resulting from experience

improvise to do or make something (when one is unprepared) with only available materials

impulsive done without thinking first

incense a substance that is sweet-smelling when burned

incomprehensible unable to be understood

independent thinking and taking action for oneself

indicate to show or signal; to say or suggest

individualist an independent person whose characteristics and ideas set him/her apart

individuality the qualities that make one different

indulge to give in to someone's desires

inexhaustible unable to be used up

infant a young baby, before the age of walking

infidelity the act of being unfaithful or disloyal to (usually refers to adultery)

infinite without end or limit

influential capable of affecting thoughts or actions; powerful

inform to give someone an understanding of

infringement going against (one's rights)

infusion a mixture of something poured into a liquid

ingenious very clever or inventive

inherit to receive something from one who has died

initial at the beginning of

initiate to begin

initiation a ceremony (often with instruction) to mark the entry of a person into a group

initiative the motivation to begin an action

insist to strongly order something be done

insistent repeatedly, firmly declaring

install to set up

instill to put into (one's mind or heart)

instinctively resulting from a natural tendency to do something

institution an organization, often public

intellectual of the mind or reason, as opposed to the emotions

interactive acting on each other; two-way electronic communication

interfere to get involved in something where one is not wanted

interminable endless

intervention the act of coming between two things, usually opposing groups or individuals

intolerable that which one cannot accept or bear

invasion the act of moving in on and attacking

inventory (*verb*) to make a list of

investigate to search for the facts about

investment the act of putting money into property or stocks, for example, to receive financial gain

invisible not able to be seen

involve to make a connection with

invulnerable not able to be attacked

ionic diffusion the spreading out of electrically charged atoms

irascible quick to anger

iridescent showing changing colors in light

irrepressible unable to be restrained or controlled

irrevocably unable to be changed

irritate to make slightly angry

Islam the Muslim religion

isolated apart from the group

itinerant moving often from one place to another

jerking moving abruptly

Jinnah, Muhammad Ali Muslim first leader of Pakistan

junk materials that are of little value—could be thrown away; a Chinese boat

karate the Japanese martial art or sport that uses sharp blows with the limbs

karma in Hinduism and Buddhism, the way one's actions in this life will affect one's afterlife or succeeding lives

kemise (chemise) a long, loose shirt or smock

kinsman a relative

kneel to bend down and rest on one's knees

lag to fall behind

Lake Malawi a lake in southeastern Africa, in the country of Malawi. It was discovered by the explorer David Livingston.

lance (*noun*) a sharp, spearlike weapon

lance (*verb*) in surgery, to cut into

land mine an explosive device put in the ground

largess great generosity

lash (*verb*) to strike with a whip; to tie down with ropes

last straw a difficulty that finally makes something unbearable

latter the second of two things mentioned previously

launch to set in motion

lavatory a room equipped as a toilet

lavish (*verb*) to give abundantly or generously

lavishly given very generously

layout the arrangement of parts, such as on a page or in a room

leak (*verb*) to pass through an opening, usually by mistake, as with water or gas

leap to jump into the air or to jump over

legend an old story about people or events long ago

legitimate lawful or acceptable

lenient not giving hard punishment

lens the round tissue in the eye that focuses light

lessen to reduce

lexicon a dictionary

liaison one who forms a connection between two groups of people

liberal given freely or generously; in politics, supporting some change or reform

lifeline a rope or lifesaving device thrown from a ship to a person struggling in the water

literate able to write and read

littoral (*noun*) coastal area

locate to find

log (*verb*) to write down, keep track of

lorry a truck (British)

low profile acting in a way that will not draw attention to oneself

lug (*verb*) to carry, especially heavy objects

lunatic a disparaging word for a foolish or mentally ill person

lustrous shiny or radiant

luxury a very expensive item or condition that provides great comfort

macrobiotics a restricted diet said to promote health and well-being

magnet piece of metal that draws other metal toward it

magnificent wonderfully grand, glorious

maintain to continue

male and female plugs electrical connectors made to fit into opposite types of connections

malign to say bad things about

malignity a feeling of strong hatred

Mandarin a dialect of the Chinese language

manioc a tropical plant with an edible root

manipulate to control with the hands; to manage or control for one's own benefit

mantelpiece the wood frame around a fireplace

manual labor work that is physically hard

manuscript the typed draft of a work

marksman a person who is accurate at shooting a gun or rifle

marvelously with great wonder or pleasure

match a competition

materials science a field within science and engineering concerned with the study of materials, their properties, composition, and use

mating the joining of male and female animals for producing offspring

matter-of-factly behaving as though something is real or factual

Mecca the center of Islamic religion (Saudi Arabia)

medium a means/channel through which something can pass

medusa the tentacled, free-swimming stage in the life of a type of ocean animal, such as jellyfish or coral

melody a tune in a musical piece

membrane a layer of tissue on the surface of an animal or plant

mercy forgiveness and kindness

merge to combine in order to become a single thing

meritocracy a system in which those of highest ability have the highest place

microgravity the reduction or absence of gravity. In an environment with reduced gravity (such as spaceships), scientists carry out experiments in which they study the effects of reduced gravity on materials and living things.

middle echelon the middle level of people in a group or organization—not workers or the executives

minimize to reduce to the smallest degree

minnow a very small fish that lives in fresh water

miraculously done by seemingly impossible action

miscreant person who does evil or bad things

misgivings feelings of doubt

missionary a person who comes from a foreign country to teach religion

moist somewhat wet

molar one of the large grinding teeth in the back of the mouth

molecular biology the field of biology in which the physics and chemistry of molecules of the subject are studied

monitor to check on through the course of events

monster a large, scary, often imaginary, creature

monstrous very shocking or bad; unusually large or strange

monument a building, tower, or sculpture created in remembrance of someone or something

moor (*verb*) to fasten (a boat or ship) to land or to the bottom of a lake or ocean (with an anchor)

mortar a bowl in which material is crushed

mosque a house of worship for Muslims

motionless without movement

motto a short sentence that expresses an ideal or principle

moustache a growth of hair, usually trimmed, above the lips

Mozambique Channel the waterway that separates Madagascar and Mozambique in southeast Africa

mug to attack and beat up someone in order to rob

Murrow, Edward R. an American radio/television broadcaster, famous for descriptions of German bombing of London during World War II

mute silent

myth an old story about a natural or historical event

nag (*verb*) to repeatedly scold someone or complain about something

nagging (*adjective*) worrying or annoying

nauseous feeling sick in the stomach, often with a foggy feeling in the head

needlefish fish that have thin bodies and narrow jaws

negotiate to work out an agreement

niche situation that is very well suited for one

nod to raise and lower the head, showing agreement

norm that which is within the range of culturally accepted behavior

North Eleuthera northern part of Eleuthera Island in the Bahamas

nurture to care for something as it develops

oars long, thin pieces of wood with a rounded end used to move a boat through the water

objective (*adjective*) having to do with an actual thing, not an idea or belief

objective (*noun*) a goal

obligation duty; that which is necessary

oblige make necessary

obligingly willingly

obstinate refusing to change

obstruction a barrier or obstacle that gets in the way

obverse opposite

obviously easily or clearly seen

occupation job

occupiers those who maintain control of an area as a result of military conquest

occur (*verb*) to happen

off limits forbidden

old maid an older woman who has never married

omit to leave out

omnivore an animal that eats other animals and plants

on board having joined with a group in the pursuit of something

opalescent softly shining or glimmering with colors

ophthalmologist a doctor who examines and treats the eyes

opportunity a favorable time/occasion to do something

option one of several choices

oral spoken rather than written

orbit the path of a planet or other body as it circles around another object in space

ordeal a difficult experience

orphanage an institution where orphans (children without parents) live

outhouse an outdoor bathroom or storage building

outlet a box (in a wall) for connecting to an electric power supply

outspoken voicing opinions frankly and without reserve

outstrip to leave behind or go past

overboard over the side of the ship

overwhelming overpowering

paganism the beliefs of those who do not believe in one of the major world religions (Christianity, Judaism, Islam, Hinduism)

pakora a dish of vegetables, fried in butter

palm the inside surface of the hand from the wrist to the base of the fingers

parachute a circular piece of material fastened by ropes to a person or object in order to slow the fall to earth from a plane or other great height

paradise an imaginary place of heavenly beauty and perfection

paramecia tiny, oval creatures (protozoans)

paralysis the state of not being able to move

participate to join in an activity

paschal concerning the holidays of Passover and Easter

passion a great, strong feeling

passive not responding when acted upon

pay dirt something useful or profitable

payload the cargo of an airplane or spacecraft

peasant a person of the class of workers, such as small farmers and laborers, in agriculture

pedigree a line of ancestors (those who came before in one's family)

peek to take a short look at

pelagic having to do with living in the open seas, not in inland water

pellet a small ball to be shot or fired from a gun

penetrate to enter into

perch (*verb*) to sit on top of, such as on a branch or wall

perchlike   similar to a perch, a small freshwater fish

perdition   a place of eternal damnation (commonly known as Hell)

perish   to die

permanently   lasting always, without change

permissive   not exercising discipline

perpetuate   to cause to exist for a long time

persimmon   a soft, orange fruit

persist   continue, despite opposition

petition   a document asking for something from those with power to give it

petty   small or unimportant

phobia   a strong, abnormal fear of a thing or a situation

physiological   having to do with physiology (the science of all the important functions of a living organism)

pierce   to cut into or through with a sharp instrument, such as a knife

pillion   second person, behind the driver

pilings   heavy beams of wood, concrete, or steel, driven into the ground as support for a structure

pinfish   a small fish with a spine and fins

pioneer (*verb*)   to be the first in developing something

pious   observing the practices of a religion with great seriousness

pitch (*verb*)   to throw or toss

pitch (*noun*)   the highness or lowness of a musical note or voice

pitcher   (baseball) the team player who throws the ball to the batter (hitter)

pivotal   important or central

plagued   being afflicted with a repeated action or condition

plank   a heavy board made of wood

plantain   a large tropical fruit resembling a banana

platter   a large, flat plate

plot   to make plans (esp. secretly)

plow   to turn over (farmland) with a cutting tool

policy   a plan of action or procedure created by an organization, such as a business or government

polymerase chain reaction   a chemical test that can amplify and identify DNA in even a small bit of material containing human cells

porcelain   very thin, fine pottery or china

portable   light enough to be picked up and carried from place to place

Portuguese man-of-war   a large, poisonous jellyfish

poverty   the state of being poor (with little money)

precedence   the right to go before because of rank

prediction   the act of saying what will happen in the future

prefer   to desire one option above others

prenuptial   coming before marriage

presuppose   to assume to be true in advance

prevail   to win

prime (*adjective*)   most important

prime (*noun*)   time of highest perfection

primitive   from the earliest stages of development

procedure   a way of performing or carrying out the steps in a process

proceed   to go ahead or forward; to continue

procrastinate   to delay doing something

prod   to push with an object or finger

profession   form of employment, especially after education or training

professor   a highly ranked college teacher

proffer   to offer

profound   deep; strongly felt

progress (*verb*)   to move forward; advance

proliferation   spread in great numbers

prominent   very easily noticeable; widely known

promote   to bring to people's notice in order to sell

prompt (*verb*)   to cause to act

propel   to cause to move

propitious   favorable

proportionality   that which makes something properly related in size to other parts

propose to suggest something; to offer to marry someone

proposition a plan that is put forward for acceptance; a sexual overture

prosperous successful and rich

protest (*noun*) speech or action showing that one is against something or objects to something

proverbs short, wise sayings

provision preparation for risks in the future

proviso part of a document that makes a condition necessary for acceptance or agreement

proximity nearness to something

psychology the study of thinking processes, behavior, and emotions

pulp matter that is spongy and soft, such as the moist part of fruit

pulsate to shake regularly

pulverize to grind into powder

pupil the black circle in the middle of the eye; a student

purport (*verb*) claim to be

purporting appearing to be

pursue to follow in order to capture

pursuit an activity; the act of following or going after

qualify to reach the required standards for something

quartet a piece of music for four instruments; a group of four

quotation exact words or phrases taken from a written work or speech

radiate to spread out in all directions from the center of a circular shape

raid to attack quickly

rally to bring or come together for one purpose

rapport sharing a relationship of trust and of similar feelings

ray a marine fish that has a flat body and tiny fins

reaction that which is done in response to something else

reality the state of actuality or truth

realize to understand completely

rear at the back of

rebel (*verb*) to act in opposition to an authority

rebel (*noun*) a person who opposes authority

recall to remember

recesses hidden, often secret, places

recoil to draw back quickly

recoup to get back

recreational done for play or fun

recruit to bring in or sign up new members

red flag a warning

reed whistle a long, round musical instrument made of grassy plants

refer to to direct attention to

reflective thoughtful

refugee a person who has to leave his or her country because of politics or war

regal looking or sounding like a king or queen

register (*verb*) to make an official record of

register (*noun*) the range of sound, from high to low

rejoin reply sharply

relief the state of being freed from pain or discomfort

rely on to depend on another person for support

remold to make again, in a new shape

remote distant in time, space, or feeling

render to give or make available; interpret artistically

repent to say one is sorry for something

repress to hold back, such as feelings

reprimand to scold or show disapproval of

reproach (*noun*) blame or criticism

research the search for facts or information about something

residential containing homes, not businesses

resigned the feeling of having given in to something or accepted something

resist to oppose

resourcefulness ability to find ways of doing things in difficult situations

respond to answer to

restraint the control of one's feelings or expressions

restriction a limitation upon

resume to begin again

retire to stop working due to advanced age

retort   to answer quickly or rudely

retrieve   to find and take back

reveal   to make known

revelation   something that is discovered

revert (to)   to go back to (something negative)

revolver   a handgun

rheumy-eyed   having eyes filled with watery mucus

rhododendron   a large bush with bright red/pink flowers

rhythmic   consisting of movement or sound occurring regularly, with long and short alternating

ridiculous   laughable

rigors   difficult conditions

riot   a wild disturbance or uncontrolled outbreak

ritual   a repeated, customary set of actions

role model   a person whose behavior others will copy

rotifer   a tiny, multi-celled creature having at one end a wheel-like ring of hairlike projections

rumblings   deep rolling sounds; at the beginnings of social disruption

rustle   a soft sound like dry leaves touching one another

sacred   of a religious nature

sacrifice   (*verb*)   to give up something (esp. for a good purpose)

saga   a very long and dramatic story

saint   a person recognized as holy

salamander   small, lizardlike animal, living on land and in water

salwar   (shalwar)   a loose trouser worn by both sexes

sample   to try a small portion of

sanatorium   a hospital for long-term treatment

sari   long, loose dress for women in India and Pakistan—consists of a length of cloth wrapped around the body and then over the shoulder or head

savage   wild or beastlike

scalpel   a small, sharp knife used in surgery

scan   to read or look quickly over

scarce   difficult to find

scarcely   hardly

scarred   marked with scars (marks from wounds)

scathing   very severe, often harmful or damaging

scholar   a person of great knowledge who studies a subject

scholarship   money given to pay school expenses

scold   to harshly find fault with

scoot   to move quickly

Scotland Yard   London, England's Metropolitan Police

scramble   to move quickly, often on one's hands and feet; to mix together

scribble   to write quickly (making it hard to read)

scrounge   to gather or get things without spending much (or any) money

scrub   to clean thoroughly, with hard, heavy strokes

scuba diving   swimming underwater, using a tank of compressed air for breathing

scummy   covered on the surface with an unpleasant material

scuttle   to sink a ship by cutting holes in it; to rush, with short steps

sea nettle   a stinging jellyfish

sear   to quickly burn the surface of with high heat

secession   the breaking away of one (group/country) from another

seclude   to hide away

secular   that which does not have to do with the religious or spiritual

seek   to try to find

segregate   to separate from the group, often by race, class, or gender

seldom   not often

seminar   a small academic class for advanced students

sentiment   a view or idea

session   a meeting

setback   something that temporarily stops progress

severity   hardness or seriousness

shallow   not deep

shark   a large ocean fish with sharp teeth that is dangerous to humans

shiver   a feeling of slight shaking, with cold or fear

shorthand   a system of signs and letters used to write something down quickly (esp. in business)

shrug   (*verb*)   to raise the shoulders to show doubt

sidetrack to move something away from the course or path it is proceeding on

silica fibers fibers made of silica, a white, crystalline substance occurring naturally in sand and other minerals

silicaceous (siliceous) like a silicate, a material in rocks (quartz, sandstone, etc.) used in making glass and brick

silt particles of material, in size between clay and sand, carried in water

simulate to make to look like or perform like the real thing

sincerity the quality of being honest

site place

sizzle to make a hissing, popping sound, like that of frying

skeleton the internal, supporting bones and cartilage of an organism

sketch to make a quick picture of or to quickly tell the high points of a story

skewer a long wood or metal pin used to hold meat over a fire for cooking

skillet frying pan

skipper the captain/leader of a ship

skulk to hide or move secretly

slang very informal speech (esp. impolite)

slap to hit quickly with the hand

slaughter to kill (an animal) for meat

sleeve the part of a garment covering the arm

slimy being similar to or covered with slime, a slippery liquid

snack a small amount of food eaten between meals

snag to quickly catch, sometimes with a small, sharp part of something

sniff to cry; to draw air into the nose, making a noise—often a gesture of disrespect

snub rude treatment

sob to cry with great sadness

sociology the study of groups in society

socket an opening, often for screwing a light bulb into

sodium beta aluminum battery a battery designed with special materials that can withstand extreme temperatures

sojourn a brief stay

solemn very serious

solution the answer to a problem

sombre serious and sad

source the place something comes from

spare extra

spark a small, lit piece of material thrown off from a fire or burning substance

spawn to lay eggs or to produce

species a scientifically defined group of animals or plants that have important similarities and that can breed together

specify to state very clearly and precisely

spectacle a public event or display

spell (*verb*) to give someone temporary relief from work

spell (*noun*) a condition caused by seemingly magical powers

spill to run out of a container

spine in animals, the bones down the middle of the back; a stiff, pointed part of an animal or plant

spinner bait that turns when pulled through the water; used by fishermen

spinsterhood the state of a female remaining unmarried

spirit away to take away secretly

splicer a machine that joins two pieces of tape

splinter a sharp, thin piece

sponsor a person responsible for another

spool a plastic or wooden object, shaped like a wheel, which tape or thread can be wound around

spouse the person one is married to (husband or wife)

sprawl (*verb*) to lie with the limbs spreading out; to spread out over a wide area

spurn to refuse or reject

squid an ocean creature with ten arms and a soft body

squirm to twist with discomfort or embarrassment

standard usual

starve made to do without food

stationery writing paper

stature the height of a person; the level of admiration a person has achieved

status   a person's position in society relative to others

stentors   tiny, trumpet-shaped creatures

stereoscopy   the viewing of things three-dimensionally (with height and distance)

sterile   unable to reproduce; free from germs

stern   firm and severe

stingray   a sea animal with a tail like a whip, capable of causing great harm to its victims

stingy   not wanting to give something (especially money)

stint   period of time, usually short, spent doing a task

stir   to mix with a circular motion

stirrings   disturbances or commotions

stoicism   the act of being patient/courageous while suffering

stock (*noun*)   the store of supplies on hand; livestock, such as cows or sheep

stoke   to build up or fill with fuel (a fire)

strand   the land or beach bordering a body of water

streak (*verb*)   to mark with a stripe; to move very swiftly

stretch   to make wider or longer by pulling; a period of time

strict   exact; kept to very narrow limits

stride (take in stride)   to accept something unpleasant without reacting negatively

strive (for)   to try hard for

strike   to hit sharply or hard; to pull on a fishing rod in order to set the hook

stroll   to walk leisurely

struck   past tense of strike (to hit sharply)

stun   to fill with shock and surprise

stupendous   of very great force or degree; amazing

subjugation   the act of forcing obedience

submerge   to make go under or hide

subsequent   coming after; later

subservience   condition of being obedient to others

subside   to settle down or sink; to be less active

substantial   solid; wealthy

subtle   not easily noticeable or obvious

succession   following one after another

suffering   physical pain and/or painful feelings

sufficiently   enough; adequately

suffocate   to cut off the air supply and thus kill or severely damage

summon   to call together or call to mind

superorganism   a group of animals joined so as to function as one

superstition   a belief not based on reason or fact

supervise   to watch over

surf   the wave action along a shore

surgery   a medical operation, cutting into the patient to take care of disease or injury

survey (*verb*)   to look over or review

survive   to continue to live

svelte   very slim (thin) and graceful

sway   swinging motion

swell   high, rolling movement of the ocean

swirl   to spin around in a circle

synonymous   meaning the same thing

tactfully   carefully and politely

take in stride   to accept (easily) something difficult

take stock   to look over one's situation or a set of items

talisman   an object thought to have magic powers

Talking Books   records or tapes of books read aloud for the benefit of blind people

tangle   to twist or entwine together into a confused mass

task   a piece of work or a job

tattered   torn and old

taut   lean, muscular

teleplay   a play written for television

temperament   one's regular ways of thinking and feeling (such as happy, sad, nervous, etc.)

tendency   a way one is likely to think or act

tense   stretched tightly

tentacles   the long limbs on certain sea animals

terminals   individual computers

terrifying   extremely frightful

thermal insulation   material used to keep heat from moving in or out

thrown overboard   rejected as useless

thrust   a driving force, such as the forward movement of an engine caused by the rearward release of fuel gases

thumbs-up sign   a hand signal using one or two thumbs pointing upward to show approval

thump   to walk heavily, making loud sounds

tier   several levels of something, one above/behind another

tilt   to lean or slope to one side

tinged   having a slight trace of color

tinker   a traveling worker who fixes pots and pans

tissue   in biology, a group of cells that are alike and may be seen as a group

toddler   a baby at the age of first walking

toe the line   to obey the given rules very strictly

toil   to work long and hard

torpedo   a cylindrical weapon released under water against an enemy

torture   (*verb*) to cause a person great pain, often to get information

traditional   having to do with beliefs/ideas passed down from generation to generation

tragedy   an event that has disastrous, terrible results

trail   (*verb*) to stream or drag out from behind

trailblaze   to be a leader or pioneer who makes a path into a new area

transfiguration   a beautiful change

transform   (*verb*) change completely

transition   a period of change from one thing to another

transmit   to pass from one thing to another or cause to spread

transparent   a material that light can pass through, that one can see through

transport   (*verb*) to move from one place to another

traumatic   very shocking to the emotions

trial run   a test of something to see if it works

trios   groups of three

triumphantly   with great pride

trust   a feeling of confidence or belief in something

tugboat   a small boat that pulls large boats in and out of a harbor

turbine blades   the blades (like those on a fan) within a type of engine in which steam, water, gas, or air is made to spin on a rotating middle stem in order to produce power

ulema   religious leaders in the Muslim religion

ultimate   final or highest

ultraviolet light   the light that is beyond the range of visible purple light in the wide range of colors that can be seen by humans

ululations   loud wailings

unable   not having the ability or power to do something

undaunted   not discouraged or without fear

undergo   to experience

undermass   the tissue on the bottom or underside of an organism

undermine   to remove the underlying supports from

uninhibited   free to act or feel without considering what others will think

unite   to join together

unpredictable   not expected

unravel   to undo the threads in a fabric; to clear up a mystery

unresolved   awaiting a decision

unswerving   staying firm and not changing; keeping to the path or course given

untutored   unschooled or without education

unwarranted   without reason

uppermost   at the highest level or position

upstanding   thought to be responsible and honest

urine   a liquid body waste

utopia   an imaginary, perfect society

vacuum   an empty area in time, space, or feeling

vague   not distinct, clear, or definite

vainly without success

valedictorian the student with the highest grades who gives a speech at graduation

vantage point a place that gives a clear, wide view of things

vast very large and great; often empty

veil (*noun*) a garment covering the face or entire head

veil (*verb*) to hide

venerate to show someone great respect

venture course of action (business)

venture out to go out bravely; to extend one's limits

veranda a long, wide porch attached to a house

veritable true or real

veterinary (*adjective*) having to do with animal medicine

vigorous very energetic and lively

virtually very nearly or almost

virtuosity very high skill in performing

vital necessary or of great importance

vitrifaction the act of making glass with heat

voluntarily done by one's choice, often without expectation of payment

volvox a tiny creature with an arm like a whip

voracious being very eager to consume or eat food or to do an activity

wade to walk through shallow water

wayfarer a person traveling on foot

weld to use high heat to join two metals

welfare help for poor people

well-tended (*adjective*) well taken care of or groomed

well-to-do wealthy

wharf (pl. wharves) a dock or landing place where ships and boats can land and tie up

whiff a short, quick smell

whim a brief or sudden idea, often not serious or reasonable

white cliffs of Dover the pale white, steep rock faces of the land on the southeastern coast of England

whittle to make by cutting small pieces out of wood

widespread occurring on a large scale

wiggle to move back and forth

wink to close one eye briefly, giving a message or signal

wisely done with wisdom or good sense

wrestle to grab and try to throw over another person

wretched miserable or extremely unhappy; unskilled

wriggle to twist and turn the body while in one spot or while moving along

writ a legal paper

xiuxi rest time

yank to pull something back quickly, with a jerk

Yiddish language spoken by Jews (esp. Eastern Europe)

zealot one who is unreasonably or fanatically committed to an idea, cause, or religion

zoology in biology, the study of animals

Writer _____

Responder(s) _____

_____

_____

1. *Central Point:* Is the paragraph unified around one central idea that is clear to the reader? _____

What is the central idea? _____

_____

_____

_____

Suggestions: _____

_____

_____

_____

2. *Details:* Does the writer use enough concrete, specific details in describing the object to give the reader a sharp, clear picture of the possession? Explain.

_____

_____

_____

What details do you find especially vivid and appealing? _____

_____

_____

_____

Suggestions: _____

_____

_____

_____

3. *Explanation:* Does the writer explain to the reader why the possession is special to him or her (why it is "prized" or "treasured")? Can you summarize this explanation in your own words? _____

_____

_____

Does the writer need to explain more to the reader or make the explanation clearer? Why or why not? _____

_____

_____

_____

Suggestions: _____

_____

_____

_____

PEER RESPONSE SHEET FOR ACTIVITY 2.5
Writing about a Special Place

Writer _____

Responder(s) _____

_____

_____

1. *Central Point*: What is the central point the writer is making about the special place being described? _____

_____

_____

_____

Does the writer make the central point clear to you, either by directly explaining and analyzing or by suggesting it? Explain. _____

_____

_____

Suggestions: _____

_____

_____

_____

2. *Specific Details:* Does the writer use enough specific and concrete details to bring to your mind a clear, sharp picture of the special place? Explain.

_____

_____

_____

Which details do you think are the most vivid and appealing? _____

_____

Which are the least vivid? _____

_____

Do all the details work together to convey the writer's central point, or do some of them distract from the central point? _____

_____

_____

Suggestions: _____

_____

_____

Writing about a Favorite Activity or Hobby

Writer _____

Responder(s) _____

_____

_____

1. *Topic Sentence:* Does the paragraph have a clear topic sentence near the beginning that announces the point—the favorite hobby or activity? _____ If not, is the point of the paragraph still made clear? _____

_____

_____

Suggestions: _____

_____

_____

Does the topic sentence answer the controlling question of the writing assignment? Explain. _____

_____

_____

2. *Evidence:* Does the paragraph have enough specific evidence (details, facts, specific examples, or quotations) to give the reader a clear, sharp picture of the favorite hobby or activity? Why or why not? _____

_____

_____

Suggestions: _____

_____

_____

3. *Analysis:* Does the paragraph have enough analysis to explain the evidence? In other words, does the writer explain how and why the activity or hobby is a favorite? Why or why not? _____

_____

Suggestions: _____

_____

_____

PEER RESPONSE SHEET FOR ACTIVITY 4.5
Writing about a Custom

Writer _____

Responder(s) _____

_____

_____

1. *Topic Sentence:* Does the writer announce the central point in a topic sentence near the beginning of the paragraph? Is it clear from the topic sentence what the custom is and who practices it? _____

_____

_____

Suggestions: _____

_____

_____

2. *Evidence:* Does the writer present enough specific, concrete evidence to give the reader a sharp, visual picture of the custom? Explain.

_____

_____

Suggestions: _____

_____

_____

3. *Analysis:* Does the writer analyze the evidence? _____

If so, which one or two of the following questions does the writer answer in analyzing the custom?

    a. Who practices this custom?
    b. How is the custom practiced?
    c. What is the origin of the custom?
    d. Why do people practice the custom?
    e. How important is the custom to these people?

Suggestions: _____

_____

Writer _____

Responder(s) _____

_____

_____

1. *Topic Sentence:* Does the writer clearly announce the central point—the one reason for choosing his or her major or field of study—in a topic sentence near the beginning of the paragraph? Explain. _____

_____

_____

Suggestions: _____

_____

_____

2. *Evidence:* Does the writer include enough specific, concrete evidence for this reason? Why or why not? _____

_____

_____

Suggestions: _____

_____

_____

3. *Analysis:* How does the writer make the paragraph's cause-and-effect logic clear? That is, how does the paragraph explain the connection between the cause (the reason) and the effect (choosing the major or field of study)? _____

_____

_____

Suggestions: _____

_____

_____

PEER RESPONSE SHEET FOR ACTIVITY 6.3
Writing about a Family or Cultural Value

Writer _____

Responder(s) _____

_____

_____

1. *Topic Sentence:* Does the writer give you a clear idea of what the value is? Or, does the writer need to further define the value? Explain. _____

_____

_____

Suggestions: _____

_____

_____

2. *Evidence:* Does the writer present enough specific evidence to give you a clear, sharp picture of the value? Or, does the writer need to use more specific detail in the evidence? Explain. _____

_____

_____

Suggestions: _____

_____

_____

3. *Analysis:* Does the writer thoroughly analyze the value, explaining in a convincing manner why he or she rejects or accepts it? Why or why not?

_____

_____

_____

Suggestions: _____

_____

_____

PEER RESPONSE SHEET FOR ACTIVITY 7.2
Writing about a Decision: Thesis, Plan,
and First Body Paragraph

Writer _____

Responder(s) _____

_____

_____

THESIS AND PLAN

1. *Thesis Statement:* Does the thesis state the overall main idea of the essay? That is, does it answer the writer's controlling question? How do you know?

_____

_____

_____

Suggestions: _____

_____

_____

2. *Subpoints of the Thesis or Plan:* Are the subpoints of the essay (the causes or effects of the decision) made clear in the thesis or plan? Explain.

_____

_____

Suggestions: _____

_____

_____

FIRST BODY PARAGRAPH

1. *Topic Sentence:* Does the topic sentence clearly announce the subpoint of the first body paragraph? Explain. _____

_____

_____

Suggestions: _____

_____

_____

2. *Cause-and-Effect Logic:* Does the paragraph present enough specific evidence as well as thorough analysis to convince the reader that the reason led to the decision or that the effect resulted from the decision? Explain.

_____

_____

If not, what evidence and/or analysis does the writer need to add?

_____

_____

Suggestions: _____

_____

_____

Writing about a Decision: The Other Body Paragraphs

Writer _____

Responder(s) _____

_____

_____

SECOND BODY PARAGRAPH

1. *Topic Sentence:* Does the topic sentence clearly state the subpoint of the second body paragraph? _____

Does it contain a transition linking it to the previous paragraph?

_____

Suggestions: _____

_____

_____

2. *Cause-and-Effect Logic:* Does the paragraph contain enough specific evidence and analysis to develop the cause-and-effect logic? Why or why not?

_____

_____

Suggestions: _____

_____

_____

THIRD BODY PARAGRAPH

1. *Topic Sentence:* Does the topic sentence clearly state the subpoint of the third body paragraph? _____

Does it contain a transition linking it to the previous paragraph?

_____

Suggestions: _____

_____

_____

2. *Cause-and-Effect Logic:* Does the paragraph contain enough specific evidence and analysis to develop the cause-and-effect logic? Why or why not?

_____

_____

Suggestions: _____

_____

_____

Writing about the Value of an Ethnic Studies Course:
The Opening and First Body Paragraphs

Writer _____

Responder(s) _____

_____

_____

OPENING PARAGRAPH

1. *Generating Interest:* Does the opening paragraph capture the reader's attention? What technique does the writer use to get the reader interested?

_____

_____

Does the opening paragraph let the reader know the subject of the essay?
Explain. _____

_____

Suggestions: _____

_____

_____

2. *Thesis:* Does the thesis directly answer the writer's controlling question?
Does it also tell the reader the main idea of the essay? If the thesis includes
subpoints, are they clear and distinct, or do they overlap? _____

_____

_____

_____

Suggestions: _____

_____

_____

3. *Coherence:* Does the opening paragraph have smooth coherence, especially from the opening sentences to the thesis? Does the writer need to provide a link between the opening sentences and the thesis? Why or why not?

_____

Suggestions: _____

_____

_____

FIRST BODY PARAGRAPH

1. *Subpoint:* Is the subpoint of the first body paragraph clearly focused in a topic sentence? Why or why not? _____

_____

_____

_____

2. *Evidence:* Does the paragraph include enough specific evidence to support the subpoint? Why or why not? _____

_____

_____

_____

3. *Analysis:* Does the writer analyze the evidence by explaining why or how students' knowledge of the culture will be valuable to them? _____

_____

_____

Suggestions: _____

_____

_____

Writing about the Value of an Ethnic Studies Course:
The Other Body Paragraphs

Writer _____

Responder(s) _____

_____

_____

SECOND BODY PARAGRAPH

1. *Subpoint:* Is the subpoint of the second body paragraph clearly focused in a topic sentence? Does the topic sentence have a transition? Why or why not? _____

_____

_____

2. *Evidence:* Does the paragraph include enough specific evidence to support the subpoint? Why or why not? _____

_____

_____

_____

3. *Analysis:* Does the writer analyze the evidence by explaining how or why students' knowledge of the culture will be valuable to them? _____

_____

_____

Suggestions: _____

_____

_____

THIRD BODY PARAGRAPH

1. *Subpoint:* Is the subpoint of the third body paragraph clearly focused in a topic sentence? Does the topic sentence have a transition? Why or why not? _____

_____

_____

2. *Evidence:* Does the paragraph include enough specific evidence to support the subpoint? Why or why not? _____

_____

_____

_____

3. *Analysis:* Does the writer analyze the evidence by explaining how or why students' knowledge of the culture will be valuable to them? _____

_____

_____

Suggestions: _____

_____

_____

Writer _____

Responder(s) _____

_____

_____

1. *Controlling Question:* Is the writer's controlling question clear? Why or why not? _____

_____

_____

Suggestions: _____

_____

_____

2. *Thesis Statement:* Does the thesis statement directly answer the writer's controlling question? Explain. _____

_____

_____

Does the thesis make clear the approach the writer is taking to the topic?

_____

_____

Is the overall main idea of the essay made clear in the thesis? Explain.

_____

_____

Suggestions: _____

_____

_____

3. *Subpoints:* Is each subpoint clear? Why or why not? _____

_____

_____

Are any of the subpoints too narrow or too broad? Explain. _____

_____

_____

Is each subpoint distinct from the others or do some overlap? _____

_____

_____

Are the subpoints emphatically ordered, with the most important one appearing last? _____

_____

_____

Suggestions: _____

_____

_____

Writing about Overcoming the Odds:
The Opening and First Body Paragraphs

Writer _____

Responder(s) _____

_____

_____

OPENING PARAGRAPH

1. *Generating Interest:* Does the opening paragraph capture the reader's attention? What technique does the writer use to get the reader interested?

_____

_____

_____

Does the opening paragraph let the reader know the subject of the essay—the odds the writer had to overcome? Explain. _____

_____

_____

Suggestions: _____

_____

_____

2. *Thesis:* Does the thesis directly answer the writer's controlling question? Does it also tell the reader the main idea of the essay and the writer's approach to the topic? _____

_____

_____

If subpoints are included in the thesis, are they clear and distinct or do they overlap? _____

_____

_____

356

Suggestions: _____

_____

_____

3. *Coherence:* Does the opening paragraph have smooth coherence, especially from the opening sentences to the thesis? Does the writer need to provide a link (such as a transition or a bridging phrase) between the opening sentences and the thesis? Why or why not? _____

_____

_____

Suggestions: _____

_____

_____

FIRST BODY PARAGRAPH

1. *Subpoint:* Is the subpoint of the first body paragraph clearly focused in a topic sentence? Why or why not? _____

_____

_____

_____

2. *Evidence:* Does the paragraph include enough specific evidence to support the subpoint? Explain. _____

_____

_____

3. *Analysis:* Does the writer analyze the evidence by explaining the subpoint of the paragraph? Why or why not? _____

_____

_____

Suggestions: _____

_____

_____

Writing about Overcoming the Odds: The Other Body Paragraphs and Conclusion

Writer _____

Responder(s) _____

_____

_____

SECOND BODY PARAGRAPH

1. *Subpoint:* Is the subpoint of the second body paragraph clearly focused in a topic sentence? Does the topic sentence include a transition? Explain.

_____

_____

2. *Evidence:* Does the paragraph include enough specific evidence to develop the subpoint? Why or why not? _____

_____

_____

3. *Analysis:* Does the writer analyze the evidence by explaining the subpoint of the paragraph? Explain. _____

_____

_____

Suggestions: _____

_____

_____

THIRD BODY PARAGRAPH

1. *Subpoint:* Is the subpoint of the third body paragraph clearly focused in a topic sentence? Does the topic sentence contain a transition? Explain.

_____

_____

358

2. *Evidence:* Does the paragraph include enough specific evidence to develop the subpoint? Why or why not? _____

_____

_____

_____

3. *Analysis:* Does the writer analyze the evidence by explaining the subpoint of the paragraph? Explain. _____

_____

_____

Suggestions: _____

_____

_____

CONCLUDING PARAGRAPH

1. Does the conclusion reemphasize the main idea of the essay? Or does it simply list the essay's subpoints? Explain. _____

_____

_____

2. Does the writer need to strengthen the conclusion in one of the following ways?

- By discussing the implications of the essay's overall main idea?
- By closing with something specific or vivid?
- By referring back to the opening paragraph? Explain. _____

_____

_____

Suggestions: _____

_____

_____

Writing about the Way Males and Females Are Raised:
Thesis and Plan

Writer _____

Responder(s) _____

_____

_____

1. *Thesis Statement:* Does the thesis make clear what two subjects are being compared or contrasted? Explain. _____

_____

_____

Does the thesis convey the main idea or ideas—that the two subjects are similar or different? Why or why not? _____

_____

_____

Suggestions: _____

_____

2. *Subpoints or Terms of Comparison* (as revealed in the thesis or plan): Is each term of comparison clear? _____

_____

_____

Are any terms of comparison too broad or too narrow? _____

_____

Are the terms of comparison distinct or do some overlap? _____

_____

_____

Suggestions: _____

_____

_____

Writing about the Way Males and Females Are Raised: The First Body Paragraph

Writer _____

Responder(s) _____

_____

_____

FIRST BODY PARAGRAPH

1. *Subpoint:* Does the topic sentence announce the subpoint of the first body paragraph—the two subjects that are similar or different, as well as the term of comparison? Explain. _____

_____

_____

Suggestions: _____

_____

_____

2. *Evidence:* Does the writer present enough specific evidence for the sub-point? _____

_____

Suggestions: _____

_____

_____

3. *Analysis:* Does the writer sufficiently analyze the similarity or difference between the two subjects? Explain. _____

_____

_____

If there is not sufficient analysis, which of the following questions could the writer answer in the analysis and why? _____

_____

- *Why* are males and females different or similar for this term of comparison?
- *How* are males and females different or similar for this term of comparison?
- *What* are the effects of this difference or similarity?
- *Which* gender (male or female) has the "best of the situation" for this term of comparison?

Suggestions: _____

_____

_____

Writing about the Way Males and Females Are Raised:
The Opening, Concluding, and Other Body Paragraphs

Writer _____

Responder(s) _____

_____

_____

SECOND BODY PARAGRAPH

1. *Subpoint:* Does the topic sentence announce the subpoint of the second body paragraph and contain a transition? Explain. _____

_____

_____

Suggestions: _____

_____

_____

2. *Evidence:* Does the writer present enough specific evidence for the subpoint of the paragraph? Why or why not? _____

_____

_____

Suggestions: _____

_____

_____

3. *Analysis:* Does the writer sufficiently analyze the similarity or difference between the two subjects? Why or why not? _____

_____

_____

If not, which of the analysis questions listed on page 255 should the writer answer in the analysis and why? _____

_____

Suggestions: _____

_____

_____

THIRD BODY PARAGRAPH

1. *Subpoint:* Does the topic sentence announce the subpoint of the third body paragraph and contain a transition? Explain. _____

_____

_____

Suggestions: _____

_____

_____

2. *Evidence:* Does the writer present enough specific evidence for the sub-point of the paragraph? Explain. _____

_____

_____

_____

Suggestions: _____

_____

_____

3. *Analysis:* Does the writer sufficiently analyze the similarity or difference between the two subjects? Why or why not? _____

_____

_____

If not, which of the analysis questions listed on page 255 should the writer answer in the analysis and why? _____

_____

_____

Suggestions: _____

_____

OPENING PARAGRAPH

1. *Generating Interest:* Does the opening paragraph capture the reader's attention? What technique does the writer use to get the reader interested?

_____

_____

_____

Does the opening paragraph let the reader know the subject of the essay—male and female upbringings in a certain culture? Explain. _____

_____

_____

_____

Suggestions: _____

_____

2. *Thesis (if not evaluated earlier):* Does the thesis convey the main idea of the essay? Why or why not? _____

_____

_____

If subpoints are included in the thesis, are they clear and distinct or do they overlap? _____

_____

_____

Suggestions: _____

_____

3. *Coherence:* Does the opening paragraph have smooth coherence, especially from the opening sentences to the thesis? Does the writer need to provide a link (such as a transition or a bridging phrase) between the opening sentences and the thesis? Why or why not? _____

_____

Suggestions: _____

CONCLUDING PARAGRAPH

1. Does the conclusion reemphasize the main idea of the essay? Or does it simply list the essay's subpoints? Explain. _____

2. Does the writer need to strengthen the conclusion in one of the following ways?

- By discussing the implications of the essay's overall idea?
- By closing with something specific or vivid?
- By referring back to the opening paragraph? Explain. _____

Suggestions: _____

Writing about Arranged Marriages:
Thesis and Body Paragraphs

Writer _____

Responder(s) _____

_____

_____

THESIS STATEMENT

1. *Controlling Question:* Does the main clause of the thesis statement—the proposition—clearly answer the controlling question of the writing assignment? Why or why not? _____

_____

_____

_____

2. *Subpoints:* Are the subpoints—the reasons for or against arranged marriage—made clear in the thesis? Explain. _____

_____

_____

_____

Suggestions: _____

_____

_____

FIRST BODY PARAGRAPH (CONCESSION)

1. *Subpoint:* Is the subpoint of the first body paragraph clearly focused in a topic sentence? Explain. _____

_____

_____

_____

2. *Evidence:* Does the writer present enough specific evidence to support the subpoint of the paragraph? Why or why not? _____

_____

_____

_____

3. *Analysis:* In analyzing the evidence, does the writer concede to or refute the point? How do you know? _____

_____

_____

_____

Suggestions: _____

_____

_____

SECOND BODY PARAGRAPH
(SUPPORTING MAIN PROPOSITION)

1. *Subpoint:* Is the subpoint of the second body paragraph clearly focused in a topic sentence? Does the topic sentence contain a transition? Explain.

_____

_____

2. *Evidence:* Does the writer present enough specific evidence to support the subpoint of the paragraph? Why or why not? _____

_____

_____

_____

3. *Analysis:* Does the writer analyze the evidence by explaining why it proves the argument stated in the topic sentence? Why or why not?

_____

_____

Suggestions: _____

_____

_____

THIRD BODY PARAGRAPH
(SUPPORTING MAIN PROPOSITION)

1. *Subpoint:* Is the subpoint of the third body paragraph clearly focused in a topic sentence? Does the topic sentence contain a transition? Explain.

_____

_____

2. *Evidence:* Does the writer present enough specific evidence to support the subpoint of the paragraph? Why or why not? _____

_____

_____

_____

3. *Analysis:* Does the writer analyze the evidence by explaining why it proves the argument stated in the topic sentence? Why or why not?

_____

_____

Suggestions: _____

_____

_____

Writing about Arranged Marriages:
Opening and Concluding Paragraphs

Writer _____

Responder(s) _____

_____

_____

OPENING PARAGRAPH

1. *Generating Interest:* Does the paragraph open with something specific and vivid to capture the reader's attention? What technique does the writer use to get the reader interested? _____

_____

_____

_____

Does the opening paragraph let the reader know the subject of the essay? Explain. _____

_____

_____

_____

Suggestions: _____

_____

_____

2. *Thesis:* Does the main clause of the thesis statement—the proposition— clearly answer the controlling question of the writing assignment? Why or why not? _____

_____

_____

Are the subpoints—the reasons for or against arranged marriage—made clear in the thesis? Explain. _____

_____

_____

_____

3. *Coherence:* Does the opening paragraph have smooth coherence, especially from the opening sentences to the thesis? Does the writer need to provide a link (such as a transition or bridging phrase) between the opening sentences and the thesis? Why or why not? _____

_____

_____

Suggestions: _____

_____

_____

CONCLUDING PARAGRAPH

1. Does the conclusion reemphasize the main idea (the proposition) of the essay instead of simply listing the subpoints of the essay? Explain.

_____

_____

_____

2. Does the writer need to strengthen the conclusion in one of the following ways?

- By discussing the implications of the essay's main idea?
- By closing with something specific or vivid?
- By referring back to the opening paragraph?

Explain. _____

_____

_____

Suggestions: _____

_____

_____

Index